Sir Clement Freud, grandson of  1924 and died in 2009. His va as one of our first 'celebrity cf face on TV in a series of dog became the Liberal MP for Ely and retained his seat for fourteen years, subsequently being awarded a knighthood. He was a much-loved regular panellist on the long-running Radio 4 show *Just a Minute*.

FREUD ON FOOD

Clement Freud

Illustrated with cartoons by
Haro

BLACK SWAN

TRANSWORLD PUBLISHERS
61–63 Uxbridge Road, London W5 5SA
A Random House Group Company
www.rbooks.co.uk

FREUD ON FOOD
A BLACK SWAN BOOK: 9780552776547

First published in Great Britain
in 1978 by J.M. Dent & Sons Ltd
Black Swan edition published 2010

Addresses for Random House Group Ltd companies outside the UK
can be found at: www.randomhouse.co.uk
The Random House Group Ltd Reg. No. 954009

The Random House Group Limited supports The Forest Stewardship
Council (FSC), the leading international forest certification organisation.
All our titles that are printed on Greenpeace approved FSC certified paper
carry the FSC logo. Our paper procurement policy can be found at
www.rbooks.co.uk/environment

Typeset in 10.5/13.5pt Giovanni by Falcon Oast Graphic Art Ltd.
Printed in the UK by CPI Cox & Wyman, Reading, RG1 8EX.

2 4 6 8 10 9 7 5 3 1

Mixed Sources
Product group from well-managed
forests and other controlled sources
www.fsc.org Cert no. TT-COC-2139
© 1996 Forest Stewardship Council
FSC

Acknowledgements

The author and publisher are grateful to the proprietors of the *Daily Telegraph Magazine*, the *Observer* and *Time and Tide*, in which the material in this book first appeared in article form. They would also like to thank Léonie Glen for her help in preparing the material for publication.

The majority of the illustrations by Haro first appeared in *Time and Tide* during 1961/2. A dozen first appeared in the 1978 edition of this title.

Contents

Introduction

Freud on Food or
'Oh God, not another cookery book' is, in fact, another cookery book.

I have always felt that a cookery book replete with recipes that began 'take two pounds of cracked wheat . . .' had no place in literature. None of my recipes begin in such a manner; my approach has tended to be a hundred or so words of waffle followed by a recipe, followed by ways you could, if you so desired, adapt it to your own taste.

What ought to be remembered is that if you cannot cook, not even the best cookery book is going to change this sad state of affairs . . . and if you are what my children used to call 'a good cooker' then a cookery book should try to give you ideas rather than blow by blow instructions.

It so happened that I started my working life as a cook, unlike the majority of cookery critics who tended to hover around the perimeters of gastronomy. But what I learnt in my kitchen was not so much the panoply of haute cuisine as the algebra thereof.

I learnt what went with what . . . and at what temperature the two remained in harmony. I achieved an inherent sense of timing . . . and after my first year in a white hat, never ever again burnt baked potatoes or forgot the toast under the grill, the bread in the boiler room or the champagne in the deep freeze.

I learnt how to handle hot saucepans, heavy saucepans, pans of smoking oil (and some cool oil) and, if my time as a professional did not do much to teach me recipes, it made me the most able follower of other people's texts.

It is astonishing how little has changed in haute cuisine. There can be few subjects in which the textbooks of seventy-five years ago are of much more than academic interest. Gastronomy is the exception.

What we have done in this century is to make life easier, with the invention of mixers and blenders, microwave ovens and all those gadgets and utensils without which the Good Housekeeping Exhibition might have to fold up.

We have not made things better. A rotary whisk gives you faster snow from your egg whites; but it is poorer in quality because the more air you beat into the whites the better the result and a handwhisk ensured the absolute maximum of air.

I do not have to tell you of the sheer nastiness of the products of microwave ovens . . . but here again, if you use it for a baked potato and serve a sufficiency of Maldon salt and Normandy butter – who will know how the tuber achieved its finished form?

My credo in cooking has always been to equate time and quality. If you can produce a dish in 20 minutes which is 80 per cent as good as something that takes an hour and a half, then the 20 minute way is to be recommended . . . unless the guest you have asked to dinner just may leave you his fortune when he dies.

The articles in this book were written over a period of twenty years, so they are uneven in prose, quality, concept and simplicity. Too often, I find on looking back, did I give recipes for, say pork, without mentioning that it would be equally delicious for veal, lamb, rabbit – even carp. When I wrote of butter, it was before the days of cholesterol (I mean the days when we started worrying about it) and, of course, my anti-margarine feelings were from the standpoint of taste and not health – and at that, the taste of margarine in the fifties and sixties. When I wrote of wine it was in the days when a bottle of plonk cost one-sixtieth of the average industrial wage. It now costs one-thirtieth – which is sufficient incentive to experiment with cider and strong ale.

For the twenty years during which I wrote about food, drink and restaurants, a steady stream of people came up to me to say how they enjoyed reading my cookery books.

For the record, this is my first cookery book, but as my life now revolves around politics, it is only fair to say that it is some three years since anyone mentioned the fact that I used to sweat over a stove with biro poised – and I miss that.

Finally, all the recipes in this book work . . . for if they did not do so in their original form, someone wrote or phoned or sent me, by registered post, the results of what they had done at my instructions, and wanted to know what had gone wrong.

'The compositor forgot to put in the line which said – "add five beaten eggs"' I would reply; these errors have been rectified. But if something goes wrong and you feel so inclined – do send me the fruits of your labour. Some response is ever preferable to none.

Much of the contents have appeared in various publications which had the good sense to employ me at some time or another . . . and I am grateful to the editors and their successors for being generous about letting me reprint such pieces to which they had copyright.

Under Starters' Orders

The relationship between private houses and public catering establishments has never been harmonious. 'You are treating the house as if it were a hotel,' girls are told if they come home after 7.30 p.m. 'Do you think this is the Bar of the Fox and Geese?' says the little woman when her husband drinks a glass of ale in the front room. And yet, for some strange reason, when people entertain in their own homes they do their utmost to give the impression that it is a restaurant or licensed lounge in which they are offering hospitality. Instead of, say, a fresh pea omelette followed by an immaculately roasted leg of pork, which you can never get when you go out, they serve supermarket pâté; then coq au vin, or duck in orange goo.

And when it comes to a pre-dinner drink, the odds are currently 11–8 on peanuts and potato crisps being served as an accompaniment. Now the reason bars serve these abominations is simple: not only are they cheap, they contain a high degree of salt, which makes you thirsty, which causes you to drink more, which increases the bar's profits. Peanuts and crisps also represent a maximum amount of stodge – which kills your appetite – which enables you to stay in the bar longer and drink more – which increases their profits. I should have thought that before a dinner party in a private home the very last thing you want is to give people an inordinate thirst and kill their appetites . . . and yet: peanuts and crisps, crisps and peanuts.

One of the mistakes is to arrange a party so that pre-dinner drinks are one thing, dinner something quite different. The reason for this is usually that the wife looks after the food, the husband is in charge of booze, and as the couple haven't spoken to each other since granny died, *he* fills you up with dry sherry before *she* brings in melon soaked in port. Ideally the whole evening, from arrival through cocktails, dinner, coffee and liqueurs to departure, should follow a pattern – and to my mind there just isn't any decent pattern in which peanuts and crisps have a part. Mind you, I like nuts; I can feel passionate about salted almonds in moderation. I am fond of hazelnuts. I eat cashews with the best of them and were it not for the high calorific value of brazils I should eat more of those than I do. But not peanuts. Oily, taste-killing peanuts . . . such as are constantly left at the bottom of bowls that contained *Mixed Nuts*. (When young I invented a patent device which was held over a bowl of mixed nuts and destroyed peanuts. It worked on gas . . . but it never caught on.) May I suggest instead that you make

Cheese straws

Most supermarkets sell puff pastry – which is excellent for savoury dishes. Roll out the pastry thinly, spread one half lightly with English mustard, sprinkle over it a thin application of grated cheese – old cooking cheese will do – and make a sandwich by folding the plain half over the filled one.

Press the layers together and cut strips of pastry about 8 inches long and ¼ inch wide.

Lightly butter a baking sheet, press down one end of

the cheese straw, twist it a couple of times and press down the other end. Repeat this action till you have a full tray of twirled, filled puff pastry strips. Dust these with cayenne pepper and bake in a mark 5 (375°F) oven for 12–15 minutes. Let them lose their first flush of heat on a rack and eat them while they are still lukewarm.

I have never made enough to taste them when they were cold . . . but there seems no reason why they should not be delicious at any temperature.

CANAPES AND TOAST

The depressing thing about an Englishman's traditional love of animals is the dishonesty thereof. Where does one draw the line between starving a dog . . . a crime punishable by law . . . and starving a duck, a normal and necessary step taken to empty the gut prior to killing it. Keep a cat in a cage too small for it and the neighbours will come round with an inspector of the RSPCA. Keep a hundred turkeys in a pen in which there is barely room for them to move and the inspector will come round and order one for his Christmas lunch. Get a barbed hook into the upper lip of a salmon, drag him endlessly around the water until he loses his strength, pull him on to the bank, hit him on the head with a stone and you may well become the fisherman of the year. Shoot the salmon, and you'll never be asked again. On the other hand it is absolutely OK to shoot a hare, but if you go after him with a fish-hook they'll say you're heartless, cruel, or mad.

About one thing the English gentleman has a particularly strict code. If a bird says 'cluck bik bik bik bik' or 'caw' you may kill it, eat it or ask Fortnum's to pickle it in Napoleon brandy with wild strawberries. If it says 'tweet' it is a dear and precious friend and you'd better lay off it if you want to remain a member of Boodles. It is delicacy

that prevents me from giving you an Elizabethan recipe for nightingales' tongues; instead I shall write of toast, on which this tit-bit might well have been served.

After an hour or two in a warm room a cocktail canapé made with bread goes stale; one with toast is soggy. Of rights the good canapé should be the size of one bite (two at the most), and have a firm, crisp base on which is placed, not balanced, a moist tasty substance. Next time you give a party at which the canapé puts in an appearance, cut your slices of bread into the required shapes (square, round or what you will) and fry them for 15 seconds on each side in a frying pan containing a shallow layer of very hot olive oil. Drain the pieces well and lay them on a cloth until quite cold. Then give them a thin coating of butter to insulate the bread against the moisture of the filling, which might be salmon in a garlicky mayonnaise, cream cheese with black olives, or finely chopped eggs and watercress with a complement of anchovy fillets.

BUTTER

Solomon in his Proverbs says: 'Surely the churning of milk brings forth butter.' And of course the old man was absolutely correct even though he is more likely to have meant the milk of mares, goats, camels and asses than that of the underdeveloped biblical cow.

Butter today has become an emulsified status symbol; delicacies are said to melt like butter, superior margarine to contain butter, cheeses to spread like butter. Butter is at the desirable end of the breadline.

The price of butter is determined by quality – salt and water content – and country of origin. There are sound reasons for buying both the cheap and the expensive: the highly priced English regional, French and Danish for spreading on good bread to be taken neat or under bland fillings; the cheaper stuff for cheese-and-pickle sandwiches or for cooking anything that has a predominantly strong taste of its own. Once butter is heated above a certain temperature, the cheap becomes indistinguishable from the expensive.

Ideally, expensive butters should be served in small individual pots – as one might present a pâté – so that participants at a gathering can seize pieces of hot French bread and suit their appetites with do-it-yourself canapés. Or fine butters can rest on a serving board, like good cheeses. Other butter techniques are listed below – and some easy mixes, plus a useful melted butter; the mixes, of course, go on bits of fresh bread.

Clarified butter

Butter melted over a very low flame, and then skimmed until it reaches the clearness of olive oil, was once much used for pouring over well-seasoned fresh shrimps, sliced breasts of chicken or any other meat, fish or vegetable. But this old-fashioned, short-term method of preserving had the disadvantage that the butter could go rancid while the contents of the pot remained basically all right. On the other hand, still a great delicacy are

17

Freshly buttered shrimps

4 oz. peeled shrimps or prawns
½ oz. butter
Salt, white pepper, lemon juice

Toss shrimps in seasoned butter in a cool pan for a few minutes, press into individual pots to eliminate moisture – créme caramel moulds are ideal for this – and seal each with a spoonful or so of clarified butter. Allow to set and turn out, heating the moulds fractionally to ease the operation.

Melted butter

There comes a time when the guests are due and the soup is thin and there seems to be nothing for it but to squander a rich packet of butter into the dismal broth. A poor sentiment this, for the melted butter rises to the top and transforms your indifferent soup into an indifferent soup with a thick, oily film. For last-minute soup rescues, cream is best. Melted butter can be made to do the job in the case of vegetables such as asparagus and artichokes, however.

Take 3 oz. of butter and divide it up into ½ oz. pieces. Put 2 soupspoons of water into a saucepan and when this boils add the pieces of butter. Leave on a full gas, and when the butter rises – it does this just as milk rises – empty into a cold container and whisk well. It can then be warmed in a double boiler and will retain its texture for an hour or two.

Fried butter

Fried butter can be served with fish or meat instead of the more mundane medallions of parsley butter that shelter under the name of *beurre maître d'hôtel* (page 101).

Cut butter into cubes, about 12 to a ½ lb. packet, roll them into marbles, coat them with crushed cereal – Weetabix is good – or very fine toasted breadcrumbs, dip in rather liquid beaten egg and roll firmly in more crumbs. Fry in deep hot fat for half a minute.

Prawn butter

2 oz. peeled prawns
juice of quarter lemon
½ small clove garlic
pinch of salt
2 peppercorns

Reduce these ingredients to complete shapelessness with a pestle and mortar and add 3 oz. of soft butter. Blend with a fork.

Egg butter

Pass 2 hard-boiled eggs through a sieve. Add salt, pepper, turmeric, Worcester sauce and 4 oz. soft butter. Pass through a forcing-bag.

HORS D'OEUVRES

In view of what I am about to write it is galling to have to admit that the best hors d'oeuvres I was ever served consisted of hard-boiled eggs in mayonnaise, sliced tomatoes in vinaigrette and sardines in oil. My theme is that hors d'oeuvres – a non-phrase if ever I heard one – do not necessarily have to contain oil and vinegar. Moreover, the best hors d'oeuvres are those made up of some succulent remnant . . . like the last quarter of a Virginia baked ham; never the top half of a tin of baked beans.

Let us start with a definition. Hors d'oeuvres, literally, means 'outside the main dish'; realistically, a side dish; in common parlance, a starter. When manpower was cheap and expertise walked the streets, it was common practice to present a dozen dishes of delicacies to complement the pre-dinner drink and take the very sharpest edge off the guests' hunger. Unfortunately, when expertise went by the board and instant cookery became the order of the day, the demon hors d'oeuvres dishes were still around. So people filled them with imitations of what they remembered seeing in restaurants, and restaurants were so impressed with this ploy that they imitated their imitators. Personally, hors d'oeuvres are words I can manage without . . . but if I had around me some ready-printed menus, I should serve under the heading a beautiful . . .

Onion tart

An 8-inch shortpastry shell, baked 'blind' (page 217), filled with ½ lb. sliced onions fried in 2 oz. butter until golden . . . then incorporated in ½ pint of milk into which 3 whole eggs have been beaten. I would season this with cayenne pepper, bake it for 20 minutes in a mark 4 (350°F) oven and drool.

I suppose the acid test of the traditionalist hors d'oeuvrier is the quality of his mayonnaise, his vinaigrette and his garnishing powers (page 137). If you have a dozen small glass dishes and an afternoon before a party on which you wish to do nothing more than fiddle, here are a few suggestions that may result in something more compulsive than turnips tossed in salad cream.

Soused mackerel

Fillet a mackerel and cut the fillets into ½-inch strips. Lay these in an oven dish and pour on them the steaming court bouillon you have made by boiling a glass of dry white wine in the company of half a glass of garlic vinegar (page 141) and a glass of water. Garnish with carrot slices and onion rings poached in the court bouillon and decorate with the best-looking bayleaf you can find.

Potted shrimps

Buy a small packet of frozen shrimps. Let them thaw gently, then toss them in a pan containing a modicum of clarified butter (page 17), a fair amount of freshly ground pepper and a little lemon juice. Fill teaspoons of the hot shrimp/butter mixture into small scooped-out tomatoes – or small dishes – allow the stuff to set in a cool place and serve strewn with chopped chives.

Beetroot

Boil beetroots, peel them and using a *pommes parisienne* spoon (or a sharp-edged teaspoon) cut out balls (or 'olives') – serve in sour cream and tabasco.

Fennel

For lovers of the aniseedy taste this is a good starter. Put the fennel to boil in a pan of salted cold water; let it simmer for 5 minutes. Then lift it out, slice it and sprinkle the slices with olive oil, salt, lemon juice and a few drops of Pernod; garnish with the demon parsley.

Cucumbers

Sliced finely, salted, drained and served in sour cream with a garnish of chives, these are another lovely starter.

Radishes

Chopped into thin slices, mixed with a French dressing and used to fill the cavity of an avocado pear is almost the only non-nibbling use to which a radish can be put. Or try nibbling with Maldon salt.

Grapefruit

Halve grapefruit and loosen segments. Mix 2 rounded tablespoons brown sugar, 3 tablespoons rum (brandy if you dislike rum) and ½ oz. melted butter. Spread this over the faces of the grapefruit halves, cook in a mark 3 (325°F) oven for 20 minutes.

*   *   *

Many years ago before the enemy invented refrigeration there were restaurants that served food: veal and lamb and beef and pork; real chickens and ducklings; lobsters and soles, scallops and mussels – all of which, if not actually alive alive-oh on the morning of the feast, were certainly kicking a day or two before that.

And if the honest restaurateur had something left over at the end of the working day, it was not frozen, thawed and called back to life. It was used as a basis for some other dish that depended more on skill than on complete freshness. Chickens might be pounded and mixed with chopped mangoes, sherry, cream and gelatine to emerge as a mousse. Meat would be sliced and chopped and mixed in mayonnaise with a julienne of apples, celery and shallots; this is called Italian salad. A sharp sauce, made of mayonnaise, ketchup, Worcester sauce and brandy – with an optional dash of anchovy sauce – was used to dress lobster, crab or prawns. Mussels were simmered in wine and garnished with mushrooms. Old soles were given to the staff.

I'd simply adore one of those Heavenly-looking savoury things

All these creations were put on a buffet and called hors d'oeuvres – and many an establishment made its name thereby. The trouble was that hors d'oeuvres, like Liebfraumilch, became the fashionable thing to order; and because, like Liebfraumilch, the word had no specific meaning, a great deal of rubbish was dispensed under that erudite name. Restaurateurs' eyes would light up at the word and they poured forth bits of potato and cucumber; cold beans and beetroot, and sausage all covered with sauces that had come out of bottles. For myself, it yearns me not whether the thing is called an appetizer, an opener, a starter, a first course or what – as long as the result is not yesterday's reclaimed veg. glaring at a sardine. If times were hard, I should settle for

Gnocchi   (as made in Genoa, for 6 people)

1¼ lb. potatoes
1 lb. plain flour

For the sauce:
a heaped tablespoon sweet basil – fresh or bottled
a tablespoon parmesan cheese
3 tablespoons olive oil
2 oz. butter
a teaspoonful of crushed garlic
the juice of half a lemon

Boil the potatoes in well-salted water and when cooked pass them through a fine sieve. Add the flour, and see that the mixture is smooth. Make it into strips, which you pinch into the size of marbles; boil them in a big pan of salted water and when cooked – about 6 or 7 minutes – drain them well. Mix the sauce ingredients together and blend well with the hot gnocchi.

If times were better, but there was not a lot of time, I should try

Taramasalata

a peerless paste to pile upon hot, crisp breakfast toast

> *6 oz. smoked cod's roe, preferably not potted*
> *4 oz. best cream cheese*
> *1 tablespoon olive oil*
> *a heaped tablespoon finely chopped chives*
> *a dessertspoon lemon juice*

Blend, and serve cold.

But if I'd plenty of time and money, I think I should choose a

Quiche lorraine (for 4)

You first make a shortcrust lining for a 6-inch flan ring, using

> *4 oz. plain flour*
> *½ coffeespoon of salt*
> *2 oz. butter*
> *2 dessertspoons water*

Sieve flour and salt into a bowl, rub in the butter, add water and stir with the point of a knife until the pastry clings together. Then flour your hands and knead it into a smooth ball. Let it rest in a cool place.

Roll out the pastry until it is an inch or two larger than the ring; ease it on and help it to settle into place. Then cut off the surplus pastry. Put the flan ring on a baking sheet, line the pastry with greaseproof paper weighed down with beans and cook in a preheated mark 5 (375°F) oven for 15 minutes. Remove paper and beans and cook for another 5 minutes.

Rest the ring on a wire tray and after a few minutes carefully lift out the flan and allow to cool completely. Then you can put it back in the ring.

For the filling:
> *4 rashers streaky bacon*

2 eggs
¼ pint cream
1 oz. grated parmesan
2 oz. grated cheddar cheese
1 medium sized onion

Grill the bacon and when crisp break it up and cover the base of the flan with it. Then sprinkle the parmesan cheese on the bacon. Slice the onion very fine, fry it in butter and when golden drain and add a thin layer of fried onion to the parmesan.

Now whisk up the eggs, cream and cheddar cheese, pour them over the flan and allow to set for 25–30 minutes in a mark 3 (325°F) oven. It can be eaten hot or cold or at temperatures in between; it is uniformly delicious.

Ideally a first course should be complementary to the meal, sufficient to awaken but not enough to blunt either appetite or taste buds for the Oeuvres, or main courses to come. Apart from that it can be hot or cold, spiced, salted, sour or sweet.

The depressing thing about most catering establishments is that their lists contain those traditional openers: melon, corn on the cob, avocado, artichoke, asparagus, all of which can be absolutely delicious. 'Are they nice?' you ask. 'Everything in this place very nice indeed,' says a British subject from Nicosia with a flashing smile and wheels on his tired array of wares that have come to him from tin, jar or ice.

The best melons, I think, are the small Israeli cherontes; chilled, cut in half, cleaned and the centre filled with a couple of spoons of castor sugar moistened with a teaspoon or two of liqueur. Curaçao or Grand Marnier, ideally. Or halved and filled with sugared redcurrants.

When you pick up a melon, whatever its colour or origin, the ends should be soft enough for gentle pressure of your thumbs to arouse a sympathetic yield in the flesh; furthermore, a ripe melon gives out a pleasantly fruity smell. Now you cannot, in all conscience, blame a green-grocer who discourages such intimacies with his wares prior to purchase; consequently the fruit you bring home may not be what you had imagined. Nevertheless, so long as you shun the over-ripe fruit that has a pungent alcoholic smell and is so soft that your fingers will break through the skin at the point where the fruit was attached to its parent branch, buying melons is a fair gamble. If the melon is as described above, it will benefit from a short (2–3 hour) stay in a refrigerator before being cut, followed by breathing a quarter of an hour's room temperature into its chilled flesh. If it is hard, if on cutting it looks more veg-etable than fruit, all is by no means lost: here is a soup for four people.

Melon soup

Cut the melon into cubes of an inch or so, dust them with well-seasoned flour and fry them gently in butter in a saucepan with the lid tightly on for 10 minutes, stirring from time to time. Now add 1½ pints of watered milk, simmer for 30 minutes, pass through a fine sieve and bind with a liaison of 2 yolks of egg beaten into ¼ pint of double cream. Decorate the soup with sprigs of chervil or tarragon and garnish further, if you like, with small ovals of melon, browned in butter in a frying pan.

Peach soup

Slice two peeled peaches thinly, refresh them with Eau de Vie. Beat 1 whole egg and 2 yolks; add 4 oz. of castor sugar, whip well and add 1 pint of milk. Keep very cold. Beat the other 2 whites stiffly, add 1 oz. of vanilla sugar (castor sugar, that has cohabited in a jar with a vanilla pod). Into each soup bowl, place some alcoholic peaches, a ladle full of iced, blended milk and on to this float some puffs of meringue mixture, shaped with two teaspoons.

Avocados

These admirable fruit are picked in countries as politically unacceptable to each other as South Africa, Israel and Madeira. Hard and light green in their various coloured shells when they leave their native shores, they mature slowly in cockroach climate until they reach a delicate softness at which a firm grip of the hand should realize a respondingly ready yield from the pear. They must be ripe but not over-ripe.

Avocados have a rich, slightly soapy, fruity, vegetable flesh equally pleasant to serve with sweet or savoury. Avocado enemies are not only those who find taste or texture displeasing; they also number those who have been given fruit that were hard, over-ripe or inappropriately accompanied. If you come under this category, give them another chance: pick your avocado carefully with greengrocery advice; try it first with granulated sugar and lemon juice, then with a French dressing. If you don't want the bother of scooping out the pear at the table, peel it, slice it and serve it in a champagne glass swimming in iced Château d'Yquem. Some of the pleasanter fillings are:

Red caviar and lemon juice
Tunny fish in aioli (mayonnaise made of 2 egg yolks,
  2 cloves garlic, ½ pint oil, 1 lemon, salt and pepper)
Crab meat in horseradish cream.

Corn on the cob

Really only worth eating fresh. These must be boiled for a quarter of an hour, no more unless they are very big, in heavily salted water. Then drain, brush with butter, grill for a minute or two under a medium grill and serve with best farm butter, which should have had no experience of a refrigerator.

Globe artichokes
Take from 25 to 40 minutes boiling, depending on their size. Cook them in salted water until the outside leaves can be removed easily from the base. Drain them very well – squeezing the artichokes to remove water – and serve hot. You need something in which to dip the leaves, such as melted butter, hollandaise (page 50) or, if you want to try a new dip, take 2 tablespoons of very fine toasted bread-crumbs and introduce them into 4 oz. of sizzling butter to which was added a dessertspoon of vinegar as the butter began to brown. Fry the crumbs for a minute and give each diner his own small bowl of the hot mixture.

Gâteau bressan
According to some people, the food from the Bresse is better than that of any other part in France. Here is a recipe which makes a magnificent beginning to a meal, hot or cold.

Take 2 oz. of green (unsmoked) bacon, 4 chicken livers, a sheep's brain or 4 oz. of sweetbreads. Chop very finely, pound in mortar, or if you have one, give a going over in a liquidizer. Add a slice of bread boiled in milk, ¼ pint of single cream and 2 beaten eggs and fill into buttered cream caramel dishes, having seasoned the mixture with salt and paprika to your taste. Stand the dishes in a tray of water and leave them in a coolish oven (mark ½–1/250°F) for an hour. Serve in the dish or ease out on to a plate with a thin coating of double cream and a good sprinkling of chopped chives.

Asparagus
Asparagus must be fresh, though tinned ones make a pleasant vegetable course heated, buttered and given

3 minutes in a hot oven under a sprinkling of parmesan cheese.

Recently, in a newish London Club which has members who are still very much better than the food, I ordered asparagus. 'Certainly,' said the highly trained waiter: 'you wante sparagus holliday or melty butter?' I said hollandaise would be nice – and we smiled at each other (there is always that moment of friendship before the first whitebait is flung into your lap). The asparagus arrived, limp, cooked to the point of submission; consequently I was unsurprised to note that the hollandaise sauce had curdled. I could have uncurdled it in my wine glass – which would have been ostentatious, though not difficult: start with a dessertspoonful of cream or dry white wine and teaspoon the well-mixed curdled sauce on to this, whisking with a fork. Or I could have made a scene and embarrassed my host . . . or have eaten the stuff and done untold harm to my *amour propre*.

In certain respects asparagus is like turkey; there are two parts to it and both need different cooking times and methods. In the case of turkey you can get string and truss the whole bird so tightly that cookery aimed midway between the white and brown meat is reasonably successful. When it comes to asparagus, you have a very much better solution. The stalks require cleaning and scraping and comprehensive boiling. The tips need to be treated with great care and should be steamed. You can cook asparagus as do the Transylvanians: cut off the tips and steam them; take the stalks and boil them. This is satisfactory but unsubtle (as, indeed, are the Transylvanians). What you should do is to cut off the very ends, scrape the stalks, if they need scraping, with a potato peeler, and stand the asparagus upright in a saucepan that is taller than the tallest spear (use a knife, if necessary, to cut down the asparagus from the stalk). Add salted, boiling water up to 1 inch from the tips and put on the lid; boil for 10 to 20 minutes depending on the thickness of the asparagus. Drain them, wrap them in muslin and keep at the bottom of a cool oven until their time comes. They can do with clarified butter seasoned with lemon juice; creamy melted butter (page 18); or, if you are enterprising, a bowl of hollandaise.

Easy hollandaise sauce

There is a very acceptable short cut to a hollandaise sauce, particularly suitable for those who are poor or allergic to eggs. Put into a pan 2 tablespoons of water. When the water boils add to it eight ½ oz. cubes of butter, and, when the whole mixture boils up, empty it into a cold basin and whisk with a rotary whisk for a few moments. Somehow this makes a sauce, thick and unoily, which can be spiked with lemon juice and pepper and will keep its texture for an hour or so.

Asparagus soup

is an almost irresistible starter to asparagus, but you must resist. On the day following the feast, however, take the water in which you have boiled the asparagus, add to it the washed parings of the stalks and boil all this until the result is a strong and well-seasoned asparagus water.

For a very beautiful soup, to 1½ pints liquor whisk 3 egg yolks in ¼ pint of double cream and add to the simmering soup, whisking the while; keep whisking as it regains the temperature of hot soup; do not let it boil . . . because of the eggs . . . and strain.

For a less beautiful soup use 1 dessertspoon of flour for each egg yolk and water for cream. In this case it is essential to add butter – like 2 oz. – else the effort is wasted and you might as well get an asparagus soup cube.

A CUBE IS ONLY THE ROOT

It is a sobering thought that if you chop an onion, a carrot and some celery; brown them gently in oil; add a pound of shin of beef; a handful of marrowbones, a bayleaf, seasoning and two quarts of water; then simmer the lot for 2 hours, the end-product will not be noticeably nicer than Knorr Suisse soup cubes dissolved in boiling water. The trouble about serving the unadulterated juice of a soup cube is that, while it makes an adequate consommé, it makes no more than that. It is also instantly recognizable and serving it neat will do astonishingly little for your standing as a great host or hostess.

The right use for soup-stock – whether ponderously manufactured or instantly produced – is as a basis. You start with the all-purpose liquid, then set about giving it an identity, an added strength and some character. Start by remembering the enigma of soup-making: small saucepanfuls always turn out better than very large quantities, even if all the ingredients are carefully multiplied the requisite number of times.

Consommé

To make a consommé, begin with stock, made either from soup cubes or:

> *1 lb. any cheap cut of beef*
> *a composite 1 lb. of chopped, cleaned onion, leek, celery,*
> *   parsnip, carrot or turnip*
> *thyme, a bayleaf and seasoning*
> *1 egg white*
> *2 quarts water*

Boil the meat gently in seasoned water, taking the scum from the top as it rises. It is impossible to clarify effectively any soup in which scum has been allowed to boil for any time. When no more scum forms, add the vegetables and herbs and the egg white, lower the flame and simmer for 2 hours or more. Then strain through a muslin cloth. You next decide on the flavour of the consommé; the garnish; the fortified wine and the accompaniment.

Chicken stock

There is something about the physical make-up of a broiler chicken that gives a soup made of its roasted carcass a richness that no mixture of flavouring and reduction can equal. These large eunuchs of the feathered world are the ideal thing to buy when you intend chicken to be eaten cold, with salad or mayonnaise; whatever your plans, get the meat off the carcass quickly – and not too completely – and then add a leek, an onion, a carrot and a bayleaf, plenty of water and boil away for an hour or so; strain the liquor, skim off the fat, season and set in a cool place around a soft poached egg in a cup, if you like.

Chicken lemon soup

To 1 pint of chicken stock – either real or from a cube – add 2 dessertspoons lemon juice and 1½ oz. butter rubbed into that amount of flour. Simmer, poach in this soup a small handful of rice and season. Finally, add a spoonful of cream to each bowl.

Game consommé

is made similarly to chicken consommé, using an old pheasant or partridge, instead of the chicken. A glass of Sercial madeira enhances the taste. Cheese straws are an acceptable accompaniment (page 14).

Vegetable consommés

can include celery, red or green pimentos, leek. Take 6 oz. of well-cleaned celery stalks, chop them finely, boil them fiercely in a pint of stock until tender, then add a further 1½ pints of stock. Simmer and serve with grated parmesan cheese.

Fish consommés

once popular but really not everybody's cup of soup – are made from fish stock, using pike or whiting instead of beef in the stock recipe. For the stock to become soup it is reduced by boiling and, classically, can be thickened with arrowroot. It should be served with a spoonful of medium sherry per person and a garnish of quenelles (page 62).

Beautiful soup was beloved by the Victorians, faltered during the reign of Edward VII, suffered between the wars, and failed to survive the peace. With some notable exceptions, soup is now either 'a bore' or, for caterers, a cheap way of upgrading table d'hôte meals by adding an extra undesirable course. Restaurateurs buy huge tins of soup-mix, a blend of flavouring, colouring, thickening, seasoning and our old friend monosodium glutamate. Add water, says the instruction leaflet, and you have a satisfying soup at a pittance per portion.

But there are some great soups that make all the difference to a meal.

Soupe à l'ivrogne

is a soup that makes a meal, a mythical 'drunkard's soup'. Plenty of books about Paris in the twenties state that cafés in the Champs Elysées served it to home-going drunks, 'belated revellers'. The name was given not so much for the effect the soup had on the man but the craving the drunk had for just such a dish . . . liquid-solid-buttery-cheesy-hot-alcoholic, with a kick like a velvet-shod mule. But, as with the Indian rope trick, one only meets people who know people who have seen it; never people who have actually had the soup themselves. However, it works and it tastes excellent.

For four people take 1 lb. of best Spanish onions and slice them very finely. Melt ½ lb. of (preferably) unsalted butter in a saucepan, add the onions, a bayleaf, a good dash of ground black peppercorns, and cook this with the lid on for 15 minutes, when the onions will be golden brown and the liquid considerable. Add a half (or a whole, if you're feeling rich) bottle of champagne – only the worst snob would recommend a brand or a year for this purpose – to the soup and let it come to simmering point, then pour it into a fireproof soup tureen. Scrape off the hard, outside rind of a camembert cheese, put what's left between two dinner plates and squeeze it to the size of the opening of the tureen. Float this on to the liquor and bake it in a hot oven (mark 7/425°F) for 10 to 20 minutes, by which time the soup will be just off boiling point, and the saucer of camembert rich, melted and yielding. Add some breadcrumbs to take up the top layer of fat if you will, and colour them under a grill. Serve at once, dividing the top layer of cheese into quarters which are served on top of the soup.

Billybi

This can be spelt many other ways. It is a soup that started life in oyster restaurants where the main ingredient was the contents of the bucket under the oysterman's feet, containing the beards and juice of a couple of hundred oysters. The juice of mussels, clams or scallops gives just as satisfactory a result, and there are on the market tinned clams which can be liquidized and passed through a sieve. It is essentially a by-product soup, but well worth creating for its own sake. For four soup cups

1 pint mussels
1½ glasses dry white wine
2 glasses water
a dozen crushed peppercorns
a few parsley stalks
a twist of lemon peel
1 oz. sliced onion

Wash and scrape the mussels. Put the ingredients into a large pan and bring to the boil over a strong flame. When the mussels have opened, turn down the flame and let them simmer for a few more minutes to flavour the liquid.

Strain off the liquid and reduce by about a quarter by boiling.

To thicken the soup:

1 oz. butter
1 oz. plain flour
¼ pint single cream
¼ pint double cream

When the soup is thus reduced, add the beurre manié (flour rubbed into butter), whisk as it simmers, and as it thickens add the cream. Season to taste and serve very hot.

Prawn bisque

Buy 1 pint of cooked prawns (raw prawns are as hard to find as untoasted bread in commercial hotels) and simmer these in oil/butter mixture with a grated onion and a spoonful of tomato purée for 20 minutes with lid tightly on pan. Take up moisture with flour, make up with a pint of water and a soup cube, stir with a wooden spoon till it comes to the boil and simmer for 10 minutes. Liquidize, sieve and serve very hot, adding a spoonful of cream – or one of warmed brandy set alight if you like food you can read by.

Artichokes and celeriac

There is no classical name for a soup made of Jerusalem artichokes and celeriac, but it is a fortuitous marriage nevertheless.

1 lb. Jerusalem artichokes
1 good sized celeriac
3 oz. butter
1 tablespoon oil
2½ oz. flour
1½ pints of water
½ soup cube
seasoning

Clean the vegetables and cut them into small pieces. Wash them and let them simmer in the oil/butter mixture over a low flame with the lid on until they are cooked. Now dust the vegetables with flour. Let them cook but do not let them brown. Remove the pan from the flame and add water and the soup cube. Stir as it comes to the boil and let the soup simmer for 10 minutes or so.

Now pass it through a sieve, if you have no liquidizer. Add more salt, pepper or lemon juice as you think fit and serve, adding a tablespoon of cream to each plate.

Spring soup

Take of onions, Jerusalem artichokes, spinach, watercress and carrots as you will. Wash them and chop them and for every pound of vegetables use 2 oz. butter to soften them in a closed pan; take up moisture with 2½ oz. plain flour, let the flour cook and add 1½ pints of water to make the soup. Then simmer for 40 minutes and either sieve/liquidize or else serve with pieces of vegetables floating about. A spoonful of cream to every soup bowl is always an advantage.

Celery soup

Cut up 8 oz. celery stalks and 4 oz. onions. Simmer in 2 oz. butter. Add a bayleaf, and take up moisture with 4 oz. plain flour. Let this cook but not brown; remove from flame and add 1½ pints of water, ½ pint at a time, letting the soup come to the boil, thicken between additions. Simmer for 10 minutes, sieve or liquidize, and serve hot or cold, with or without cream.

I have long felt that the man who could patent the perfume of the Mediterranean would make a great deal of money, always provided one can draw royalties on a smell. Ideally, I suppose, it should be available as an optional extra with air-conditioning plants but could profitably be sold in spray form for smaller houses or coffee bars striving for atmosphere. It is a subtle blend of sweat, garlic, Gaulloise Bleu and Pernod and must come in various strengths, delicate for the early evening, stale and acid at closing time or when you want guests to leave. I stumbled upon the formula by accident, trying to get a smell back to my family who cook the dog's dinner at me; I suppose I am fortunate in having a basement kitchen which makes it possible for my daughter on the first floor to come running down and tell me the toast is burning. Those less fortunately placed will have to improvise with a bunsen burner in the coal cellar. Remember, smells rise; some of them alarmingly.

Rub the bottom and outside of an enamel saucepan generously with crushed cloves of garlic and place into it four broken aniseed balls and a pint of water. Place the pan on a good flame and engage over it a steamer containing several pairs of well worn socks. Concentration of odour may be achieved by pressing down and suddenly removing the lid of the steamer and in this way blasts of smell in the form of signals can be sent around the house: long, short, long . . . dinner is spoilt; and so on. The drawback of the Mediterranean perfume is that it has no end product; all that work and nothing but atmosphere. Here is how to make an appetizing smell and one of the nicest, quickest onion soups at the same time. It is popularly known as 'French'.

Onion soup

Skin and slice finely 1 lb. of onions, cook gently in 3 oz. of butter in a covered saucepan for 10 minutes (stirring now and then), take off lid, season, turn up flame, add 1½ pints of water, bring to the boil and simmer for 10 minutes. Serve with a coating of grated cheese and croutons of garlicky bread if you care for it.

Delicious as this soup may be there is a certain thinness about it and if you add burnt onion stock instead of water this will be largely eliminated. Take an onion and cut it into ½-inch slices which you press firmly to the bottom of your toughest metal saucepan. With lid off, put this on to a fierce heat and let the onion burn without actually carbonizing. Remove from fire for a minute, add water, simmer for 10 minutes, season gently and you have the quickest and simplest basic stock that will improve and colour any non-delicate soup.

Borsch

Bottling, preserving, pickling – that whole range of husbandry practised by careful wives – was an excellent thing to do if there was a glut of inexpensive food, you were in possession of unlimited time and had a store of jars and rings and wax-papers and screwtops and shallow pans. On

the credit side the finished homemade produce could be served with pride; silenced, or at least embarrassed critics; and never was there the shame of having alien names like 'Heinz' to sully the larder shelf.

Less happily, you pickled small beetroots in distilled vinegar and sugar and after a glumptious pickling day you finished up with row upon row of dark red jars which saw you through the year. There you were munching away, steadily conscious of the number of jars remaining, the ETTC (expected time of total consumption) never seeming to get any closer.

Freed of the bottling urge, I now buy beetroots in a tin, one at a time; serve them as a vegetable, drained and boiled in cream with a pinch of cayenne pepper – and the juice in which they wallowed is added to a similar quantity of chicken stock, brought to the boil, seasoned and served dramatically as borsch, garnished with small islands of sour cream. And nowhere around the table does one notice that strained apprehensive look of 'only another five months of this and we shall be able to start on the flageolet beans'.

ICED SOUP

There is something so British about a steaming bowl of broth that the suggestion of any cold soup other than jellied consommé is regarded with suspicion – like the iced tea they drink on the Continent. This is unfair. An iced soup is an excellent opening to a meal – and there is no reason why it should not be sweet. You start meals with melon; with grapefruit. Try

Vanilla milk soup
1 pint milk
4 eggs

4 tablespoons vanilla sugar (page 26)
3 egg whites
2 oz. sugar

Whisk the eggs and sugar, or put them into a liquidizer. Add milk and whisk again. Beat egg whites until they are stiff; add sugar and then beat until they are stiff once more. Serve the chilled egg-milk in soup-plates and decorate with floating islands of egg white shaped with two dessert-spoons. (Cold soups must be served chilled, just as hot soup must be served hot.)

Double consommé – jellied – with soft poached egg

(for 6)

1 marrowbone
½ lb. shin of beef
1 onion cut in half
6 eggs
a small muslin bag of herbs
2 pints water
1 envelope (½ oz.) gelatine
salt
crushed black peppercorns

Place the chopped-up marrowbone and the onion halves in a roasting tray on the top shelf of a mark 9 (475°F) oven for 20 minutes. Let the tray cool slightly. Pour off any fat, then pour in 2 pints of water to loosen deposits, and transfer the bone, onions and water into a saucepan. Let it boil and skim off fat. Add beef (chopped-up), herbs, gela-tine, and seasoning and let the stock reduce by a third. Allow to cool before straining the mixture through a couple of layers of muslin.

Very lightly poach the eggs by tilting them from a ladle into a pan of fast-boiling water to which a dessertspoon of vinegar has been added. Let them cook for 1½ minutes. Place one poached egg – neatly trimmed – in each bowl.

41

Top up with lukewarm consommé and let this set in a cool place. Garnish with cream and cayenne pepper.

Iced watercress soup

Simmer in oil/butter 1 shredded potato, 1 grated onion, 2 bunches of watercress cleaned and chopped. Season well, let this cook for a few minutes and then take up liquid with plain flour. Add 1½ pints stock, boil for 10 minutes, liquidize, sieve and serve very cold with cream and chopped chives.

Fish

CHOOSING FISH

Fresh fish is firm of flesh and lustrous of eye. The White Fish Authority says that if the imprint of your finger remains when the fish has been handled, this is a bad sign. I have yet to meet a fishmonger who lets you squeeze fish before you buy it – but it's an idea.

Look for closeness of texture in the flesh of large fillets such as cod, haddock, red fish and coley. Mackerel when fresh is rigid, and fresh herrings have a sheen, and the scales do not drop off. In plaice and sole look for brightness of skin (North Sea plaice has orange spots that fade with staleness), and remember that stale fish begins to 'go' at the edges. Fishmongers open the flap from which the gut has been removed to assess freshness. The discoloration of fins is also a bad sign for which you should be on the alert. The flesh of the turbot and halibut should strain at the skin, for in all cases shrinking of the flesh and consequent flabbiness of skin denote stale fish. In trout and whiting look at the brightness of the eyes and the sheen of the skin. Skate is the only fish in this list that tastes no worse after three or four days on the slab; but the colour should still be white.

Armed with this information, go to a fishmonger and buy what seems good value rather than deciding on a certain fish and purchasing it regardless.

COOKING FISH

To generalize: if it's oily, grill it; if it's dry, boil it; if you can't stand the smell, fry it.

Boiling

Fish should never actually be boiled. Ideally, it should be simmered in a court bouillon – the liquid should be brought to boiling point and left to shiver. In practice, even the water in which you have boiled the vegetables (but not cabbage) is better than the tap variety, although nothing is quite as good as a properly made

Court bouillon

> 2 carrots, chopped
> stalk of celery, cut up
> medium onion stuck with cloves
> (or, these ingredients, minus cloves, sliced and fried lightly in oil)
> 2 bayleaves
> 1 teaspoon of salt
> half a coffeespoon coarsely ground black peppercorns
> 1½ lb. fish trimmings
> 1 pint water
> 1 pint dry white wine

Put all these ingredients in a pan or fish kettle and boil for 30 minutes, then strain. It will keep in a cool place for a day or two. The nearer you can get to the classic court bouillon, the better your fish will be. But water with some sliced onion and a dash of tarragon vinegar is a great improvement on just water.

The duller the fish, the better the stock should be. Stock reduced by boiling can be incorporated in fish sauces. For instance: take 2 egg yolks, 2 tablespoons reduced fish stock, lemon and seasoning. Whisk this in a basin over a pan of boiling water and add, ½ oz. at a time, 6 oz. of butter or margarine, using the fat to cool the mixture as it thickens. When the sauce is the consistency of thick cream, stop whisking and pour it extravagantly over the meanest cod fillet to make it fit for a property tycoon. It can also be used, with a good dash of added vinegar, to prepare soused mackerel or herring.

Poaching

Butter a fireproof dish; put in the fish, season it and cover with equal quantities of milk and water. Top with buttered paper and cook in a medium oven.

Grilling

Brush with fat, season and cook under or over a preheated grill. Cook slowly, turning up the heat at the end if you want the fish coloured.

Steaming

Season the fish; place on buttered paper to facilitate the lifting out, and put into the steamer. Alternatively, make your own steamer. Put the fish on a buttered plate. Place plate on an empty pudding basin, which you stand in a large pan of boiling water that comes halfway up the side of the basin. Cover the pan and refill with more boiling water as the water boils away.

Baking

As a process, this is much the same as poaching but for the fact that you bake fish with the herbs, vegetables and liquid which will fashion the sauce and the accompanying garnish. If you have both a large fish kettle and aluminium foil, bake those that are bright of eye and firm to the touch – what's called in their first flush of death. Pour oil on the foil, rub the fish with salt and pepper and put into it a sprig of rosemary or other herb; raise the edges of the foil, anoint the fish with a little dry white wine, and fold the foil to make a loose parcel – which can be put straight on to the oven shelf. This will need about 13 minutes to the pound on mark 4 (350°F). The fish will keep hot in the foil until you are ready for it; and the longer it remains in such liquor as came forth in the oven, the better will be the taste. Put the fish on a handsome dish, skinned if you don't like skin. Pour the juices into a parsley sauce (page 47), heat and serve. If you want cold fish, leave the fish in the foil for the required time, then unwrap, skin, and serve with watercress mayonnaise (page 48).

Frying

The fish is dusted with seasoned flour, brushed all over with beaten egg and then fried in toasted breadcrumbs, which are patted down. Alternatively, dust it with seasoned flour and dip it in a batter, remembering to smooth off the excess before frying.

Batter

> *3 oz. self-raising flour*
> *¼ pint milk – or Guinness, which makes excellent batter*
> *salt and white pepper.*

Fish that is crumbled or battered can be cooked in a deep fat pan, or in a shallow frying pan in oil and butter or pure clarified butter (page 17). If the smell of frying fish worries you, use the oven. Put a roasting tray of fat in the top of a mark 8 (450°F) oven and do your frying behind the oven door.

I even have a certain respect for fish fingers, and consider frozen fillets of breaded plaice a convenience food with a distinct edge over blotting paper similarly prepared. But real fish is better. And the laws of gastronomy state that the bigger the fish, the better the taste – which is fair if you discount the odd giant whale who died of old age. But the important thing is to keep the fish whole. Remove the head and tail; scrape off the scales; take out the guts if the fishmonger failed to do so; and then decide how to cook it.

Timing fish

The majority of fish served in this country is overcooked. While this may be the lesser of two evils it is still very far from ideal. Cooking time depends on the thickness of the fish and, naturally, the process of cooking. You will have to experiment and remember. As a guide: an 8 oz. fillet of plaice can be deep fried in 5 minutes, shallow fried in 8 minutes (4 on each side); boiled in 5 minutes, and improves by being left for another 5 minutes in the court bouillon; steamed in 15 minutes; poached in 7 minutes; or baked in 20 to 25 minutes, depending upon the accompanying vegetables. Fish is cooked when you can move the centre bone without tearing the flesh. In the case of fillets, pierce the thickest part with a needle and it should come out clean.

SOME SAUCES FOR FISH

Parsley sauce

is not a white sauce enriched with a carefully measured spoon of parsley flakes. What you do is to pick the blooms from the parsley stalks, crush the stalks in a mortar, pour a coffeecupful of boiling water into the mortar and incorporate the resultant green liquor in a sauce fashioned of butter, milk, cream and flour. Freshly chopped parsley is added 2 or 3 minutes before serving.

Watercress mayonnaise

If you chop finely a handful of watercress, put it into a bowl with 2 egg yolks, a speck of English mustard, salt, pepper and a teaspoon each of lemon juice and wine vinegar you need do no more than mix this well and trickle in ½ pint of salad oil as you whisk to obtain an impeccable watercress mayonnaise.

Cucumber sauce

Ask your fishmonger for some turbot bones and boil these with sliced onion and lemon thyme for 20 minutes or so. To ½ pint of strained stock add 2 oz. of butter and 2 oz. of flour whisked into ¼ pint of single cream.

Let this sauce cook for a few minutes, whisking the while; if it should get lumpy pass it through a sieve. This fish béchamel will keep for a day or two. When required, dice half a cucumber, simmer it in butter and after a few minutes add the cubes of cucumber to the sauce, which you will have reheated gently, will you not?

Cucumber-and-champagne sauce

1 cucumber
2½ oz. butter
1 tablespoon plain flour
2 egg yolks
¼ bottle champagne
¼ pint double cream
1 dessertspoon chopped chives

Peel the cucumber and grate it on the half moons of your

grater; add salt and press out a little of the excess water. Melt butter, add cucumber mush and a pinch of cayenne pepper and simmer with lid on for 3 to 4 minutes. Add flour, and cook, but don't brown; remove pan from flame, add champagne and bring gently to the boil, stirring it as you do so. Boil gently for 5 minutes.

Now beat egg yolks into cream and add to the sauce; reheat, but make sure it does not boil again. Just before serving, add the chives. This is especially good with salmon.

Bonne femme

½ pint court bouillon (or a similar quantity of fish stock
  with a dash of wine)
1 oz. butter
1 oz. plain flour
2 oz. button mushrooms
1 oz. butter
⅛ pint double cream

Reduce the court bouillon or fish stock by about one-third, and thicken it with flour and butter kneaded into a paste and dissolved in the reduced liquid. Slice mushrooms and cook them in a closed pan with 1 oz. of butter, salt and pepper. After 2 or 3 minutes, add mushrooms to sauce; add cream and cook to the consistency you care for.

Anchovy sauce

Make a rich white sauce using:
¼ pint milk
¼ pint fish stock
2 oz. butter
1½ oz. plain flour

Add to this eight tinned anchovy fillets passed through a sieve and some of the oil from the tin. Boil gently for a few minutes.

Italian sauce

1 oz. butter
2 tablespoons oil
1 tablespoon each:
  chopped onion
  chopped peeled tomato
  chopped sweet pepper (fresh or tinned)
  chopped lean ham or bacon
a little crushed garlic
1½ oz. plain flour
1 glass white wine
½ pint fish stock
fresh chopped parsley for garnish

Let onion and sweet pepper cook in butter and oil mixture until soft, add garlic, tomato and ham, and let this simmer for a few minutes before adding flour. When the flour is cooked but not too brown, remove from flame, add wine and fish stock, and let it simmer on a low flame for 20 minutes, or more.

Hollandaise sauce

1 egg yolk
2 oz. butter
a few drops lemon juice
salt and white pepper

Put egg yolk, salt, pepper and lemon juice into a pudding basin and suspend this over a pan of boiling water. Whisk well and drip in hot clarified butter (page 17), beating it into the sauce well.

A hollandaise will keep in a warm place for an hour or two; if it should get too hot, and separate, simply spoon the curdled sauce into a clean basin containing a spoonful of cream, whisking the new sauce as you do so.

Tartare sauce

2 egg yolks
1 coffeespoon French mustard
1 teaspoon each:
 chopped chives (or parsley)
 chopped capers
 chopped or grated onion
juice of half a lemon
1 dessertspoon wine vinegar
8 oz. oil

Beat egg yolks and other non-oily ingredients into a paste, then drip in oil while you whisk and the sauce thickens.

Shrimp sauce

2 oz. shrimps or prawns (fresh, frozen or tinned)
3 dessertspoons flour
1 dessertspoon paprika
1½ oz. butter
1 oz. grated onion
1 level tablespoon tomato purée
1 liqueur glass brandy
½ pint fish stock
salt, ground pepper

Melt the butter in a pan, add the grated onion and sizzle. Dust the shrimps in flour and paprika, put them into the pan and cook for 3 minutes over a low flame, with the lid on, stirring from time to time. Add the brandy, light it, and then remove the pan from the flame; put in the fish stock, tomato purée, salt and pepper. Put the pan back on flame, stir until it comes to the boil and simmer gently for a few minutes. For celebrations add a whosh of double cream.

WHITING

An all-the-year-round fish, probably best from November to March, though the flesh is so tasteless it is hard to tell between good and indifferent whiting. Its utter fatlessness made it a favourite fish to give to invalids, and it used to be a popular breakfast fish served *en colère* – angry – with its tail between its teeth, but few fishmongers these days seem able to curl a whiting. Its price and its popularity as a fish for cats have done little to make it irresistible. Boil it to eat with anchovy sauce (page 49), or fry it with no sauce.

HERRING

Another all-year fish, best from June to December. One of the most nutritious, and probably the cheapest fish to come out of the sea. The only real disadvantage of a herring is the many small bones. If care is taken and the fish is not overcooked, nearly all of them will come away with the central bone. Grill it.

Soused fillet of herring

Take equal parts of dry cider, water and distilled vinegar; boil this to reduce the quantity by one-third. Add onion rings, peppercorns, a chilli pepper and bayleaf, boil for 3 minutes and pour immediately onto herring fillets. Arrange in a single layer on a fireproof dish. When cold serve with fresh brown bread and butter. If you care for that sort of thing you can add a little powdered gelatine to the marinade.

Herring à la lorraine

Clean the herrings; flour them and brown them lightly in butter. Season with garlic salt and white pepper, and when they are cooked, add a squeeze of lemon and a tablespoon of double cream for each fish. Serve the fish on a bed of fine brown breadcrumbs.

HALIBUT

This is the largest flat fish found in the Atlantic. Usually a little cheaper than turbot, its natural taste is less desirable, though a considerable improvement on cod. It is the ideal fish for exotic salads. Steam it to eat with anchovy sauce; eat it poached with Italian sauce; grilled with anchovy sauce; or steamed with shrimp sauce (page 51).

Greek fish salad

The halibut is simmered in good court bouillon until cooked and then allowed to cool in the liquor. Remove ½ pint of court bouillon, reduce it by a half and flavour it with lemon juice and olive oil. Pour this over the flakes of

halibut in a salad bowl and decorate with shrimps, onion rings and watercress.

TURBOT

A large European flatfish, best from March to August. It is distinguishable from halibut by its dark skin. The flesh is excellent, and it is an ideal fish to steam and serve with lobster, mussel or shrimp sauce; or, as with halibut, steamed or grilled with anchovy sauce, or poached with Italian (page 50).

Baked turbot

Wrap pieces of turbot in buttered foil, bake them in a low oven until cooked – a 6 oz. piece will take 25 minutes in a mark 4 (350°F) oven – serve with maître d'hôtel butter: butter blended with chopped chives and lemon juice. For special occasions make a sauce using per person a dessert-spoon of peeled prawns simmered in a tablespoon of cream, a tablespoon of sweet wine and a dash of Tabasco. This can be kept hot in a double boiler.

Turbot cooked in cream

Butter a flat tin, put 1½ lb. of turbot into it and anoint it with the juice of half a lemon, some salt and white pepper and ½ pint of double cream. Stand the tin in a roasting tray of water and let it bake slowly in a medium oven, basting it every 5 minutes or so. When it is cooked serve with the cream liquor poured over it and with mashed potatoes.

ROCKEEL

This is also called variously huss, dogfish, rockfish or rock salmon. He is ugly of face and shaped like an eel. His edible bones and delicate flavour are too often hidden in soggy batter anointed with an overflow of fish and chippery vinegar. Provided the rock salmon you get is rockeel, he is a delicious fish, one of the best to serve cold, as an hors d'oeuvre, and particularly well suited to salads. Available throughout the year, eat him boiled with tartare sauce, poached with Italian, or fried and left to cool.

Rockeel ramekins

Poach ½ lb. of rockeel in good court bouillon; remove flesh from bones and incorporate this in a thick mayonnaise garnished with capers and slices of small gherkin. Dissolve a packet of gelatine in a very small quantity of water and add this to the fish mayonnaise. Mix well and set the mixture in individual dishes. Turn out when cold. Garnish with chopped chives and paprika.

REAL EEL

As must have been said before, if eels only looked a little less like eels, more people would eat them. King John, as many readers will recall, died of a surfeit of lampreys . . . and while a surfeit was clearly excessive, and the consequences suitably dire, a sufficiency of lampreys can be a most excellent thing. Lampreys were small eels and as whatever went for one goes for the other, let us continue by using the name eels. An eel has long been considered very low-class fare. This is nothing to do with the delicacy of the flavour, the elegance of its design or the amazing depth of its birthplace (all eels are spawned in the Sargasso Sea). The fact is that small delicious pieces of eel (such as are jellied and available on good racecourses and from barrows in some parts of London) contain in their centre a spiky bone about which you can do nothing much but suck the flesh from its exterior and expectorate.

Mayfair hostesses reluctant to coexist with carpets

decorated with spat-out eel bones were probably the first to demote the fish from its former Royal position . . . but over the years the word 'eel' has evoked back streets in Lancashire, barrows in the East End of London, and serious men surrounded by equally serious spitters at Brighton, Yarmouth, Redcar and wherever else in England thoroughbred racehorses run for the greater glory of the punters' indigestion. If only CAEKS (the Council for the Appreciation of Eels and Kindred Serpents) could achieve the introduction of jellied eels into the more civilized enclosures of English racecourses, it would be a considerable feather in their caps. You cannot imagine the trouble I have had getting commissionaires to believe that my reason for going from the 'members' into the silver ring was a sudden yearning for a basin of Josh Isaacs' best, with a shot of chilli vinegar on top. This is unfair, especially unfair as smoked eel is considered a delicacy. I know of no other food that manifests so wide a range of social acceptance between its raw and its cured stage.

A quick word about availability. Eels are available; costers have them and barrowboys; fishmongers tell you they do not have them because there is no demand; so, ask for them and create a demand; there are plenty of eels in the sea and a fair quantity of eels in fishmarkets. If you are squeamish it would be as well to get a middleman to see to the actual slaughter, cleaning and cutting up into 1½-inch lengths, because it is an eel-family trait that they go on slithering around long after they are dead, which has caused the odd twitty lady to banish them from her house.

I am fond of jellied eels but my favourite mode of preparation is to stew them and serve them with parsley sauce.

Stewed eel

Prepare a court bouillon by boiling together a quart of water with a wineglass of dry white wine, a tablespoon of tarragon vinegar, half an onion spiked with cloves and a few bayleaves. Remove onion and bayleaves after 30 minutes' boiling, and introduce the pieces of eel – say 1 lb. – which should see to four people. Let the pieces simmer for about 20 minutes.

Take ¾ pint of this stock and ¼ pint of single cream; add 2 oz. of butter into which you have rubbed 1 oz. of flour . . . and let this thicken while you whisk.

Fish the pieces of eel from the broth, slip them (or in the unlikely event that they are still showing signs of life, let them slither) into the sauce and garnish this with freshly chopped parsley.

There are recipes that call for eels with red wine: stews and *matelotes* and *salmis*. I am not at all in favour of this marriage. And yet I did once have eels wrapped in vine leaves, and roasted over an open charcoal range. They were absolutely delicious – and as I was a guest I drank the wine served by my hostess which was red. It was what the old Wine and Food Society Magazines used to call 'a memorable meal' though I cannot but think of fish and claret as an unnatural alliance. I suppose, as my daughter put it, 'life is whatever grabs you'. I suggest you grab an eel . . . and to be on the safe side, grab tightly, holding it with your index and third finger below the brute, second (or long) finger above it, else he will get away.

PLAICE

Gastronomically speaking, plaice is probably the most interesting flatfish. It is in season from May until January. Larger plaice should be filleted and grilled, or deep fried, and the smaller ones grilled whole, for this fish is always better on the bone. Watch for the orange spots and the very white underside. Poach fillets of plaice and eat them with

Italian sauce; or steam them to go with anchovy sauce; fried, they are delicious with hollandaise (page 50).

Plaice meunière
Fillets of plaice dusted with well-seasoned flour and fried in butter to which, as it begins to turn golden brown, is added a squeeze of lemon juice. This dish should be garnished with chopped parsley.

MACKEREL

An all-year fish, best in April, May and June. It must be fresh. Beware the limp mackerel which is usually bad and can be poisonous. Watch for bright, protruding eyes and bright red gills, which denote freshness. Because of the oil in them mackerel are best grilled; or smoked.

Soused mackerel   (page 20)

Mackerel with gooseberries
It is essential to have very fresh mackerel. Clean them and poach for 15 minutes in salt water that is almost boiling; drain well and serve with a sauce made of equal parts béchamel and sieved gooseberries.

COD

Cod are all-year fish, but best from October to February. They can be used for all general recipes. Steam and eat it with a bonne femme sauce, have it baked with Italian sauce (page 50), or fry it.

Cod custard
Lay 1 lb. of flaky codfish in a baking dish. Beat 3 eggs and add ¾ pint of milk and a half teaspoon of celery salt. Pour

this over the codflakes and bake in a low, mark 2 (300°F) oven for 45 minutes.

COLEY

There is nothing wrong with coley, except that its black skin looks faintly unappetizing. It is insipid when boiled or poached, but is good fried, although it needs rather more vinegar than other fish.

HADDOCK

This northern Atlantic fish is best from September to February. It's an exceedingly useful all-purpose fish and most excellent in quenelles – pounded and mixed with cream and egg yolks and poached in white wine. Also eat it baked with Italian sauce or steamed with hollandaise (page 50).

Creamed haddock au gratin

Make ½ pint of good white sauce and cook this slowly to reduce it by about half, stirring constantly. Then add ¼ pint of double cream, and add the sauce to the flakes of poached haddock. Put this mixture into a baking dish and pile on top ¼ pint of white sauce into which you have whisked 1 whole egg, 2 tablespoons of grated parmesan cheese and another of whipped cream. Sprinkle with fresh breadcrumbs and paprika, dot with butter and bake for 5 minutes in the top of a hot oven.

Omelette Arnold Bennett

(4 small portions: for a main dish, double the quantities.)
4 oz. cooked smoked haddock
2 oz. butter
6 tablespoons double cream

4 eggs (separated)

2 oz. grated cheddar cheese

Heat 1 oz. butter and 2 tablespoons cream in a pan and put into it the flakes of haddock. Let this cool. Beat the 4 egg yolks, season with ground black pepper, add half the grated cheese and mix with the fish. Whip up the egg whites and fold them into the mixture.

Make an omelette pan very hot, put in 1 oz. of butter and as soon as it has melted add the omelette mixture. Move the mixture about as it cooks and when the base is set slide it onto a heatproof dish. Sprinkle with the remaining cheese mixed into the rest of the cream and brown under a hot grill.

SKATE

This is a coarse October to January fish, excellent for children as it has edible bones. It is very much an all-purpose fish but finds its place in the classical haute cuisine through black butter. Otherwise, poach it or fry it.

Skate with black butter

Cook wings of skate in a court bouillon; place them on a serving dish and keep them hot. In a pan brown some butter until almost but not quite black, remove it from the flame and add to it a tablespoon of good wine vinegar. Mind your clothes as it splutters. Pour this black butter over the fish and decorate with whole or chopped capers and chopped parsley.

SOLE

Fish at its finest. Dover sole is the name given by retailers to the real sole, to distinguish it from inferior flatfish which they call lemon sole, Torbay sole or something similar, in search of a little ill-deserved glamour. The flesh of real sole remains firm, fragrant and resilient, which makes it the ideal fish for banquets or unpunctual guests, as it does not depend on split-second timing. It also means that the asking price is high.

The difference between *haute cuisine* treatment and *basse cuisine* is probably greater with fish than with any other food. There is, for example, no quick, cheap substitute for a classic court bouillon in which you poach the fish. You can, for this, use cider instead of wine; or you can use one part vinegar, one part wine and four parts water. But the results will be cheap and only fairly satisfactory. What is important, however you make your court bouillon, is that the fish should spend the maximum time in it, consistent with not overcooking, and that the court bouillon should be well cooked and fragrant before you put the fish in. It is infinitely better to simmer a large fish for 5 minutes and let it cool gently in the liquid for an hour than to give it '25 minutes in a pan of shivering water drawn to the side of the fire', as is so frequently advocated. Good fish stock, an essential base for fish sauces and soups, should come from the slow infusion of the flesh, bones and skin of fresh white fish in simmering water, skimmed occasionally. Stock made of job lots, such as are swindled from fishmongers by means of the open sesame 'fish for the cat', is entirely unsatisfactory. It is a far, far better thing to use a fresh whiting than to try to squeeze goodness out of the entrails and trimmings of a tired Dover sole.

For the cook/hostess as for the caterer, a Dover sole is a godsend. At its simplest grill it or fry it whole. Poach the fillets to eat with hollandaise sauce, or eat them fried with sauce tartare. But for something a bit more special, try

Filets de sole veronique   (for 4)

two 1 lb. Dover soles
some peeled, halved, stoned, white grapes
¼ bottle dry white wine
2 oz. chopped onion
1 bouquet garni (bayleaf, thyme, parsley stalks)

Ask for the soles to be filleted, and take home the trimmings. Boil these in a pint of water with salt, pepper and chopped onion to make ½ pint of fish stock. Butter an oven dish, put the fillets in it. Season and cover them with equal parts of stock and white wine, adding the bouquet garni and covering the fillets with buttered paper. Bake in a mark 4 (350°F) oven until just cooked – about 15 minutes.

Take out the fillets, and put the liquid in a pan, add the rest of the wine and a walnut of *beurre manié* (equal parts of flour and butter mixed) and boil until the sauce thickens. Then add the halved grapes.

The fillets can be cooked and the sauce made an hour or two before the dinner. Bake the fillets for 7 or 8 minutes, drain, and replace the liquor with a little warm milk. Reheat the fillets in the milk, in the oven; pour on the sauce and colour the dish for a few seconds under the grill.

Quenelles de sole dijonnaises

For the quenelles: the mixture may be made at any time and kept on ice. The fish stock, equally, can be made on the morning of the party. The garnish alone must be made at the last moment but the sauce is of such quality and richness you may feel that it needs no help.

1 lb. fillets of Dover sole
3 egg whites
⅓ pint double cream
salt and ground white pepper

Pass the fillets of sole twice through a mincer, put them in a bowl perched over another bowl filled with chipped ice, and slowly add the egg whites, stirring each into the minced fish before adding the next. Season with salt and white pepper.

Let this mixture rest on ice for half an hour or so.

To make satisfactory quenelles it is absolutely essential to pass some of this mixture through a sieve, or all of it through a mouli. A liquidizer won't do. Get a large sieve, press through a minimum of one-third of the quantity, using a wooden spoon or mushroom, and then add the contents of the sieve to the purée that has been passed through it. Shape the quenelles with two teaspoons or dessertspoons and poach them in fish stock for 5 minutes.

For the fish stock: use the trimmings of the soles that have provided the fillets.
> *½ onion, sliced*
> *1 carrot, sliced*
> *bouquet garni*
> *1 pint water*
> *salt and pepper*

Put all the ingredients into a pan. Bring to the boil and simmer for 20 minutes. Strain the stock.

For the sauce:
> *¼ pint fish stock*
> *¼ pint medium white wine –*
> *or dry white wine plus a spoonful of sweet sherry*
> *¼ pint cream*
> *2 oz. butter*
> *1½ oz. flour*

Boil together the fish stock and wine until the quantity is reduced by about a third. Rub the flour into the butter and stir it into the stock. Add the cream. Let this sauce simmer for a few minutes. Dilute with fish stock if it gets too thick.

For the garnish:
  some strips of filleted Dover sole, say 3 oz.
  3 oz. button mushrooms
  2 oz. peeled prawns
  2 oz. butter
  1 tablespoon oil

Melt the butter and oil in a pan, and fry in these the strips of sole rolled in seasoned flour, the mushrooms, quartered, and finally the prawns.

Poach the quenelles, drain them, place them on a warmed serving dish and cover them generously with sauce. Use the garnish if you so desire.

This dish can equally well be made with *pike*, a fish that is easier to pass through a sieve, though the bones give a less pleasing stock.

TROUT

Broadly speaking, the name trout includes all the small members of the salmon family who live it up between the river and the sea. A trout's popular size has made it an ideal banquet fish and the price is consequently high. Rainbow trout, probably the most popular, contain a certain amount of oil and, like herring and mackerel, can be grilled without being brushed with butter. They are also delicious baked and served with Italian sauce; or done with almonds.

Trout with almonds

Clean the trout, remove the head and tail, dip them in milk, then dry them in seasoned flour. Fry them in a mixture of oil and butter until they go golden brown on both sides (tug at the protruding bone to determine how easily it comes away from the fish to tell you when it's cooked), then place them on a warm dish. Chop some blanched

almonds and cook them in the fat from which you have taken the trout, adding a little more butter. Add lemon juice and finely chopped parsley and pour the sauce over the trout.

I am much surprised at the growing popularity of trout tanks in restaurants. Recently in the Midlands I was asked if I cared for trout – and when I nodded, the waiter waved his arm towards a dank pool of slithy pescs wallowing in water that I would not care to have had my daughters swim in. 'He looks nice,' said the manager, who had crept up behind me . . . and we stood, the two of us, looking into the moronic eye of a fat brown fish.

Perhaps the most attractive thing about cannibalism was that by the very nature of the exercise the consumer had ample opportunities for becoming closely acquainted with his dinner. This made for an extra dimension in gastronomic enjoyment . . . an approach that is now much discouraged. But the bull point, the very motivation of cannibalism, was the belief that you took on the qualities of those you ate, and in view of our friend's unprepossessing countenance I asked for black pudding and mashed potatoes instead. I suppose it is cowardly and ostrich-like, but even those of us who call vegetarians cissies prefer not to be reminded of the living element of our meal. I am convinced that if an eating house showed pictures of frolicking lambs to each prospective consumer of a best end, it would be mushroom omelettes all round.

To return to the trout tank . . . trout, unlike mackerel, taste every bit as nice the day after they are caught. I will eat trout pulled from a stream, tickled in a lake, stolen from an aquarium or purchased, headless if need be, from the fishmonger's slab.

In view of the fact that trout is considered a restaurant fish, the 8–10 oz. single portion size will always be more expensive than the less fashionable smaller or larger fish; these, then, are better value.

Baked trout

If you should come across small trout, bake them and serve them as a cold starter. Remove the head and tail-fin and wipe the fish well, inside and out. Put into a fireproof dish with some chopped peeled tomatoes, small onions cut into rings, a bayleaf, a dozen juniper berries, and 3 tablespoons of olive oil; add a wineglass of dry white wine boiled together with a tablespoon of wine vinegar until it has reduced in volume by about a quarter. Add salt and pepper, cover with greased foil and bake in a mark 3 (325°F) oven for 30 minutes; then turn off the oven and let them cool in the liquor . . . in which you serve them, accompanied by lavishly buttered wholemeal bread.

SALMON

The time is past when discriminatory bodies can urge the masses to boil black lobsters in order to turn them a more acceptable shade of red. Salmon is pink, and Pacific frozen salmon is equally pink and costs about half the price of its eclectic Scottish cousin, or its relatives who are pulled from the Wye in late January; it is none-the-less excellent. A lovingly simmered quick-frozen fish, headless, gutless and hoiked out of the ocean a year ago, can be made succulent and infinitely desirable. I have partaken of the more expensive variety, shot or whatever by a belted earl, and it was boiled until it was fit only to be forked into grains of glutinous rice. I speak truth; good natural ingredients can be ruined by a poor cook. Proper care bestowed upon less immediately appealing food can produce dishes out of all proportion to their cost. Frozen salmon then . . . Thaw the fish gently, like overnight in a cool place, and never use the wine butlers' trick of plunging a cold body into a hot basin.

When the fish, or piece of fish if your trust in me is only limited, is restored to pliability, you have two choices. Ideally, if you possess or can borrow a pan or kettle of a size to fit snugly around the fish, poach it.

Poached salmon

Prepare a broth, flavoured with wine vinegar and crushed peppercorns. Boil in it some onion rings, shredded carrot, a pair of bayleaves, and two dozen dill seeds tied in a muslin bag, and let it have an hour on a medium flame, so that it becomes properly aromatic, for broth must boil; fish must never do more than just 'draw'.

Now turn off the flame and when the contents are no warmer than a cup of railway tea when the cleaners get round to cleaning the empties, introduce the salmon.

Bring the pan very slowly to boiling point, let it hover for 10 minutes and then remove from the flame so that the broth can cool around the fish. It will now be perfectly cooked and when cold the fish can be easily skinned and the fillets eased from the bone and rewarmed in the fish stock when required. Or, if you intend to eat it hot, leave it in the liquid for about half an hour.

The reason for this no-cooking-time phenomenon is that if you have a 9 lb. beast the warming-up/cooling-off time of a gigantic fish kettle is about eighteen times longer than that involved in heating/cooling a 6-inch pan containing a ½ lb. salmon steak. To put it another way, if you use the method to cook a sprat in a bathtub, success will elude you.

Baked salmon

The alternative to poaching is a slow bake in an aluminium jacket. Brush the foil with oil and in a saucepan boil together a pint of ingredients, similar to those used in the fish stock. When the amount of liquor is reduced to half its volume, place the fish on the oiled foil, fold up the edges and pour the broth over the fish. Completely enclose the salmon in foil, place it on a baking tray, provide a few discreet holes through which the steam can escape and bake in a mark 4 (350°F) oven for about two hours if you have a whole fish. Eat poached or baked salmon with cucumber, or cucumber and champagne sauce (page 48).

Salmon steaks

Place salmon steaks on a sheet of buttered foil, add salt and pepper, brush fish with melted butter, sprinkle with a dry white wine, cover with more foil and bake in a medium oven for 20–30 minutes. This will give you time to make a very beautiful mousseline sauce: 3 egg yolks and a teaspoon of lemon juice blended in a basin engaged over a pan of boiling water. Add 6 oz. melted butter, a spoonful at a time, whisking as the sauce thickens, then add to it ¼ pint lightly beaten double cream and juices from the foil.

Salmon croquettes

To 1 lb. of flaked boiled salmon add 3 oz. soft white bread-crumbs, 2 beaten eggs, salt and white pepper. (Black pepper looks ugly in light-coloured food.) Mix well, shape the mixture into rounds or ovals about 1 inch thick, dust with seasoned flour and fry in shallow fat for 5 minutes on each side. Serve with cubes of cucumber dusted in flour and fried in the same fat and decorate the dish with slivers of toast spread with anchovy butter: 2 oz. butter, 2 anchovy fillets passed through a sieve; blend.

LOBSTER

A book rather ambiguously entitled *All About Cookery* published in 1961 by the late Mrs Beeton (deceased 1865) gives one absolute gem of information, which might well have been inspired by the council for clean food. Writing of shellfish, she states: 'Choose a crab, around which there are no flies. Flies will always go for the bad crabs, especially around the mouth. They ignore the fresh ones.'

Armed with a matchbox full of flies then, you must go into the lobster-shops and let loose your hordes. Clearly this is a more tactful way of choosing fish than raising it to your nose, as well as being a useful deployment of insects which were previously thought to have only nuisance value. Moreover it is a powerful argument for the reduction of the asking price. Victorian actors used never to go touring without carrying a bedbug in a matchbox which was brought down to the landlady of theatrical digs on the last morning to enforce a lowering of the bill. If you cannot marshal enough flies to do your dirty work for you, choose a lobster that is alive, or, if the fishmonger has precooked all his stock, one that is heavy for its size.

Don't be cruel, people will tell you . . . don't plunge a live lobster into boiling water; I mean, how would you like it if someone plunged your daughter into boiling water? (There, that's made you think.) I think it's high time it was realized that for those of us who care deeply about the finer feelings of crustaceans there is the simple alternative of a mushroom omelette. For the rest, the don't cares – and I have this on the most excellent authority – the lobster who has been kept alive for four hours in a lobster pot, three more in a fisherman's wooden box, half a day in a goods truck on the way to Paddington, and then spent anything up to another twelve hours shadow boxing with tied claws in the back of a fishshop, yearns for a quick death; the greater the speed with which he is cooked and eaten, the happier he is; honestly. And yet, however little one cares for cruelty to animals, to plunge a live lobster into boiling water is an unnecessary refinement, rather like going to bed in an electric chair when you could use an electric blanket. Put the animals into lukewarm water and heat this; the gradual increase in temperature is said to cause the lobster a pleasantly comfortable demise.

You begin by simmering them in a court bouillon, half water, half dry cider, with sliced shallots, bayleaf and peppercorns swimming attendance. Give about 15 minutes to the pound – a little less if they are very large – twist off the tail and the claws for another occasion, and pound all the coral and other non-white flesh as well as you can in a mortar – or simply put it in a good strong cloth and bash it a few times against an outside wall: this is for the soup.

To make any lobster dish without using the liquor is a fearful waste. To the pounded flesh you could add grated onion and a good spoonful of tomato purée, salt and pepper, then simmer all this in butter. After some minutes with the lid on, add flour and make a roux. Fill this up with the stock in which the lobster was cooked, and reduce it by boiling until it is as strong as you want. (If you add gelatine, this makes a splendidly original setting for a soft poached egg.)

Or you could simmer all the legs, and the carcasses with their interesting contents, in a saucepan in half oil/half butter, well seasoned and with a pinch of saffron. Add a grated onion, let it brown slightly and sprinkle with as much plain flour as will take up the liquid. When the flour is cooked, make up with the stock, stirring until it comes to the boil. Let it simmer and then reduce until it has reached the lobstery strength that pleases you. Strain the bisque into bowls containing at least 2 tablespoons of cream, then warm and light some domestic brandy and spoon a measure of the flaming spirit to float on each bowl. This glows handsomely as it burns on the thick red bisque.

Having satiated your immediate crustacean needs with this nectar, you can now spend your time browsing amongst the cookery books to find the best deployment of the lobster meat. Try as you might with butter and cream, truffles, mushrooms and chilli peppers, it is hard to better the thinly sliced white flesh piled on to a bed of corn salad, covered with a mayonnaise of your own making and decorated with fillets of anchovy, whole capers and halves of hard-boiled eggs, yolks removed, mixed with cream and chives and piped back into place. Just that, fresh whole-meal bread spread thick with Normandy butter and a bucket or two of a suitable wine.

Lobster croquettes

*8 oz. lobster meat or (taking a leaf out of the book of my
    least favourite restaurateur) 8 oz. tinned crab meat*
1½ oz. butter

3 oz. button mushrooms
½ oz. grated onion
¼ pint cream
1 egg yolk
salt
paprika
seasoned flour, beaten egg, toasted breadcrumbs for coating

Melt the butter; sizzle therein the grated onion and add button mushrooms, thinly sliced. Then add lobster (or crab) meat, well drained. Blend and cook it with the lid on over a low flame for 5 minutes, stirring occasionally. Season well, add egg yolk beaten into cream and remove from flame. Let this mixture cool, set it in deep freeze or top of refrigerator and shape it into balls or barrel-shaped croquettes, coating these in seasoned flour, beaten egg and toasted breadcrumbs. When frying in breadcrumbs the fat should be a little cooler than for batter. In emergency, many cereals, notably Weetabix, make good instant breadcrumbs – use a rolling pin.

SCALLOPS

January is the best month for scallops – sometimes called scollops; the spelling is immaterial. What *is* important is that they should be freshly opened, so that their flesh is white and the coral tongue moistly orange. You may even be able to buy them closed, in which case they open under their own steam after a few minutes at the bottom of a cool oven.

Take the scallops from their shells and remove the black thread that encompasses the white flesh. There is no reason why you should not scrub the shells themselves and keep them as ashtrays. But I can think of no *good* reason for using the shells for the actual serving of molluscs: a scallop shell makes a rotten plate. If the dish is cooked properly the shell should be too hot to steady with your left hand while you fork away with your right. (There is, however, a case for serving frozen scallops or tinned crayfish under a sauce and on shells – possibly surrounded by mashed potatoes bound with egg yolk. One does this rather as one burns two coffee beans under the grill while instant coffee is served in the next room.)

The French name for scallops is coquilles St Jacques. The trouble is that if you air your French upon a waiter . . . ask him 'how are the coquilles St Jacques?' . . . you do not receive information about the well-being or otherwise of bivalve molluscs. You get the standard 'everything on the menu is very nice' sneer, and soon afterwards you receive a scallop shell ringed by mashed potato, containing under a crisp formalogical exterior some creamed crustacean. This is absolutely correct . . . because coquille St Jacques is not merely the name of the animal; it is the dish: scallops sliced and poached in a court bouillon, the liquor reduced, thickened with cream and flour rubbed into butter, garnished with parmesan cheese and grilled under the salamander. It is served in the shell decorated with the border of potato.

One of the reasons why I feel that the classic coquille St Jacques is unsuitable for the cook/hostess is that reheating a scallop shell with potato, filling, cheese topping and all, is liable to present major problems: making them *à la minute* would take the good lady from her guests for an unconscionable time. Preparation should be governed by the number of guests. If you are alone or have one guest with a small appetite, then anything goes.

Coquille St Jacques mornay (for 4)

8 scallops
2 oz. peeled prawns (optional)
¾ pint white sauce

1 oz. toasted breadcrumbs
2 oz. grated cheese
½ oz. butter

Poach the scallops in court bouillon and slice them. Make a smooth, rich, white sauce and add to it grated cheese and a little English mustard. Put in the sliced scallops, and, if you care for them, peeled shrimps or prawns.

Pour all this into an ovenproof dish, sprinkle with toasted breadcrumbs, dot with small pieces of butter and bake in a medium oven for 15 minutes; if the crumbs don't begin to colour use the grill momentarily.

You can surround the dish with duchesse potatoes – the classic accompaniment of this confection – but the only virtue of these mashed-potatoes-mixed-with-egg-yolk is that the mixture withstands intense heat. In taste it is inferior to old potatoes – steamed, passed through a sieve and blended with good butter. Add sufficient hot milk to attain the texture you prefer, and salt, pepper and nutmeg.

Scallops and parsley sauce (for 4)

6 scallops
chopped parsley
¼ pint single cream
1 tablespoon flour
1½ oz. butter
with mashed potatoes

Clean and poach scallops for 6 or 7 minutes in as little prepared court bouillon as will cover them (2 parts of water to 1 of white wine, a sprig of thyme, half a bayleaf, 1 stick celery, 1 shallot stuck with cloves, all simmered for 20 minutes). Strain off ½ pint of the liquid. Add to this cream into which flour has been smoothly whisked. Season and simmer the scallops in the sauce for 10 minutes or so, before adding chopped parsley 2 or 3 minutes before serving in soup plates.

Scallops in white wine and cream   (for 4)

Cut 8 scallops into 3 or 4 slices and simmer 12 minutes in
½ pint dry white wine with lid on. Remove pieces to a buttered oven dish and add to the fish stock ¼ pint double
cream and a level dessertspoon cornflour. Blend; put in ¼
lb. halved button mushrooms and bake in top of mark 4
(350°F) oven for 10–15 minutes.

Scallop meunière

Cut scallops into slices, dust with seasoned flour (1
rounded tablespoon flour to ½ teaspoon salt and three
turns of the white pepper mill), fry gently in half butter
half oil for 4–5 minutes. Turn up flame, give a last squeeze
of lemon, spoon scallops onto the plate, anoint with
butter and lemon, and garnish with chopped parsley.

If the solitary guzzler is impervious to the smell of the
deep fat pan, flour, eggwash and breadcrumb the halved
molluscs, fry them in deep fat and serve with an exquisite
tartare sauce.

Scallop pancakes   (for 4)

Beat together 3 rounded tablespoons flour, ½ pint of milk,
1 whole egg and 1 tablespoon melted butter, season well.
Add to this the chopped raw tongues of 4 scallops and
let the mixture stand while you cut the white domes of
scallop flesh into slices.

Put into a pan 1 glass water, 1 glass wine, 1 teaspoon
wine vinegar, 1 bayleaf and half a finely chopped onion.
Let this boil fiercely for 5 minutes and then turn down the
heat and simmer the sliced pieces of white meat in this
broth. Remove slices after 6 minutes, reduce the liquor in
which they were cooked by fierce boiling, thicken with
double cream and flour rubbed into butter and incorporate
the thick, smooth sauce (you can always use a sieve if there
are lumps) with the scallop meat. Keep in a covered oven

dish in a mark 3 (325°F) oven. Make 7-inch pancakes in a very hot 7-inch pan . . . and garnish each with a heaped spoonful of the mixture.

Fisherman's breakfast

Take 4 scallops, cut them into smallish pieces, dust them in flour and fry gently in butter for 5 minutes or until tender. You may taste one. Add to the pan 8 small new potatoes cut into similarly small pieces, 4 oz. of streaky bacon, grilled until pleasantly crisp and loosely crumbled. When all is sizzling add 6 whole eggs and a sherry glass of water whisked together with a fork. When the mixture at the base of the pan is set, shake the pan to make sure the omelette slides around, then put under a grill to set the top. Serve in slices.

Skewered scallops   (for 6)

Prepare skewers of scallop quarters, mushroom, bayleaf, bacon and onion segments. Sprinkle with black pepper and garnish with melted butter. Bake the skewers in an oven dish at mark 6 (400°F), brushing with the attendant juices every few minutes. The skewers should take about 20 minutes (longer if they are very tightly packed). Serve on a bed of rice.

MUSSELS

The reason why mussels are sometimes succulent morsels of delicate tenderness and on other occasions taste remarkably like an old boot has little to do with culinary skill. For mussels are either wild – and pounded to leathery toughness by the sea – or cultivated to plump tenderness on wooden hurdles in mussel beds. Larousse says you can tell the tender ones because the shell opposite the hinge is convex – the tough ones are concave here; but it really isn't as simple as that. However, since fishmongers are faithful to their suppliers and consequently sell either one kind or the other, all you have to do is simply buy and try a sample before you buy a gallon.

Mussels must be cooked live. When you get home, pick up the mussels in your hands, individually, and discard all those which are not tightly closed. The remainder you put into salt water in a cool, dark place, feeding them twice daily on small quantities of porridge oats until you decide to use them. They will be quite content on this, for a day or two; begin to smell regardless after that period, even if you change their diet to grape nuts. Before using them scrub the shells or scrape them if necessary and remove the protruding beards.

As mussels need only the minimum amount of cooking time – 10 minutes with the lid on is enough to open the shells – it is essential to use the proper liquor to cook them.

Mussel soup   (for 4)

1 large grated onion
1 bouquet garni
1 glass dry cider
1 pint water
1 quart mussels
1 sherry glass brandy
saffron, salt, black pepper
lemon juice
¼ pint cream
2 oz. butter
¼ pint milk
3 egg yolks
chopped parsley

Simmer the onion in butter, add bouquet garni, salt, pepper, cider and water. Bring this to the boil and leave it there for 10 minutes. Now add the mussels, and remove them from the shells when they open; keep them in the brandy in a soup tureen at the bottom of a cool oven.

To the stock now add a little saffron and a teaspoon of lemon juice; and when the saffron has turned the soup yellow, beat 3 egg yolks into the milk/cream mixture and whisk into the soup, stirring as it thickens over a low flame. Strain into the soup tureen and decorate with chopped parsley.

Moules frites Ostend

These are cooked mussels rolled in seasoned flour, dipped into an eggwash – made by beating an egg with a teaspoon of wine vinegar – and dried in toasted breadcrumbs. Then brown in half butter, half oil in frying pan (infinitely better than suspended in deep fat). Decorate with sprigs of deep-fried parsley and serve with tartare sauce.

Moules marinière

To make the best possible moules marinière, put 1 quart of well-scrubbed mussels into a saucepan containing 1 pint of dry cider, or a similar quantity of half dry white wine/half water. Season well with coarse salt, crushed black peppercorns, the juice of half a lemon and a finely chopped or grated shallot. Cover the pan, let it boil fiercely for 6 or 7 minutes when death will have relaxed the mussels' muscles and the shells await your pleasure, conveniently open. Now strain the liquor from the pan into another saucepan containing 1 oz. of plain flour whisked into ½ pint of milk to which you have added 3 oz. of butter and a generous handful of parsley. Let this come to the boil as you stir, simmer it for 10 minutes and pour the sauce generously on to soup-plates in which you have arranged the mussels on their half shells. The Italians, who call mussels marinière 'marinara', add 3 tablespoons of chopped tomatoes cooked with crushed garlic.

Classically the shells must make their appearance at the table (the poor quality of the bottled mussels makes this a guarantee of authenticity), but if you know your guests well they will greatly appreciate their complete removal and being left to eat decorously and in peace nothing but plump amber molluscs swimming lazily in a sauce fit for the most discriminating reader of independent weeklies.

It is extraordinarily difficult to recommend a drink other than white burgundy or Guinness to serve with moules marinière, though I know a man who accompanies it with long gulps of hot sweet cocoa . . . but then he takes long gulps of hot sweet cocoa with everything.

OTHER FISH DISHES

Red mullet

Make a few incisions in side of fish, brush with seasoned butter and grill, 5–6 minutes a side. Make a white sauce, add

Dijon mustard and a few fillets of anchovy passed through a sieve and pour into it butter remaining in grill pan.

Fish pie (for 4)

1½ lb. cod or fresh haddock fillets
6 oz. onions, sliced and simmered in butter
¾ lb. boiled potatoes
1 pint well-seasoned white sauce

Mix fish, potatoes and fried onions and blend with sauce. Turn into buttered oven dish, sprinkle with grated cheddar cheese and bake in a mark 5 (375°F) oven for upwards of 40 minutes. This is a humble but very worthy and comforting dish.

Kedgeree

4 oz. rice
1 lb. cooked fish
2 oz. grated onion
3 oz. butter
2 hard-boiled eggs
½ pint mustard sauce

(make as anchovy sauce, page 49, substituting a dessertspoon or less of made mustard for the anchovy fillets and adding salt)

Boil rice in salted water until tender; meanwhile, flake the fish, removing skin and bones, and toss it gently in the butter in which grated onions have been simmering for 5 minutes. Combine rice and fish in a preheated serving dish, fold in the hot mustard sauce and decorate with hard-boiled eggs passed through a sieve and sprigs of parsley.

Koulibiac

8 oz. puff pastry
5 oz. cooked patna rice
5 oz. flaked fish

Basically this is a dry kedgeree baked in puff pastry. Roll out some puff pastry into two rectangles, one ⅛ inch thick and the other a little thinner. On the thicker one spread the cooked rice, cooked as for paella (start rice in fat and then, adding 2 cups of stock to 1 cup of patna type rice, cook it with the lid on).

You can mix into the rice some fried onion, mushrooms, shrimps, chopped, hard-boiled eggs, and pounded anchovy fillets. Put small pats of butter on the rice and lay the flaked fish on top. Damp the edges of the puff pastry rectangles and lay the thinner on the thicker, joining the edges firmly.

Put this on a baking tray and keep in a warm place for half an hour so that the pastry begins to rise a little; then brush with cream or egg yolks; make a few incisions into the pastry and bake for 40 minutes in a mark 5½ (385°F) oven till golden.

Whitebait

Dip the whole fish in milk, dry in well-seasoned flour and fry in hot fat until brown. Drain well and serve with deep-fried parsley and half-lemons sewn in muslin to prevent the pips shooting across the table.

You might like to know something about the way catering establishments deal with the problem of preparing the same predictably flaccid flesh in different and compulsive forms.

A hotel kitchen, like an army brigade, is divided up into departments, like regiments. The veg. is like the Pioneer Corps; pastry akin to the Corps of Signals, hors d'oeuvres comparable to REME . . . until you finally get to the aristocratic sauce department which has the hardest, most important work and from whom the next commanding officer (or chef) is chosen. On a Monday morning – or every other day if the place is huge – the basic sauces are prepared . . . and there is no reason why a housewife catering for a fair number of weekly meals should not do likewise.

Sauce Portugaise

Oil and butter are heated, chopped onions and tomatoes added, then thyme, bayleaves, rosemary, and when all has simmered in a closed pan for 10 minutes or so, flour is added to take up the liquid. When the flour is cooked and begins to brown, take the pan from the flame, add meat stock a little at a time allowing each addition to come to the boil before adding more. Then reduce by boiling, season diligently and strain the result into a basin.

Sauce béchamel

is sometimes known as white sauce. They tell you to make it with a roux of butter and flour; I maintain that it is definitely better made by dissolving butter in milk – 2 oz. to 1 pint – adding flour whisked in water – 3 tablespoons to a teacup – and whisking while the sauce comes to the boil and thickens. Then season. This method causes the sauce to retain the buttery taste by virtue of it never having been heated beyond the boiling point of milk, but it must boil until the taste of flour disappears.

Sauce diable

is dark brown and owes much to Lea and Perrins Worcester Sauce and pepper. In 1843 a crazed French evangelist, half-way through preparing his coq au vin, gave way to sudden temptation and *drank* the brandy and the wine. He then forgot about the pieces of chicken browning in the pan for 20 minutes (though he turned them absentmindedly once or twice). Jealous of his professional reputation (as a cook), he added cream and Worcester sauce to the mush-rooms, onions, and gammon, and served it in a sauceboat as an accompaniment. He called it *poulet sauté: sauce diable*. Thus are the world's great dishes invented – at least by food writers.

Demi-glace

is a meat sauce, which, if all goes well, resembles nothing so much as the meat jelly you find under the fat after roast-ing a joint in the oven. You make it by putting into an oven dish scraps of meat and bones and minced beef and sugar and onion and garlic . . . and leave it for 20 minutes on mark 6 (400°F) or thereabouts.

Then when all is brown and tacky wash out the oven dish with meat stock, reduce the result by boiling, check seasoning, strain and add a packet of gelatine. This last step allows the demi-glace to set when cool and will also tell you when it has ceased to be good and strong – gelatine declining to keep in jelly form any foodstuff that has gone off.

CHICKEN

For *Poulet sauté chasseur*, take three parts Portugaise, one part diable and garnish with mushrooms cut into slices and tossed in sizzling butter. To give it more fully:

Poulet sauté chasseur

a 4 lb. chicken
2 oz. butter
½ oz. flour
1 oz. grated onion
1 oz. tomato purée
6 oz. mushrooms
1 bouquet garni
1 wineglass cider
½ pint stock
water and soup cube

Put the butter into a good pan or cast-iron casserole. Rub the chicken with salt and pepper and brown it all over in the butter. Put the lid on the pan and let the chicken simmer in the butter for about 15 minutes.

Now take out the chicken and put into the juices of the pan the flour, grated onion and tomato purée; let this brown slightly and add the stock and cider. Joint the chicken and replace in casserole. Add the bouquet, cover tightly (if necessary paint a badly fitting lid with a thick flour-and-water paste) and cook in a mark 5 (375°F) oven for just under an hour.

Remove from oven, open casserole, remove joints of chicken and reduce the sauce by boiling fiercely. Quarter the mushrooms, simmer them in butter, add to the chicken and cover with strained sauce.

To serve: this durable dish will mature happily in a slow oven for half an hour or more and can be warmed up again.

Optional garnish: a dozen chipolata or cocktail sausages baked in a medium oven in a tablespoonful each of oil and red wine.

Poulet poché à la crème

requires a basis of rice and the sauce is prepared by adding béchamel in equal quantities to chicken stock and white wine boiled together. But perhaps my favourite way of producing the battery bird broiler is to make

Poulet grillé à l'americaine

With the wishbone hard against your apron, slit a filleting knife either side of the breastbone, open up the chicken, remove the ribcage and flatten what remains with a rolling pin – there should be two breasts and two legs attached to the vertebrae.

Paint all over with a goo made of English mustard, oil, salt and pepper and grill on each side under a medium grill for 10–15 minutes, depending on the size of the bird. Garnish with rashers of crisp bacon and serve with a sauce-boat of sauce diable – the hot mahogany-coloured one on which you do not spend a great deal of time because the overall taste is pepper and Worcestershire sauce.

The ideal accompaniment to grilled chicken is

Croquette potatoes

peeled, steamed, sieved, seasoned with salt and pepper and 2 beaten egg yolks added per pound of tubers. The resulting mass is shaped into small barrels which are dried in flour, dipped in eggwash and rolled in toasted breadcrumbs before being deep fried. Tomato salad is excellent with this.

That afternoon they came unto a land, in which it seemed always afternoon . . . Tennyson might so well have been writing of the new intake at a broiler house. The stability of temperature, consistency of feeding, predictability of light; all these must make it impossible for a chicken to know which is the seventh day and when it shall rest. Undoubtedly lack of life with a capital L translates itself into tender and unexciting meat; flesh devoid of the flavours that rotting grains of corn, bacon-steeped peas and twigs of wild garlic give to the more wordly farmyard bird. But there is no question of the fact that this lack of flavour is vastly exaggerated by the food-snob. After all, we now get cheaper chickens, meatier chickens, more chickens, and if in their short and uneventful life they don't achieve a lot of flavour, why then, they must have flavour thrust upon them.

So don't knock the poor battery-chicken. As I wrote to 'mother of three, Runcorn', only the other week, 'how would *you* taste after nine weeks of enforced apathy in the oyster light of a broiler house?' What people actually get when they buy an antiseptic fowl is quite a lot of tender brown and white meat quite cheaply. This should be a challenge to chaps rather than spark off yet another letter from 'discontented, Macclesfield' to the Ministry of Ag. and Fish.

If a chicken rubbed with salt and coarse pepper, trussed with streaky bacon, roasted in butter and anointed with mild red paprika 10 minutes before it leaves the oven bores you; bores you even when it is accompanied by a sauce fashioned from 1 grated onion, simmered in ½ pint of milk, 6 cloves and 1 oz. of butter, to which is added a sufficiency of coarse-chopped rindless white bread and a tablespoon of Noilly Prat vermouth; bores you even if the roasting-tray is washed out with a bottle of Guinness and a dessertspoon of cornflour to provide gravy . . . then all is still not lost.

Chicken in mushroom sauce

Joint the chicken – two legs, two breasts. This is really not difficult: an incision of the skin between leg and breast; a sharp knife run along either side of the breastbone down to the side of the wishbone, some intelligent pulling and the thing comes to pieces in your hand. Some supermarkets even sell the beasts ready jointed. Take 2 tablespoons of flour, 1 teaspoon each of garlic salt, paprika and dry mustard; coat the pieces with this mixture.

Now take a large frying pan, brown the pieces in olive oil for 30 seconds on each side, add 4 oz. of butter and turn down the flame. The pieces will appreciate about 20 unattended minutes on each side before they are due to be lifted from the pan and placed in a heatproof serving-dish in the oven (mark 2, 300°F).

Now cut 6 oz. of mushrooms into halves – quarters if they are very large – fry them in the pan and add the juice of a quarter of a lemon; when they are tender (3 or 4 minutes on a medium flame) add ¼ pint of milk into which you have stirred a dessertspoon of plain flour. Deploy this liquid for melting all the chickeny deposits from the frying pan before pouring sauce and mushrooms over the chicken in the oven-dish.

When you come to serving this – to the accompaniment, I imagine, of new potatoes sprinkled with chives and a salad of tomatoes and sliced shallots – you may find that the fat has detached itself from the body of the mushroom sauce. If that is the case, pour all that is liquid in the dish into a bowl containing ⅛ pint of double cream, stir, and pour back. This remedial exercise costs, but is worth considerably more in resultant deliciousness.

Here are two more possibilities:

Roast chicken with bread sauce

Simply, rub your chicken with well-seasoned oil, and put a walnut of butter and a dessertspoonful of brandy inside it. Roast him in good fat in a moderate oven, giving him half his cooking time with the breast pointing to his maker, the second half equally divided between the two sides on which he can lie.

Serve him with crisply grilled streaky bacon and gravy, made by pouring off the surplus fat and adding to the roasting tray a glass of stout and half a glass of stock, which are allowed to boil for a minute before straining the liquor into a sauceboat.

For the bread sauce, chop a shallot finely, boil for 5 minutes in ½ pint of salted, peppered and cloved milk, to which you have added 1 oz. of butter, then add enough chopped crustless white bread, to give it the consistency of which you approve, simmer for a few more minutes and add a dash of double cream before serving.

Chicken casserole

Less simply, joint the chicken (2 legs, 2 breasts), dust the pieces with seasoned flour (some paprika if you like) and fry them lightly in half oil, half butter in the frying pan for 5 minutes. Lay these pieces in a casserole, and introduce into the hot fat of the pan a chopped onion, some button mushrooms, and after a few minutes of tossing, a skinned crushed tomato and a squeeze of lemon. Pour the entire contents of the pan on to the chicken. Now bring ½ pint of burgundy to the boil and add this also to the casserole.

Cook in a medium oven for 45 minutes and serve croutons of garlic-rubbed bread and diced fried gammon and chopped parsley. With it, give them mashed potatoes with a small grate of nutmeg.

If you should have a 2 lb. battery chicken, cut it into quarters, brush the pieces with a marinade of: 3 tablespoons oil, 3 tablespoons lime juice, 1 tablespoon grated onion, 1 teaspoon salt, 1 teaspoon dried tarragon, and a long dash of Tabasco. Roast in a tray in a mark 6 (400°F) oven, basting with the marinade. Serve with pilaff rice and tomato salad.

Coq au vin (for 4)

1 jointed chicken
½ lb. pickling onions
4 oz. button mushrooms
a 4 oz. slice of gammon
½ bottle red (or white or pink) wine
1 liqueur glass brandy
⅛ pint double cream
2 tablespoons oil
1 oz. butter
1 oz. flour
Salt, paprika, black pepper

The broiler chicken is a challenge to the cook as well as an object of sympathy, and one very good way to treat it is with wine. While I am impressed by men who take a mouthful of Madeira cake and mutter 'late landed Bual 1922 – probably matured in the cask for ten to twelve years', it is their courage rather than their expertise that gets me. Wine used for stewing ought to be of reasonable strength and unvinegary; no more.

Coq au vin is an excellent marriage of wine and chicken and the ideal party dish: it can be prepared in the morning and left to cook itself in the calm of early evening. Its cooking time is an elastic 'not less than an hour and a half'. And the end-product is spectacular and delicious.

Heat oil and butter and gently fry the peeled whole onions, quartered mushrooms and diced, lightly floured gammon. After about 5 minutes – when the onions begin to become transparent – lift gammon, onion and mushroom from the pan and place them in a casserole.

Dredge the chicken pieces in a mixture of 1 oz. flour, 1 coffeespoon each salt and mild paprika, and some black pepper. Brown the pieces in the fat in the pan; when they are coloured all over, lower the flame. Add brandy and ignite it. It will flare suddenly, then burn unspectacularly for about a minute. When the flame has gone out, add the wine, stir pan with a wooden spoon to loosen the deposit, and pour the contents of the pan into casserole. Cover with a lid and put into a mark 4 (350°F) oven about 1½ hours before it is due to be served at table. Prepare a saucepan containing the cream, and as you go into the kitchen to fetch the coq au vin to the table pour the juices of the casserole into the cream, let them boil for 1 minute and pour them back over the chicken. This takes care of any surplus fat which might otherwise spoil the appearance of the dish.

OUT FOR A DUCK

Factory farmers, who have succeeded in robbing the chicken and turkey of their free-range flavour, have been less successful in this respect with duck. No matter how uneventful has been its short, synthetic life, it still retains (glory be) something of that desirably duckish taste – somewhere between poultry and game.

The free-range duck is flesh-coloured, usually rough-plucked, and looks as if it might once have clucked attractively in a farmyard. The broiler duck is white and plump and anonymous; it is wrapped in plastic. The broiler duck tends to be frozen – which does it no harm. Thaw it gently and do not bother to keep the reddish water that it renders. When the duck is soft, cut out the wish-bone – making it much easier to carve; wipe the bird inside and out with a clean cloth and pierce the skin with a carving fork, paying particular attention to the fattest parts.

Roast duck

Sprinkle salt and freshly ground pepper inside the duck. Melt 1 oz. butter and dissolve in it 1 teaspoon salt and ½ coffeespoon of ground black pepper. Place the duck on a rack in a roasting tray, the breast pointing upwards, and paint the outside with seasoned butter. Cook in a steady mark 4 (350°F) oven, allowing 20–25 minutes to 1 lb. I have never found any virtue in underdone *roast* duck, nor is it at all necessary to effect subtle changes in oven temperature. Baste the bird from time to time; if the skin becomes darker than you think it should, cover it loosely with foil – but let it have the final 10 minutes uncovered.

The bird is cooked when a fork plunged deep between breast and thigh brings forth white rather than pink juice. The skin, if you have followed these instructions, will be crisp and desirable.

Besides gravy, the classic accompaniments for duck are:

Apple sauce:
　　½ lb. peeled cooking apples
　　2 tablespoons cider
　　garlic salt
Simmer the apples in cider (in a pan with the lid closed), pass through a sieve and season to taste.

Stuffing:
　　The duck's heart and liver and 2 oz. streaky bacon (all
　　　　finely chopped)

4 prunes, soaked, stoned, chopped
3 oz. white breadcrumbs
1 oz. grated onion
1 tablespoon chopped parsley
1 beaten egg
seasoning

Mix the ingredients well, wrap them in aluminium foil and bake them with the duck for about an hour.

Peas: Peas are the classic accompaniment. There is an old myth about serving turnips with duck; the best that can be said for it is that a turnip roasted with a duck loses most of its turnipy taste. This seems a weak argument for the marriage.

Braised duck with orange sauce (for 4)

1 duck, 4–5 lb.
4 oz. butter
1 teaspoon sugar

Remove the wishbone, wipe the bird and season it inside and out. Use as small a casserole as will accommodate the bird. Melt the butter, add sugar and sauté the duck on all sides until it is brown. Then reduce the heat, put the lid on the casserole and simmer gently for about 1½ hours on top of the stove, turning the duck over now and then. Remove the duck to a warm place.

Orange sauce:
3 tablespoons bitter orange marmalade
3 oranges
2 dessertspoons tarragon vinegar
1 teacup chicken stock
1 oz. plain flour rubbed into 1 oz. butter

Now put the casserole on the flame (or if you are cooking roast duck remove the duck and put the roasting tin on the flame), add 1 chopped orange, vinegar and marmalade.

Let this boil fiercely for 2 or 3 minutes, then add chicken stock and simmer for another 5 minutes. Skim the fat from the surface, thicken the sauce with flour and butter, strain it and season. Before serving add to this sauce segments from the remaining oranges.

For a simple, extravagant and absolutely smashing sauce for duck, melt ½ lb. of redcurrant jelly in a pan, add to it a wineglass of brandy and garnish this with the peel of pithless orange skin cut into thin strips and boiled in water until soft.

If you want a newish vegetable accompaniment, boil 1 lb. of Brussels sprouts, chop them up, put them into a liquidizer with ¼ pint of double cream and serve with a topping of crisp streaky bacon cut up or crushed by hand.

Cider duck

Place the duck in an oven tray and pour over it a wineglassful of sweet cider. Roast on mark 4 (350°F) for 30 minutes to the pound, covering the bird lightly with foil when it gets brown enough. You may crisp it by removing the foil and the best sauce is made by removing most of the fat from the juices in the pan and using what remains to make a rich sauce with the aid of flour, black treacle, celery salt and single cream.

Garnish the dish with segments of apple fried in a caramel of 1 oz. of butter and 1 dessertspoon of oil, 1 oz. of sugar and 1 teaspoon of lemon juice. Stir the ingredients and when the mixture turns to a pale shade of mahogany put in the lightly floured apple segments and cook them on both sides.

Smoked duck is a splendid delicacy.

Duck stew has none of the goodness of a *cassoulet* – viz. goose and pork and bacon and goosefat and haricot beans.

Duck Soup is the title of a very funny Marx Brothers film; it has no gastronomic entity.

HARE AND RABBIT

In January, a hare is cheap and large. Sometimes he is large because he is old; as he is old he is tough; and for that reason you cook him for a long time. Such a process renders the meat stringy and you become sorry you didn't leave him hanging face down on his hook where the butcher should have been. However, this is negative stuff.

Ideally, a hare should be a yearling – a tender age in the full meaning of the word. If this then is his first winter, his paws are slender, the fur has not yet grown completely over his claws and the hair on his back has an even sheen without wave or bristle. Skin him, joint him, and he is fit to roast.

Roast hare

Go and buy yourself a larding needle. Cut bacon or salt pork into thin slices and make these into strips the thickness of two or three matches; thread them in your needle and practise your embroidery on the back and two plump rear legs of the animal – the other joints are best given to slaves or children. Dust the joints with well-seasoned flour, fry quickly on all sides in shallow fat in a pan, tip into a baking tray and, provided no one piece weighs more than a pound, roast in a medium oven for 45 minutes. It needs no basting because of the lardons, you see? Now lift the pieces on to your prettiest dish, pour cream into the juices of the baking tray and blend during a hasty boil before straining this over the joints. Next, in a frying pan of hot oil, crisp three or four slices of diced cut white bread and some bacon or gammon similarly shaped; this last garnish is best drained of fat and given to each guest in an individual bowl ready for sprinkling over the sauced meat.

Let redcurrant jelly attend the feast, which needs a good, coarse red wine: one of the Northern Italian Fellowship, a Chianti or one of his friends, you may well find especially

pleasing, and as the oven takes 15 minutes to warm, the hare 45 minutes to cook, why not baked potatoes?

So much for a hare at the age of one. At two the doe is better than the buck (a hare is easily sexed), and at three or more, when the fur is speckled with grey he needs loving care, and that, as often as not, is wasted.

But if you've got him, and it's too late to send him back, and you realize in time that he is old, cut him into pieces and he may well turn out to be a happy companion to a casserole that you intended leaving in the oven for some hours in any case. Especially if it is filled with leek and onion, wine and herbs, Jerusalem artichokes, pimento and peeled tomatoes and slices of belly of pork; this latter ingredient is important for a hare who leads a fast life retains little fat on his bones.

Jugged hare

Fry pieces of hare rolled in seasoned flour in a frying pan containing butter and oil. Put into a casserole. Add the blood of the hare. Heat 2 glasses of red wine; 2 teaspoons of French mustard; 4 oz. grated onion; 4 oz. redcurrant jelly; 2 tablespoons oil in a pan. Add 12 (optional) juniper berries. Pour this over the hare. Close the casserole tightly and cook for 3 hours on mark 4 (350°F). Remove the lid and thicken the gravy with cream or cornflour; pour it over the meat and garnish with cubes of fried bread and slices of fried bacon.

A casserole is a flameproof dish of sufficient beauty to appear at table. It also can be a foolproof, timeproof stew of meat and vegetables. It is a modern answer to the servant problem, a money-spinner for the Gas Board and a boon to the unpunctual. It is a perfect excuse for another drink before an unspoilable meal.

The ideal casserole should not only consist of a vessel in which ingredients are cooked and served, but also should contain food that will keep full quality for hours. That means the ingredients of a casserole should hold their characters and shapes even when subjected to long punishment in an oven.

Mushrooms, onion, pimento and carrots are usable. Potatoes, tomatoes, marrows and courgettes are not.

The following recipe for a durable casserole could be readily adapted to other game or fowl, including chicken, but I chose rabbit because the sturdy post-myxomatosis rabbit is an underrated and economical delicacy. It feeds six.

Rabbit casserole

5 lb. rabbit jointed into four leg pieces and the saddle (or 2 medium sized quartered chickens)

2 oz. butter

2 tablespoons oil

8 oz. carrots

8 oz. pimento

3 small onions

2 cloves of garlic

1 bouquet garni. It consists of 1 leek, 1 stick celery, thyme, bayleaves and marjoram, tied together in a tiny muslin bag

½ lb. streaky bacon

1 calf's foot

1 bottle claret

salt and black peppercorns, roughly crushed

Prepare a small mound of eight parts flour, one part salt and half part paprika and roll the rabbit pieces in it.

Now put butter and oil into the casserole, brown the rabbit pieces all over and add finely chopped streaky bacon, roughly chopped onion, carrot, garlic and pimento. When the vegetables begin to lose their resilience, add the remaining ingredients, cover the casserole and cook very slowly for at least 2 hours.

Then take the rabbit from the dish and remove the bones. Also remove the calf's foot, which will have done its work, and the bouquet garni. Serve the rabbit hot, with new potatoes, and a salad of tomatoes dressed with olive oil, sliced shallots and salt.

Should your guests never actually get round to eating, the rabbit will set in a firm jelly if left in the casserole and will make an excellent terrine.

Roast pheasant

Put into your pheasant 2 oz. well-seasoned butter. Drape slices of streaky bacon around the breast. Roast for 40 minutes in a pre-warmed mark 6 (400°F) oven and serve with toasted breadcrumbs, and gravy made by loosening the deposits in the roasting pan with brown ale – and bread sauce (page 310), to which you can add a dash of cream.

QUAIL

A quail is a luxury. It looks like a mini-chicken – and tastes like unhigh partridge. In cases of acute hunger one would hesitate to recommend it. The average bird weighs 3½ oz. dressed and if eaten sensibly – that is to say ultimately in one's fingers with finger-bowls provided – it yields only about 2½ oz. of meat. But it is excellent meat, and it also can provide the quail-serving hostess with much subject for conversation and a reputation for high living.

A quail is a migratory game-bird. Before the war the majority of quails eaten and served in this country were caught in Egypt on migration, imported live, fattened and then killed. I mention this to still cries of 'shame' and 'cruelty' when I say that quails are now reared in English farms, where they lead lives embarrassingly similar to those led by battery chicks. If your diet is motivated by love of God's creatures there is little hope for you, gastronomically . . . Your butcher can obtain quails from wholesale poulterers, and you can buy them, inevitably, at Harrods. They gain nothing by being left to become high and should be eaten within a day or two of being killed. As an alternative they can be kept deep-frozen and slowly thawed when required for the table.

The classic way to cook a quail is to season it with salt and pepper, put into it a hazelnut-sized piece of butter, wrap it in a slice of streaky bacon and roast for about 25 minutes in a mark 5 (375°F) oven. Serve on a square of fried bread spread with pâté. Garnish with watercress. But this is pretty unenterprising. It has earned the ultimate in French insults: the appellation *caille à l'anglaise* (*choux à l'anglaise* is boiled cabbage, *pouding à l'anglaise* – custard).

Quails in casserole

6 quails
1½ oz. butter, 1 tbs olive oil
4 oz. redcurrant jelly
2 oz. glacé cherries
juice of half a lemon
1 wineglass port
½ pint stock
chopped rind of half an orange
salt and pepper

Take the eviscerated quails, melt butter and oil in a casserole, and brown them all over on top of the stove. Then put on a lid and cook them in a moderate oven for 25 to 30 minutes. Lift them out, drain most of the fat from the pan, add stock, wine and orange rind and allow to simmer for 10 minutes before stirring in the jelly. Put back the quails, add chopped cherries, season with salt, pepper and lemon juice and leave in the oven for 10 minutes.

Grilled quails

Split open as many quails as you wish to serve; flatten them and marinade for 2 hours in a dish containing

2 teaspoons olive oil
juice of half a lemon
a bayleaf
some onion rings
salt, ground black pepper, a pinch of mixed spice and some thyme

Lift out the quails and roll each bird in toasted breadcrumbs, seasoned with salt, pepper, spice and thyme. Cook under a slow grill, turning the birds every few minutes and moistening the breadcrumbs with drops of melted butter. Serve up on rings of pineapple fried in butter and decorate with grilled rashers of streaky bacon.

Meat

BEEF

For too long meat-starved Englishmen were so willing to say 'Oh good a steak', that anything red from the right animal that compared favourably with the sole of a boot was acceptable fare. Now your standards should – and can – be higher. Price is usually a guide to quality. By and large the lighter the shade of red, the fresher and tougher the meat is likely to be. Obvious sinews and gristle should be avoided, and fat surrounding the meat must be white – never yellow.

The grilling cuts are fillet, which is expensive, tender, and has not a great deal of natural flavour, rump and sirloin, which are a little less expensive, a little tougher, and at their best considerably more delicious. The point about steaks is that the more you fiddle about with them the less desirable they tend to become.

A steak should be cooked under or over a hot grill until it is sealed on both sides, then more gently until it has reached the desired colour. Before it is grilled it should be brushed with melted butter, seasoned with salt and ground or crushed black pepper. No more.

Steaks for a dinner party are a bad idea; not only do different people like their steaks cooked differently, but steaks cooked in advance and reheated or left to fossilize in an oven should be given only to guests you really dislike. If you are determined to serve steaks to guests, take thick slices or barrel-shaped tournedos and seal them under a very hot grill – cooking those that are to be well done for 3 or 4 minutes each side. They can then be set under a red wine sauce in the bottom of a low (mark 2/300°F) oven for 15 minutes. But confining yourself to serving something that *must* be eaten 15 minutes from the time it has been put in the oven is not the way to make a dinner party a success.

Steaks can be drowned in sauce, anointed with pâté, spiked with garlic, or hotted-up under a bountiful coating of roughly crushed peppercorns. But the following accompaniments may be better suited to a steak of quality:

Beurre maître d'hôtel

½ small clove of garlic
juice of half a lemon
2 tablespoons chopped parsley (washed and squeezed out in
a cloth)
4 oz. soft butter

Crush the garlic against the sides of a bowl and add lemon, a good pinch of white pepper, and parsley. Blend well and add butter. Work with a wooden spoon until the parsley is evenly distributed and then pile the mixture on to the wrapping-paper of a ½ lb. packet of butter, roll to a sausage shape, set in the refrigerator, and cut into medallions that ride upon the steaks.

Sauce Béarnaise

1 shallot finely chopped
1 sherry glass dry white wine

101

1 *sherry glass tarragon vinegar*
1 *level dessertspoon each chopped tarragon and chopped*
   chervil
2 *egg yolks*
6 *oz. butter*

Boil the chopped shallot in wine and vinegar until the liquid is reduced by half. Strain this into a bowl and set over a pan of boiling water. Add yolks and herbs (use less if herbs are dried) and beat with a whisk as you add the butter, ½ oz. at a time – the final piece just before the last one has totally melted. Whisk the sauce until it reaches a thick creamy consistency, making sure that there is no deposit of egg solidifying at the base of the bowl.

Béarnaise can be kept for an hour or two; you stand the bowl of sauce, covered, in a pan of hot water. Should it separate you can save it by spooning the curdled sauce into

a clean bowl containing a tablespoon of cold water, whisking it as you do so.

Beurre de Montpelier

1 heaped dessertspoon of chervil
6 sprigs of tarragon
a small bunch of chives
3 fillets anchovy (tinned)
1 dessertspoon of capers
2 cornichons (small pickled gherkins)
half a small clove of garlic
2 oz. soft butter
salt, black pepper and nutmeg
2 hard-boiled egg yolks
2 tablespoons olive oil
dessertspoon wine vinegar

Wash in water chives, chervil and tarragon (use less if herbs are dried). Drain and blanch using salted water in a copper pot so that the herbs keep their colour. Cook for 5 minutes, remove with a skimmer, and cool in clean water.

Now press water from the herbs and pound them in a mortar with the anchovy fillets, capers, cornichons, and garlic. When you have a fine purée add the butter, the hard-boiled egg yolks passed through a sieve, salt, a good pinch of ground black pepper, and as little nutmeg as will cover a sixpence. Pound once more and add the olive oil and wine vinegar. Work this up with a pestle until the paste becomes not only smooth in texture but also entirely perfect in taste.

(To clean a copper pan, take equal portions of salt and flour. Add enough vinegar to make this into a thick cream and apply to the copper pan with segments of lemon, pressing just hard enough to brighten it. Messrs Lea and Perrins' Worcestershire sauce is almost as good for this as my mixture, though somewhat more expensive.)

Of all the prestigious dishes served in restaurants, Chateaubriand is the prestigiousest. The asking price is high, but it will suffice for a brace of consumers; halve it and you will find the cost not very much more than a fillet steak – to which it is immeasurably superior. A Chateaubriand is the thick end of the fillet, immaculately roasted, with Béarnaise sauce and accompanied by soufflé potatoes – perhaps the ultimate in culinary confidence tricks.

Soufflé potatoes

You take an old potato, preferably a waxy Dutch rather than a White or King Edward – which means nothing to you if you are not a potato buff, but could make sense if you have a switched-on greengrocer. Peel the potato, regardless of expense, with a smart sweep of the knife so that you are left with a barrel shape from which you cut perfect elliptical, ⅛ inch-thick slices. You discard the ends – I am sorry about that.

Dry the slices well and deal them into a pan containing oil just hot enough to sizzle when you splash into it a drop of water. Keep the oil at this un-hot temperature and agitate the potato slices continually with a wooden spatula or similar undamaging instrument and after 3 minutes or so you will see blisters form on the skin of the potato slices. That actually is what we are after: blisters. In fact, that is why we have been doing all the agitating. When most of the slices are well and truly blistered remove them on to a piece of foil and raise the flame under the fat pan.

When it is really hot, shortly before it bursts into flames, and shows a good heat-haze hovering over the oil, redeal the potato slices; the shock of contact with the very hot fat causes the blisters to open up and present you, the maker, with a wondrously round potato soufflé, which you flip over and remove, via a grease-consuming paper napkin, on to the serving dish. Inside there is air; around it, properly cooked, lightly salted potato. The cost is negligible, the sense of achievement enormous, and a good soufflé will stay up for all of 3 minutes – longer, even permanently, if the potato slice is thinner. In fact, this is just the sort of dish that you should order in restaurants – which, I always maintain, ought to be used for the provision of difficult and time-consuming confections.

Chateaubriand

For the Chateaubriand itself, you need a good butcher, such as used to prefix his trade with the word 'high class'. If the name Chateaubriand does not mean anything to him, explain that you want a thick piece of fillet weighing 1½ lb. to 2 lb. – firmly tied with string. Season it well, brush it with melted butter and 'seal' the piece of fillet by letting the outside of it come into contact with the inside of a very hot pan. When it is mildly coloured all around, so that the juices remain therein instead of trickling out, place the Chateaubriand on a buttered roasting tray in a hot oven allowing between 9 and 15 minutes to the pound, depending on your preference for rare or well-done meat. Remove string and carve at table.

If you want to make this dish at home, there is really no great problem. The first stage of the soufflé potatoes, the blistering part, can be done in the afternoon. The Béarnaise can be made in the early evening and left over a pan of warm water to be given a final application of double-boiler heat. And the meat can be sealed an hour or two before the meal and placed in the oven just before the guests sit down to their first course of moules marinière. I am afraid you might have to employ someone to come in and make that.

Boeuf à la mode

3 lb. top rump, or topside, or eye of silverside

At least 1 day before the meal – preferably 2 days – the meat should be put into a marinade:

½ bottle red wine
2 tablespoons olive oil
10 crushed black peppercorns
1 crushed clove of garlic
4 oz. onions, finely sliced
bouquet of herbs

With plastic bags, it is now possible to marinate a great deal of meat in a very little marinade; in this case the marinade forms part of the sauce, so such economy is unnecessary. Turn the meat in the preparation from time to time, and take it out on the afternoon of the dinner.

To garnish:

1 calf's knuckle
2 oz. bacon fat
1 pint water
2 soup cubes
12 baby carrots
12 small onions
½ pint water
1 oz. sugar
1 oz. butter

Rub the meat with a cloth, dust it lightly with seasoned flour and brown it all over in the bacon fat. Pour off the bacon fat, add the marinade passed through a sieve, the water and the soup cubes, and the calf's knuckle, chopped up. Bring to boiling point and simmer gently for upwards of 3 hours, skimming off any surface fat. For the garnish, simmer the carrots and onions in water, butter and sugar until tender.

*   *   *

To serve: take the meat from its sauce, cut it into thick slices and keep in a warm place. Add the garnish to the sauce, boil up together for a few minutes, strain and pour over the sliced meat. The meat sauce and garnish may remain in the bottom of a low oven for another hour without any detriment. The dish can also be served cold – in which case the skimming off of fat should be scrupulously done.

Gravy

It would be lovely to be able to give quick, accurate definitions of the words sauce and gravy. Dictionaries, never keen to hand out free publicity to other words in their run-down on the main issue, seem to me to be missing the point – which is that gravy is gravy . . . and somewhere along the line gravy reaches the stage at which it becomes so overloaded with additives that one has no alternative but to change the appellation to the rival five-letter word. To put it another way, gravy from the goose given the full treatment becomes sauce for the gander. Basically, gravy is what the French call *'jus'* which is rather more than the English equivalent 'juice'. *Jus* is concentrated aromatic juice, more like juices. *Jus* is what gels in the dripping pan underneath fat. Melt this, and you obtain an immaculate gravy; unfortunately insufficient of the stuff runs out of properly roasted meat to give you more than a mouth-watering idea of what gravy should be. The reason for this is that if meat is properly roasted – by which I mean that the outside is sealed by direct contact with a hot pan, or started off in so hot an oven that this sealing process is simulated therein – the juices that emerge are very much scarcer than those of a cool piece of meat started off in a tepid oven and brought to roasting temperature.

Now I realize that the man who eats meat and gravy does not greatly care whether the goodness of the dish lies in the solid or the liquid. But there are those of us who indulge in cold meat sandwiches and care for dipping crusts of wholemeal bread into the gravy bowl, and to us both flesh and juices must be perfect. Let us take roast beef and gravy. Ideally the beef is cooked in such a fashion that there is very little juice and the joint retains the maximum moisture and flavour. We now have two alternatives for the provision of gravy: the first is to pour a sufficiency of hot water on to a modicum of Bisto and stand by to hear our guests say 'Ah!' It will come as small surprise to you that this is not what I had in mind. Sauce for beef could be fashioned of horseradish and cream; plum jelly, English mustard and port; tomato purée, Worcestershire sauce and béchamel. Gravy can afford no such embellishments.

The perfect solution that springs to mind is to purchase two identical pieces of beef and roast one perfectly; skewer the other frequently before baking it shoddily and erratically so as to produce the maximum amount of succulent liquor. There is no doubt about the effectiveness of this method; unfortunately it is nearly as uneconomical as was Charles Lamb's system of burning down houses containing pigs in order to partake of roast pork. Lamb's solution was to build ever smaller pighouses. Mine is to purchase less expensive cuts of beef for the sole purpose of providing gravy.

Take your piece of topside (or sirloin if you are rich), rub it with oil and salt and pepper and mustard and seal it most carefully. Allow it to cool and place around it in the roasting tray some scraps of meat and gristle, a few thin ends of oxtail, a bone or two and occasional pieces of mince and fat.

When the meat has been put back into a hot oven and received its allotted span of cooking time, the accompanying bits of what were once beef will have provided the most excellent basis for gravy and need no more than a glass of red wine, a touch of browning and a correction of seasoning. Boil up and loosen the deposits and strain into a gravy bowl.

Naturally, if you want to add redcurrant jelly and cream and Tabasco and a glug or two of Cumberland relish the end-product will be delicious; alas, it no longer qualifies under the heading of gravy, and if you care deeply about things like that, you must act accordingly.

Fondue bourguignonne

For my guests who have variously permuted tastebuds, I give a fondue bourguignonne. Expensive rump steak, cut in single-bite squares, marinaded overnight in red wine, grated onion and olive oil. On the table there is a pan of olive oil on a stand over a methylated spirit burner. Each guest has a fork, long, with insulated handle. (You can buy these or adapt them.)

Also on the table, a selection of hypodermics, and bowls containing oil of garlic, brandy or Pernod. Squares can be injected as desired. (Hypos are optional.) Having done this, fit one or two squares to the end of a fork, cook for 15 seconds or 10 minutes in the olive oil and eat with any of the accompaniments thoughtfully provided: fresh horseradish grated into a mixture of well-whipped half-double half-single cream; Kraft tomato chutney; chopped gherkins; curry sauce; aioli (page 146).

Catering supply shops sell whole fondue bour-guignonne outfits, pan, burner, forks and all; until you become an addict they don't appear to be a profitable investment, though they make a useful present to bad cooks who owe you a meal.

Hang the beef, make venison

After the war one ate horse; I do not mean to imply that chaps went to the Savoy and ordered the maître d' to produce a fillet of the chestnut which was tailed off in the

Cesarewitch. What happened was a shortage of beef – and by what we call professional resourcefulness and you will insist is dishonesty we bought horsemeat and made it taste as much like beef as our skills and the sweetish flesh permitted. On the menu was written 'steak' and when someone got suspicious and asked what it was, we said, 'Oh, that's horse'. So customers, knowing that no one admitted to the dastardly crime of cooking brother H., thought it must be all right.

Recently, in a seventeenth-century cookery book, I found a recipe for 'making venison taste nearly as palatable as beef' and my wife said that the process would have to be reversed to get anyone remotely excited. It was a challenge: buy a piece of top rump on Tuesday; serve it as braised venison for Sunday lunch. After all, the Lord will provide. What's in a name? You can own up afterwards. Basically, what makes 'game' different from domestic animal is an absence of fat and the presence of taste which actually owes more to the decomposition of the entrails than the quality of the flesh of the beast. So, cut the fat from the beef . . . and marinate it in a

Game marinade

¼ pint of oil
1 tablespoon crushed peppercorns
a dozen juniper berries
1 teaspoon rosemary
bottle brown ale

There was a time when marinading was done in an enamel pan with large quantities of oily, vinous goo . . . and the meat was placed in it and turned every 4 hours . . . for which purpose dutiful wives spent much time and money on alarm calls from the Post Office's telephone service. All this has changed with the deterioration of the alarm service and the advent of the plastic bag – into which you put the meat and the marinade, withdrawing the air. Thus a pint will suffice for any but the very largest joints, and you need only give the bag an occasional twirl in the tumble drier or tie it to the minute hand of a sturdy kitchen clock – if such a thing still exists – to achieve fair distribution. Give it about four days in a cool place – like the drawing room, if your drawing room is like that of most people I know. Then fry the outside gently in bacon fat, add the marinade and braise in a mark 4 (350°F) oven for 35 minutes to the pound. Add a slice of game pâté to the finished product, though this may produce the uneasy feeling that gameyness in the pâté has been achieved as fraudulently as has your joint of ex-beef.

Chilli con carne

I first came across this dish in Mexico City where I ordered it because of some dimly remembered Hemingway reference. I took a forkful of the stuff and then ordered six bottles of cold beer in quick succession. In the fullness of time I mentioned to the proprietor that it might be advisable to warn strangers about his speciality; he replied that it was *chilli con carne* . . . the ratio was about one to one – which turned out to be a pound of meat to a pound of chilli peppers. Had I wanted *carne* with a little *chilli*, he said, there was an American place just down the road.

Now the joy of this dish is that you can spice it to the extent where the fury of the pepper limits the amount that a man can consume . . . and for a restaurateur harassed by customers who demand larger portions there is a certain oblique pleasure in watching a man with watering eyes and set lips staring at a BEA basin of food that is wholly delectable and totally uneatable.

But enough of getting one's own back; as my mentor Mr James Young is wont to say: 'What's the recipe?'

You begin with 1 lb. of coarsely minced beef. You put this into a pan in which you have fried a large onion, minced together with 2 cloves of garlic, in a tablespoonful of nut oil until golden. Now lower the heat and add a small tin of peeled tomatoes, a green pepper, minced; 1 teaspoon of thyme; a bayleaf; 1 teaspoon of celery salt, and stir until the mixture simmers. Then cover tightly and cook gently for 2 hours while you decide how many chilli peppers or handsful of cayenne you are going to put in. Whatever your decision, remember that the longer you cook chillis, the hotter the stuff gets.

Steak-and-kidney

A steak-and-kidney pie is beautiful. With its covering of flaky pastry – brushed with milk or cream or beaten egg – it is started in a hot oven and finished in a rather cooler one. It attains a shining golden splendour. It bristles with pastry leaves. It can even wear a ruff.

But the plain, paler, unphotogenic steak-and-kidney *pudding* tastes even better.

A pie is an assembly job – cooked meats marshalled into a pie dish, anointed with a crust and finally baked all together: a pudding, on the other hand, is an entity throughout. In the process of steaming, each of its ingredients spends 3 or 4 hours quietly enhancing the delicacy of every other ingredient. There are no vents to permit steam to escape, no funnels to allow you to pour in afterthoughts. A pudding is conceived and built, closed and cooked. It is then opened and eaten and talked about. Rules Restaurant in Maiden Lane, London, WC2, makes puddings every Thursday. On that day one may observe complete strangers beaming genially at one another over their pudding basins.

The diameter of the basin you use is immaterial; one can always eat more than one gets. But whatever size pudding you choose to make, be sure that you have a saucepan, complete with lid, big enough to conceal it.

The perfect steak-and-kidney pudding has a golden sheen with each component part cooked to perfection. As the pastry is white and takes 90 minutes to steam, the meat needs 2 hours of simmering and the kidney requires about 45 minutes, this would appear to be like getting a tall ship into a thin bottle. Not so. As Kate and Sidney deserves a smooth red Burgundy, let us economize on the meat. Buy shin of beef, which is cheap predominantly because it is tough and gristly. Remove the gristle with a knife and help the toughness by leaving the small squares of meat (for 6 you will need 1½ lb.) in a marinade of 1 bottle brown ale, 2 tablespoons corn oil, 1 coffeespoon chopped dried tarragon and 1 minced onion of medium size. Clean and cut up the ox kidney (¾ lb.) and keep it overnight in milk.

Fry a medium chopped onion in fat until it is golden brown; fish the marinaded pieces of beef from their bowl, dredge with well-salted flour and add to the pan; when slightly coloured, add the marinade plus ½ pint of stock or water. Simmer for 1 hour and add the kidney to simmer for another 40 minutes. Add gravy browning if the colour does not please you.

You make the pastry by sieving 1¼ lb. of flour into a basin; adding ½ lb. chopped or shredded suet (a packet thereof will do well) and moisten with a coffeecup of milk into which you have beaten the yolk of an egg, and a teaspoon of black treacle to achieve the honey colour. Add salt and pepper, and an optional dash of Worcestershire sauce. Mix well, adding more water if the mixture is too dry (more flour if too moist) and let it rest in the refrigerator for half an hour. Roll out so that you have sufficient to line the pudding basin with enough left to fashion a lid.

Having lined the basin, pour in the meat and gravy, flavoured with English mustard if you like mustard; pinch on the lid and wrap the basin in a piece of well-greased foil before steaming it for 90 minutes. Remember to refill the saucepan as the water boils away. If you like suet crust very much you might care to make individual puddings; in fact I cannot understand why some enterprising food manufacturer has not flooded the market with these.

LAMB

In a cookery book bearing the sophisticated title *Meat* I read with a degree of agoggery about the author's proposed treatment for a leg of mutton. You grasp the well-hung limb, wrote the late Ambrose Heath, scrape the meat thighward from the extremity and repeatedly plunge into it a thick skewer. In the course of the next week or two you pour into the resultant apertures the contents of an entire bottle of dry port, massaging the joint to permit liquor to permeate flesh. The result, he promised, is sensational – a wise comment to commit to the printed page as I seriously doubt the existence of many men, women or horses with sufficient courage to try the receipt for themselves.

I would be less than honest if I did not state here and now that this type of gastronomic advice seems to me to epitomize all that is worst in cookery writing. In a nutshell, the rewards are out of all proportion to the time employed and the work entailed; the chances of ending up with an inedible, possibly crawling, piece of meat are strong, and I reckon that if you are going to give a recipe for mutton, the cost of the principal ingredient should contribute the major part of the cost of the dish. For this last reason I have never written about baked potatoes stuffed with Beluga caviar – excellent though the baked potatoes are.

Let us return to our mutton – a name that currently appears to be given to any lamb that has ceased to gambol

– though for this depressing state of affairs the Gaming Board is not responsible. The flavour of lamb – and this gem of information applies to all animals – is better from parts of the body situated close to the head: thus shoulder is more delicate than leg . . . and tail is ever the least subtle cut of all. But delicacy apart, eat meat as it was originally intended to be eaten – roasted, or possibly boiled, with accompaniments that complement rather than drown.

Butchers do not look down on people who buy cheap cuts of meat. Prices are governed by demand. Fillet steak is not intrinsically a more expensive cut than flank, but it is more tender and quicker to prepare, so more people ask for it. And as the butcher pays a given price per pound for a carcass he will charge four times that price for fillet, somewhere around half the carcass price per pound for flank. It is time to take advantage of this.

Best end of lamb

Lamb is the most difficult meat to spoil. Get a best end from your butcher, and prepare:

1 tablespoon English mustard
1 dessertspoon gravy browning
1 rounded tablespoon golden syrup
1 teaspoon salt
1 tablespoon wine vinegar

Mix well and, using a pastry brush, spread it all over the best end which you have conveniently placed in a roasting tray. It would be lovely if you could roast this for 25 minutes to the pound in a mark 7 (425°F) oven which you turn down to mark 5 (375°F) after the first quarter of an hour. After an hour it will still be pink. For the next hour it will be well cooked and after that it will be rather over-cooked – but perfectly edible.

Roast breast of lamb

Ask for the meat to be boned – the loss is about ½ lb. in a 1¾ lb. breast. Cut off surplus fat, wipe with a damp cloth and paint both sides with a solution made of:

1 level teaspoon English mustard
1 level teaspoon salt
ground black pepper
1 tablespoon of water

Put the meat in a baking tray (it will produce its own fat) and roast it for 50 minutes in a mark 6 (400°F) oven, basting now and then.

Boned breast of lamb

can also be stuffed and rolled. Stuffing for one breast:

3 oz. minced pork
3 oz. white breadcrumbs
½ medium grated onion
a small fistful of chopped sage
1 teaspoon French mustard
1 beaten egg
salt and fresh-ground pepper

Spread the stuffing on the inside of the breast of lamb to within an inch of the edges. Roll it lengthwise, tie it in three or four places and roast in 1 oz. fat in a baking tray for 1¼ hours at mark 4 (350°F).

Sweet and sour spare ribs of lamb

Take a whole unboned breast of lamb (about 2 lb.), cut off surplus fat, season well with salt and pepper and roast in a baking tray for 40 minutes in a mark 3 (325°F) oven. Pour off the fat. Into a pan put

2 tablespoons of the fat
1 tablespoon golden syrup
1 dessertspoon wine vinegar

and bring this to the boil. Pour the contents over the breast of lamb in the baking tray and let it wallow in a mark 2 (300°F) oven for half an hour or more, basting it or turning it as you please. The breast is then cut cross-wise to make cutlet-like strips. Baste with the liquor before serving.

In spite of the fact that you can now obtain pretty well any food at virtually any time of the year – what might be called a ham for all seasons – cookery calendars continue to ride high in popularity. January was for cod, February for red cabbage, and so on. 'June,' I recall writing, 'is a good month for intensively reared chickens.' The sentiment was eagerly endorsed by the trade, those bland, short-legged, firm-breasted men who bear out Brillat Savarin's statement: 'Tell me what a man eats and I'll tell you what he is.'

But there are exceptions to my first sentence, and milk-fed lamb is among the most notable. The lamb is of tender age and its meat of similar consistency. Sheep's milk is not commonly consumed because it is thin and strong and aromatic. It is this very quality that makes the meat so desirable . . . a regurgitated, second-udder version of the green fields of England and Wales. Baby lambs are killed; soon after that the meat appears in butchers' shops and if you do not buy, someone else will. For a sizeable leg of lamb such as comes, on ice, from what the Queen Mother used to call 'our New Zealand people', there is every incentive to lard the lean side with strips of bacon fat and inject slivers of garlic deep into the fattier parts. No such aids are required for baby lamb.

Roast lamb

The joint, be it leg, shoulder or best end, is brushed with melted butter, salted, given a thin sprinkling of fresh-ground white pepper (black pepper on pastel-coloured food looks like grit) and roasted. An initial 15-minute blast in a pre-warmed mark 7 (425°F) oven is followed by a thoughtful sojourn on mark 3 (325°F), to make the total time up to 15–19 minutes per pound, depending on whether you like your meat pink or cockroach-grey.

Or, rub the outside of the shoulder with salt and pepper, flavour it with a little lemon thyme (a herb it probably consumed during its lifespan) and allow 20 minutes in a mark 6 (400°F) oven before basting, turning down the temperature to mark 4 (350°F) and giving in all 20–30 minutes to the pound depending on how chunky is the joint and, again, your preference for either pink or grey meat.

For gravy I use a pipette to syphon some of the fat from the roasting tray and add strong ale and double cream to the juices that remain. There are those who use Bisto-like substances, of which I find Instant Gravy Mix the most acceptable, especially when used in conjunction with meat juice.

It is not quite enough to say I have bought good meat and cooked it as instructed. There are a number of obligatory side-dishes. For contrast: mint and sugar and vinegar. This runs under the name of mint sauce or perches on the side of the plate as mint jelly. The difference is achieved with a few grains of gelatine, a tasteless substance. It is therefore a question of whether you want the pungent sauce to lap around your plate, embracing all that it touches (which I humbly submit is a mistake when you have food of quality), or provide a harbour of pungent jelly with which to sharpen your taste-buds (which I reckon is the right thing to do).

If you do not much care for the taste of roast lamb or mutton, *then* is the time to make

Mint sauce

Ideally you need a mortar and pestle. Take a good handful of washed mint leaves, put them into a mortar, add 1 tablespoon of granulated sugar and pestle, crushing together mint and sugar until you are left with a green goo. Add to this ⅛ pint of boiling water, then just less than ¼ pint of cold distilled vinegar . . . and let it cool.

Mint jelly

Put into a mortar a handful of mint leaves or dried mint and a dessertspoon of granulated sugar. Work with a pestle until you have a green mush, add to it one part boiling water, and when this has made an infusion add two parts cold distilled vinegar. Add sufficient gelatine to set this amount of liquid and leave in a cool place.

To complement the meat, serve redcurrant jelly. Buy this; the more you pay for a tin the better are the contents likely to be, unless, of course, you shop in the wrong place. Wilkins of Tiptree make a particularly good one, or you can make your own by boiling redcurrants, sieving them and setting the unsweetened juice with gelatine for short-term use. If you want to go in for large-scale redcurrant jelly-making it requires more care plus sterilization, pectin, wax paper *et al.*

And there are people who like port wine with their mutton, I suppose. If you have this pioneering spirit, why not get a hypodermic from your neighbourhood junkie and blow the leg full of Croft's 1955. Another equally good way of permeating meat with liquid is to pump it full of holes with a larding needle and place it in a plastic bag containing half a bottle of the liquor of your choice – be it wine or ginger cordial. Tie the plastic bag tightly with quadrupled elastic bands, push out such air as got in on the act and turn the bag for a day or two when you are passing. The problem here is that as often as not the goodness of the meat runs into the booze – which makes the system more useful for a stew than a roast.

The classic potato accompaniment is *Pommes Sarladine* – slices of new potatoes and truffles cooked in meat stock in a low oven and brushed with cream before the dish is lightly coloured under the grill. Single or double cream, did you ask? The answer is double; I do not recognize single cream.

Crowning glory – crown roast of lamb

For Easter try a crown of lamb. Not untypically, a crown roast is the invention of the monarchless Americans. As a dish – and a very pretty dish it is – it became popular in this country before the war; then went the way of all large joints during meat rationing. The reason why it has failed to regain its former popularity is principally because of the decline in privately owned butcher shops – and the reluctance of streamlined multiple firms to waste time on fiddling jobs for the exacting customer.

A good butcher should be pleased to provide you with a crown of lamb. He will want a little notice and may well charge you a penny or two for the trouble of removing the backbone from two best ends, trimming the scraping the upper portions of the cutlet bones and folding and tying the loins into shape. He will also expect you to pay for each cutlet frill used in decorating the joint. A crown of lamb is an ideal dish for a party of six or eight – or twice that number of midgets – and if your butcher won't or can't oblige, it is well worth finding one who is willing and has learned his trade.

Or you can do it yourself by taking two best ends of English lamb, trim them well to give the scraped chop bones a 2-inch clearance, and make incisions into the meat to separate the individual chops so that they are held together only by the fat and the fragment of backbone at the base of the triangle of meat. Now place the two loins next to each other to make one long loin and join them by sewing or wiring the two ends together, once at the top, once at the bottom. Rub the meat all over with seasoned olive oil into which you might like to crush a small clove of garlic, and bend the long loin gently into a ring, the solid wall of fat on the inside, the chunky parts of the chop pointing out to all the directions of the compass. Secure the joint downwards with a skewer, and tie a piece of string around the outside to retain the shape of the crown. Remove from the centre of the crown any fatty scrag-ends. Stand the joint in a roasting tray and with a pastry brush paint it thoroughly with the following mixture:

2 dessertspoons water
1 dessertspoon French mustard
2 teaspoons salt
1 teaspoon coarsely ground black pepper

Preheat your oven to mark 6 (400°F), put the joint in for about 10 minutes and then reduce the heat to mark 5 (375°F). Cook for just under 1 hour if you like your lamb underdone, about 1¼ hours if you like it pink. Serve it on your best round dish.

It is customary to stuff the centre of a crown with forcemeat, mashed potatoes, peas and carrots or mushrooms in a cream sauce. However pretty this may look when you bring the dish to the table, the image crumbles if, the moment you remove the first portion of meat, there is a cascade of vegetables over the tablecloth. So decorate your crown with parsley or watercress and bring your vegetables to the table in containers designed for that purpose.

Other good vegetable partners are new potatoes boiled in their skins, peeled immediately and left in a covered dish on the side of the stove while they melt the butter you have allocated them; and very fine, young French beans.

Decorate the chop bone spikes with frilly paper hats, inverted bluebells or Union Jacks on pins according to the allegiance of your house.

To make gravy, pour off the surplus fat and loosen the deposit in the baking tray with a glass or two of strong ale. Boil and strain and serve – and forget neither mint sauce nor redcurrant jelly.

For a different kind of sauce, throw a good handful of sorrel leaves into 1 pint of stock, boil to reduce this by a quarter, add a coffeespoon of French mustard and a similar quantity of redcurrant jelly, pass through a fine sieve and incorporate the liquor left in the roasting tray. Thicken this with an egg yolk whisked into ⅛ pint of cream.

Basically there are two ways of cooking meat or fowl: frying or roasting in hot fat – so that the outside is sealed and the flavour remains within, or boiling, braising or slow-roasting (casseroling) so that a fair proportion of the flavour finds its way into the sauce . . . which is then incorporated into the dish. It is the latter section, not dependent on accurate-to-the-minute timing, which contains dishes most suitable for the cook/hostess.

Boiled leg of lamb with caper sauce

(Boiled leg of lamb may not sound 'haute cuisine', but it makes a splendid dinner dish.)

4–5 lb. leg of lamb

thyme, bayleaves, marjoram, etc.

a butter muslin big enough to be doubled up and envelop the joint

Use a dessertspoon each of crushed thyme, broken bayleaves, marjoram and such other herbs as are available or pleasing. Sprinkle one side of the doubled muslin generously with the herbs. Wrap the joint in the muslin and sew up tightly. Put it into a pan, with enough cold water to come to an inch over the top of the joint. Bring the water to the boil and simmer for a good 40 minutes to the pound, skimming from time to time.

For the sauce:

¾ pint lamb stock

¼ pint cream

1½ oz. butter

1½ oz. flour

2 tablespoons capers

Bring the stock and cream to the boil, add the flour worked into the butter and whisk while the sauce thickens. Add the capers, and check the seasoning; there are those who prefer the capers chopped, but the flavour of the sauce is more delicate if they are left whole.

To serve: take the leg of lamb from its broth, cut open the muslin and wash off excess herbs and pepper with a ladleful of broth, judiciously wielded. Cut the meat into thick slices and serve sauce liberally. The meat will remain happily in hot broth for an extra hour or so – and will stand being warmed up in it a number of times.

VEAL

Roast veal

is much neglected. Veal is so expensive that one has got used to buying small quantities, beating what one gets into escalopes and cooking them in any one of the seven hundred ways. A joint of veal is expensive, but it is uncommonly delicious. Ask for boned and rolled shoulder; it should be Dutch rather than English. Spread it lightly with French mustard, salt and pepper it and seal the joint in butter in a roasting tray on top of the stove. Let it cool. Start it off in a preheated oven on mark 7 (425°F) and then lower the temperature to mark 5 (375°F) allowing about 25 minutes to the pound. If the meat is ready before you are, turn the oven down to a lower setting, put the meat on the bottom shelf, baste it now and then, and no harm will come to it.

To serve, put the meat on a dish, pour off some of the excess fat from the roasting tray and mix into the juices that remain as much double cream as it will accept without spoiling the mahogany colour of the gravy. If you have meat cooked to perfection with an immaculate sauce and a few buttered new potatoes by way of accompaniment, it is lunacy to slosh on to your plate a salad swimming in no matter how delectable a vinegary sauce. Use another plate for, say,

Salad of French beans

Boil your beans in well-salted water; drain them, and while they are still warm mix them into a dressing made of

1 tablespoon tarragon vinegar
1 tablespoon lemon juice
3 tablespoons olive oil
1 teaspoon sugar
1 sieved hard-boiled egg yolk
salt and pepper

Blanquette de veau   (for 6)

2 lb. shoulder or boned breast of veal cut into 1-inch cubes
3 tablespoons oil
4 tomatoes peeled and liquidized
1 crushed clove garlic
salt
1½ pints water
1 onion spiked with cloves
1 leek
1 piece celery
1 bayleaf
salt
pepper
¼ pint cream
1½ oz. butter
1½ oz. flour
8 oz. button mushrooms simmered in a wineglass of dry
   white wine

Fill a pan with the water; bring it to the boil and poach the cubes of veal for 5 minutes. Strain, reserving the water.

Heat the oil, liquidized tomatoes and garlic in a saucepan. Add veal cubes and let this cook with lid on for 1½ hours stirring occasionally – until the veal is tender.

Meanwhile add to the water the spiked onion, the leek, celery and bayleaf (tied together), salt and pepper and any scraps or bones of veal. Reduce by boiling to about a pint. Add flour rubbed into the butter and cream. Let this simmer for a few minutes and strain.

The dish is an assembly job: the garlic-simmered veal being poured into the cream-thickened sauce and made fragrant by wine-soaked mushrooms. It will last well in a slow oven, can be warmed up without detriment and may – if you feel dashing – be garnished with squares of bread fried golden in olive oil.

Veal pie

A different sort of veal pie for winter.

Step one:
   1½ lb. Jerusalem artichokes
   3 oz. butter
   ¼ pint cream
Scrape the artichokes, cut them into slices, and simmer these slowly in butter over a low flame, in a pan with a lid tightly in place; stir now and then to make sure they do not burn. When the artichokes are soft, pour contents of pan into a large pie dish.

Step two:
   2 lb. stewing veal
   clove of garlic
   2 tablespoons of tomato purée
Cut veal into small pieces and simmer in a quart of stock for 1½ hours. Season to taste; remove the veal into the pie dish, reduce the liquor by half and add tomato purée and garlic. Pour this into pie dish.

Step three:
   ½ lb. button mushrooms
   a wineglass of Pernod
Cut mushrooms in half and simmer very slowly in Pernod. Add this to the pie dish. Mix contents of pie dish; if it is too thin, thicken a little with cornflour (remove all liquid, add cornflour, simmer, strain back) then cover and decorate pie dish with puff pastry and bake in a mark 6 (400°F) oven for 45 minutes, painting the puff pastry with cream 15 minutes from coming-out time.

Veal cutlets

Dredge with seasoned flour, liberally sprinkle with dried rosemary and fry in hot butter. There is no advantage in underdone veal; if in doubt, cook it for a longer rather than a shorter time.

HAM AND PORK

A ham is a leg of pork – salted and smoked. As such it weighs between 10 and 16 lb. Only limited quantities can be consumed at one sitting – try as you will with mousses and terrines, ham by any other name goes on tasting quite remarkably like ham. Nevertheless – boiled, braised or baked – an entire ham on its first appearance at table is delectable.

Ask for it to be boned. Soak it in water for at least 24 hours, changing the water at half-time. Then boil in plain water: seasoning and aromatics are wasted on such meat. As soon as it boils, turn down the flame so that the water does no more than shiver, and allow 20 minutes to the pound. Let it cool in its own liquor if you are having it cold. Hot or cold, the brown rind will peel easily.

For the first meal from the ham, cut medium slices and serve with no other garnish than a tablespoonful of champagne (for children and teetotallers use a similar quantity of white sauce, with cream, butter and parsley). Subsequently you can serve slices braised in madeira and accompanied by leaf spinach; cold ham and salad; cold ham and salad; cold ham and . . .

Cumberland sauce

is custom-built to accompany ham, and one of the few classic English sauces. To make it, cut the pithless rind from a lemon and half an orange, chop finely into strips and boil for 10 minutes. Dissolve 2 tablespoons of English mustard in 4 tablespoons of port. Add 4 tablespoons of redcurrant jelly. Add the chopped rind and bring to the boil, slowly stirring while the sauce becomes smooth and thick. Serve it – and the ham – at any temperature.

One answer to the old ham problem is

Ham mousse

Chop and pound – or liquidize – 1½ lb. of lean ham; add ½ pint of thick white sauce seasoned with mustard. Pass this through a sieve. Now dissolve as much leaf or powdered gelatine in a teacupful of water as promises on the packet to 'nicely set 2 pints of liquid' and add this to the mixture. Beat together ¼ pint of single and ¼ pint of double cream. Add this, too. Mix well and let the mousse set in the refrigerator in a mould, a pretty dish, or, if you prefer, a number of individual dishes. This serves eight.

Perhaps the noblest ham is

Virginia baked ham

a process that is equally practicable, if slightly less impressive, for smaller cuts or even thick slices if they are rolled and tied. Take the ham from its liquor when three-quarters cooked. Remove its rind and spike the outside with cloves. Add a small coffeecup of pineapple juice to 1 lb. of brown sugar. Put in another small cup of rum, blend, and spoon over the ham in an oven tray. Cook the ham in the bottom of a mark 3 (325°F) oven for 90 minutes, basting frequently. Decorate *à la porcupine* with maraschino cherries and pineapple chunks mounted on cherry sticks, and use the juices in the pan for gravy.

Boiled ham

For something a little less noble, buy a piece of boiling ham (or bacon). If it is packed in cellophane, ignore the advice to cook it in its wrapping. Soak it overnight to remove excess salt (alternatively, buy 'green' bacon which is milder and may be cooked at once). Bring the joint slowly to the boil and simmer it gently, allowing about 45 minutes to the pound. Alternatively, take off the rind after soaking, put it into an oven tray fattest side up, cut out little strips of fat cross-wise so that the surface looks like the outside of a pineapple and spike it here and there with cloves. Blend ½ lb. of Demerara sugar with 2 tablespoons of white rum and the same quantity of water. Pour this over the ham. Cook in a low oven for 35 minutes to the pound, basting every 15 minutes, adding a walnut or two of butter and an additional spoon or two of water if the basting liquid becomes too thick. Serve the ham with slices of pineapple baked in the basting liquid.

Roast pork

In a word, the difference between the French and English approach to roast pork is crackling. The French remove the skin and much of the fat, and cut it into strips called *lardons* for lacing into lean joints. We leave it on and make it crisp. As crackling is, for many people, the cardinal reason for preferring pork to other meats it is important to go about it the right way. It is the butcher's job to score the rind. After that it is up to you. If you have time, rub the skin with a mixture of salt and oil and leave this to soak in overnight. Otherwise, put a breakfastcup of water and 2 tablespoons of salt into a roasting tray, boil gently on top of the stove and give each section of the scored rind half a minute or so in the bubbling brine. Let the rind dry before you start to cook it.

The joint should be brushed with fat and given a second sprinkling of salt, put into a prewarmed mark 7 (425°F) oven for 15 minutes and then roasted at its appointed temperature. Pork requires a good 30 minutes to the pound in a mark 5 (375°F) oven, for there is no virtue in underdone pork. Baste frequently. If the crackling looks as if it is beginning to get too dark, protect it loosely with foil or paper, which must be removed 10 minutes before the joint leaves the oven. If, when the joint is cooked, the crackling is still soggy – which will be your fault and not mine – pour off the fat and raise the oven temperature for about 10 minutes.

Roast stuffed belly of pork

is an excellent, much neglected, economical, family joint, ideal for those who care for crackling, of which there is a lot. It can be served hot or cold. The belly should be boned by your butcher, excess fat removed, and the rind scored. Then, for a 4–5 lb. piece of belly, take:

   8 oz. minced pork
   8 oz. minced liver
   4 oz. breadcrumbs
   3 oz. grated onion
   2 beaten eggs
   1 tablespoon each chopped sage, chopped parsley, salt,
   pepper and an optional crushed clove of garlic

Make a shallow incision down the centre of the belly, cutting towards but not through the rind with a knife, and create two side pockets between meat and rind, into which you place the stuffing. Roll the joint, so that the two long ends of rind meet around the stuffing, and tie it firmly at 1-inch intervals; prepare the rind for crackling and roast it as already described. Normally, the skin will never become crisp at the point of contact with the roasting tray. So if you are jealous of every square inch of crackling, 15 minutes before roasting is completed pour off the fat and stand the joint on a wire tray.

For the sauce, add to the deposit in the roasting tray some soured cream and as much again of stock or water, a little flour (if you like your sauce thick) and a spoonful of marmalade; boil and strain.

130

Roast pork normande

This recipe uses hand of pork, which is the trade name for the foreleg. It weighs around 5 lb. and tends to contain 20 per cent of bone. The asking price is around half that of the more popular hind leg; as it is more than three-quarters as nice, you are already showing a considerable profit.

Like its rich relation at the other end of the pig, a hand can be roasted, boiled or minced. The disadvantage is that you cannot obtain from it the large lean slices by which some people set such store.

hand of pork, boned
1 teaspoon salt
a little ground nutmeg
2 tablespoons oil
1 wineglass cider
4 oz. brown sugar
segments of apple
a little flour
butter

Ask the butcher to bone out a hand of pork. Rub it all over with a teaspoon of salt and a little ground nutmeg dissolved in 2 tablespoons of oil. Start it off in a hot – mark 8 (450°F) – oven and after 10 minutes reduce the temperature to mark 4 (350°F) and add the wineglass of cider and 4 oz. brown sugar. Roast for 1¾–2 hours, basting from time to time. (If you particularly want crackling, omit the brown sugar and give the meat a final 15 minutes in a hot oven.) As a crowning flourish, decorate with apple segments dusted with flour and simmered in butter.

Pork cheese

is an excellent Sunday morning breakfast dish, or was considered so while breakfasts were fashionable. To make it, take:

1 lb. cold roast pork, about 12 oz. of which should be lean
1 breakfastcup of strong gravy seasoned with Worcester
  sauce
1 dessertspoon chopped parsley
pinch nutmeg
1 teaspoon grated lemon peel
coffeespoon of ground mace

Cut the pork into small, very thin slices, season with pepper and salt, mix in the other ingredients, blend well and put into a mould. Add the gravy, cover with foil and bake in a medium oven for about an hour. When it's cold, turn it out of the mould.

Devilled pork chops

Dredge pork chops in flour, salt, and dry mustard, dip in beaten egg and then in toasted breadcrumbs, fry in a mixture of oil and butter. Garnish pork chops with a pineapple ring fried and seasoned with Tabasco.

A sausage in my schooldays seemed to me a rarely delectable fruit. I remember it well – so peppery hot that I could scarcely manage another bite, so good that I couldn't bear to leave it uneaten. I have experimented copiously of late trying to emulate this gastronomic beacon of my youth, but without avail. Perhaps 7–12 years is a human's optimum era for sausage eating, just as 18–23 is the time one most enjoys revues in the theatre, comparing (in my case) for the rest of one's life *Sweet and Low* to what appear to be its lukewarm and inferior imitators.

Hamburgers

Inspired by a friend who sells Hamburgers in a Discotheque – I have a wide circle of friends – and complains about having to buy pre-shaped 2 oz. mounds of Hamburger meat at 18p a go, I tasted his wares. They were

Hamburgers in the loosest sense of the word.

I gave him the following recipe which cut the cost to just under half: 1 lb. lean pork, 4 oz. pork fat, 3 oz. rusk (untoasted crumbs turn mixtures sour sooner), 4 oz. water, 1 egg. Mince the first three ingredients, add water and beaten egg, season with salt, coarse ground black pepper, a heavy pinch of mace and mix well. The resulting mass will compare favourably with the filling of most pork sausages.

Sausages

If you insist on the snap and crackle of the sausage skin, all need not be lost. While it is unlikely that a butcher will make up the mixture, stuff it into casings and sell it to you at a fraction of his usual price, you could buy the ingredients at one butcher's shop, mince them in the privacy of your own four walls and then ask another butcher to fill it for you into Cambridge or chipolata gut. By these somewhat devious means you will be able to reduce the cost-of-living index by 1¼ points.

This excerpt from my soon-to-be-published 'I was a teen-age night club owner' forms the basis of a good substantial meal such as one human might prepare for his mate in 5 minutes after a lawn-mowing session. You need: a small tin of frankfurter sausages, 6 oz. self-raising flour, 2 eggs, ½ pint milk, 1 teaspoon of grated horseradish, 2 oz. good dripping.

Add egg yolks to sieved flour, adding milk as you beat. Whisk egg whites and fold them into mixture to which you add horseradish, salt and pepper.

Melt the fat in a large frying pan and pour in the sausages, cut into 1-inch lengths. After a minute's sizzling, distribute the sausage pieces evenly over the pan, turn up the flame to its top limit and pour in the pudding mixture. Let this cook for 2 minutes or a little more, shaking the pan to stop it from sticking and burning; then engage under a very hot grill or toaster to set the top. Reverse on to a preheated serving dish and cut into slices or fingers.

We who cook for what is loosely called a living try hard to create the impression that we are artists rather than trades-men. To this effect we write that sirloin is 'stripped', as is a canvas; ingredients, like paints, are 'blended'; soups are 'constructed'; sauces 'fashioned', a menu 'designed'. 'Carve an ounce of butter from a block', I have written with my best you-and-me-together-Henry-Moore look. After this I selected a fine brush and painted the outside of a jam tart case, coloured the onions, chiselled the guests. The lan-guage is flowery, the argument impressive and still people will insist on shouting, 'Hey, you with the white hat.'

If there is one confection that smacks even more of artistry than others, it is the raised pie . . . such as, in its most basic form, you find on the outside of veal, ham and egg or your actual pork.

Pork pie
The crust of such a pie is made by pouring hot liquid on to flour . . . so that you are in fact sculpting partially cooked

pastry; the substance could also be used for lino-cuts, mezzotints, etc. To get to the basic facts, you make your hot water crust by donning an old smock, pulling a navy blue beret over your right eye, screwing a Passing Cloud cigarette into your ebony holder . . . and putting into a pudding bowl

½ lb. plain flour
a fair amount of salt, like half a teaspoon
1 beaten egg

Throw some flour over the beaten egg and pour on to this mixture 3½ fluid oz. of boiling water in which you have boiled 1¼ oz. each of butter and cooking fat. Mix the pastry with a wooden spoon until it is cool enough to handle . . . when you handle it. Knead and mix until the egg streaks have disappeared and the pastry is smooth . . . at which point you leave it for half an hour in a warm place. It is now that you don your sculptor's outfit, comb the hair over your eye, affect a wild look and remove from the pastry ball one-third of the volume from which you will be constructing lids.

Divide the rest into six even parts and roll each piece into a circle which, when draped over an inverted, floured tumbler, will reach two inches down. When six tumblers have been thus adorned, put them into a refrigerator for a while to set. Meanwhile, roll out six lids and make the filling:

12 oz. lean coarse-minced pork
1 medium size onion, finely chopped
salt and pepper
2 tablespoons cider
1 tablespoon sieved apple

Blend well and divide this mixture into six equal parts . . . stand back and measure them for regularity by lifting a thumb and closing an eye . . . fill the cases and then cover the pies with the lids. Moisten the joints and pinch them together. Brush the outside with beaten egg and cut a small cross into the top of each pie to enable the steam to emerge.

Bake for 25 minutes at mark 7 (425°F) when the case should be brown; then turn down the oven to mark 4 (350°F), cover the pies with greaseproof paper and bake for another hour or so to cook the meat.

If you are a perfectionist, if you want to hang or exhibit rather than eat the pork pies, then you can cut some pastry leaves and place them gently over the steam escape hole prior to cooking. Later, when the pies are cooked, remove the bud of leaves and funnel on to the meat inside the piecrust some port jelly . . . just 2 tablespoons warm water to dissolve 2 teaspoons of gelatine crystals and a glass of port to flavour the stuff. Syphon a little into each pie.

A garnish should be a trimming or accompaniment to fish, meat or fowl that blends in flavour and complements in colour. It is infinitely depressing that in this country it is more often chopped parsley scattered to hide the blemishes of boiled potatoes around a stew. In the classic French cuisine an inordinate amount of time is spent giving each dish its authentic garniture. A Chateaubriand without its accompanying soufflé potatoes (page 104) would be as unthinkable as a kitchen without its chefs. But while it may be interesting for readers of menus to know that *à la financière* means that the dish will abound with quenelles (fish or meat balls), that *princesse* denotes the presence of asparagus tips, that *bonne femme* includes mushrooms and that *St Germain* encompasses dried peas, this knowledge is of no more than academic use to the cook/hostess. The ideal garnish for a home-cooked meal must be quick to make, or capable of being prepared in advance, or cookable in the same oven as the dish it is going to support.

Take first the quick-to-make category: cucumber diced, dusted with seasoned flour and sautéed for 2 minutes in sizzling butter – is a pleasant garnish for a veal cutlet fried in olive oil and butter and rosemary.

In the ready-made group, you can use coarsely chopped chives to decorate a garnish of young French beans dressed in 2 tablespoons of olive oil, a teaspoon of lemon juice, a good pinch of salt and a coffeespoon of granulated sugar. (Pour it over the beans while they are still warm.)

But the most satisfactory garnishes are those that share the last 20 minutes of oven-time with the joint. For example, small skewers of alternate pieces of mushroom, kidney and pimento cooked in bacon fat can be stuck into a leg of lamb to make it look like a porcupine – and taste better.

Chicken garnish

To sound the deathknell for soggy chipolatas, take

7 oz. minced beef
2 oz. minced pork
1 oz. grated onion
a beaten egg and a sherry glass of soda water

Season with mustard and salt and black pepper and shape into small marbles. Roll in flour and cook with a chicken for 15 minutes.

Provençale tomatoes

An excellent, all-purpose garniture for baked meats can be Provençale tomatoes.

3 oz. white breadcrumbs
½ oz. chopped parsley
1 small grated shallot
1 or 2 crushed cloves of garlic

Season well, add a spoonful of olive oil and heap on eight halves of tomatoes in a buttered oven dish. They require 25 minutes in a medium oven and can be parsleyed before serving.

The great restaurants still make their weekly pans of 'mother sauces' (foundation sauces from which others are blended), but the pans are smaller; it is no longer a matter of course for the chef to pour into the meat juices of a pan a ladleful of *Notre Espagnole*. Sauces have become thinner, lighter, subtler – altogether less elaborate works of art.

Today the French leave Dover after a day-trip to the emporia around Piccadilly Circus and report that we have bottles and bottles of A1, HP, OK, Daddy's . . . but no religion. It is sad that among all this array of well-adjusted, ready-mixed sauces and relishes we have nothing economically available that can be used as a foundation sauce, which is the function of the *grandes sauces* of the Haute Cuisine. Here, then, is an enormously useful foundation sauce you can make: Sauce Espagnole. The uses are infinite. Reduce a pint of it to half that quantity, add a glassful of port and you have the perfect sauce to rejuvenate a slice of tired ham. Or reduce it by about one-third, add a sliced truffle – if you can afford it – and some poached button mushrooms, and adorn an escalope of veal or glaze an egg softly cooked *en cocotte*. Or incorporate it with the butter in which steak or cutlets have been fried, adding French mustard.

The sauce will keep almost indefinitely in a refrigerator; if surface mould appears, remove it and boil up what remains.

Sauce Espagnole
2 oz. good fat – lard or dripping
4 oz. chopped salt pork or diced fat green bacon
6 oz. each carrots, onions, celery, all coarsely chopped
1 crushed clove of garlic
3 rounded tablespoons flour
2 oz. tomato purée
3 pints water
2 soup cubes
1 bouquet garni

Melt the fat in a heavy saucepan and put in onion and bacon; cook for a minute or two before adding the garlic and vegetables. Stir for about 5 minutes in a medium flame, then cover and cook slowly for about 20 minutes, to give a rich brown gravy. Now add the flour and tomato sauce and brown the mixture – making sure that it does not burn – before adding water, soup cubes, bouquet garni, salt and pepper. Stir the mixture until it comes to the boil and cook on a very low flame for 2 hours. Skim off the surface fat, remove the bouquet garni, and pass the contents of the saucepan through a fine sieve or liquidizer. Boil the resultant sauce in a clean pan until the quantity is reduced to approximately 2 pints. Finally, cool and store it.

There is still something to be said for buying bottled sauces, pickles, chutneys and relishes: you have the chance of a variety that is denied the lady who makes 28 lb. of mushroom ketchup and has to live with it. But the price grocers would have you pay for the necessary flavoured vinegars really seems out of all proportion to the work involved. If you are going to make your own pickles and chutneys, you can get distilled white malt vinegar at any decent shop. Buy a quart and you can divide it into four parts.

VINEGARS

Tarragon vinegar

a good handful of fresh tarragon, or a rounded tablespoon
  of the dried herb
½ pint vinegar

Lightly chop the tarragon leaves, put them into a beer bottle or kilner jar and pour on the vinegar warmed to the temperature of a cup of buffet-tea. Cover it, and you will find that over the weeks the tarragon flavour becomes increasingly strong. If it is too herbaceous, make up with a little more vinegar.

Garlic vinegar

3 cloves garlic
good pinch salt
½ pint vinegar

Crush garlic and salt in a mortar, pour on the vinegar just off boil, sluice out the mortar and bottle all the contents in a kilner jar. After a week or two, strain and rebottle.

Apple vinegar

It is pointless to make this in small quantities. Take 14 lb. or more sour apples, cut them up, put them in a tub in the basement or potting shed, pound them with a hammer, and when they begin to fizz add some water, which they will assimilate. After three weeks strain off the juice and for every gallon of liquor add ½ pint of white vinegar – reduced from a pint by boiling. Keep this in the bottle for a few weeks before using.

Chilli vinegar

is not to be despised. It is as hot as you care to make it and is produced simply by pouring ½ pint of boiling vinegar over anything from ½ oz. to 2 oz. of dried chillis.

CHUTNEYS

These are marriages of sugar and vinegar built on a base of fruit or vegetable and flavoured with the contents of small jars and packets that have lost their labels. A chutney requires long, slow cooking and, as it tends to dry over the months, jars for future use should be bottled in a more liquid form than those designed for immediate consumption.

For your own house recipe, a fair guide is to take 2 lb. of fruit to 1 lb. of sugar, 1 lb. of onions, 1 lb. of raisins, 1 pint of vinegar and 8 oz. of assorted flavourings. The method of preparation generally is as for . . .

Pear chutney

3 lb. peeled, cored, sliced cooking pears
1 lb. chopped seedless raisins
4 oz. sliced, crystallized ginger
2 oz. crushed garlic
1 oz. salt
grated rind and juice of 1 lemon
1 lb. brown sugar
1½ pints white distilled vinegar
a muslin bag containing 2 dried chilli peppers, 6 cloves,
    12 juniper berries and such herbs and spices as you
    choose

Mix together the pears, onions, raisins, ginger, garlic, lemon and salt and pour over them the sugar and vinegar boiled for 15 minutes in the company of the spice bag. Leave this overnight. Cook gently for 3 hours when you should have the right rich, dark consistency. Remove spice bag, and then bottle.

PICKLES

To pickle is simply to preserve something in spiced vinegar. The social overtones are working class; if that puts you off there is little hope for you. Pickling is ideally achieved in two operations:
1 The careful preparation and seasoning of the fruit, flesh, fish or vegetable.
2 The creation of the pickle in which it is to be cooked.

Sweet cucumber

  2 lb. peeled, sliced ridge cucumber
  12 oz. finely sliced onions
  1 large finely sliced sweet pepper
  1 oz. salt

Put the cucumber, onions and peppers into a bowl, sprinkle with salt and mix from time to time. After 2 hours put them into a colander and rinse them gently.

The pickle:
  8 oz. brown sugar
  ¾ pint distilled white malt vinegar
  1 tablespoon pickling spice (or your own concoction of garlic, mustard seed, mace and turmeric)

Bring this liquid to the boil for a few minutes, making sure the sugar has completely dissolved. Then add the vegetables and let it come back to the boil. Bottle in the usual manner. This is the most satisfactory filling I know for plain pickle sandwiches.

PARSLEY

Parsley is green and coarse and harsh; chop it and sprinkle over a dish and it adds colour and unsubtlety. Deep fried and served with fish or what, it is no better than the fat it has been cooked in. Pounded in a mortar and mixed with butter it makes a less pleasing spread than would watercress treated in the same manner, while the omelette fines herbes made with parsley alone is one of my least favourite confections.

It is the delicatelessness of the herb that makes it so unacceptable. New potatoes blossom into fresh glory with a few sprigs of fennel or dill; soups benefit from sorrel or cress; a mayonnaise from chopped chives; a good sauce deserves chervil; small tarragon leaves are happy in young

143

green lettuce hearts and sliced tomatoes; rosemary loves veal; lamb goes with bay. All these have a purpose and give a message, while parsley grows unfriended and uncompromisingly green with only the grace to turn yellow overnight by way of an excuse.

It is the strength of parsley that is its weakness and its undoing. While other herbs suggest, parsley submerges all that it approaches. If you use it, do so with this in mind: add it to a dull potato soup, a steamed fillet of cod or an overboiled turnip; in fact, like anyone who overacts give him a bigger part. Parsley has an undeniable freshness which might make one forget the chromium plated origins of cube, packet, tin or dehydration, but, generally speaking, to add parsley is a sign of failure.

Why not fail magnificently and do what an old Park Lane veg. cook used to do (I've gone too far by now to tell you where he actually worked). For special customers he would chew a clove of garlic in his yellow teeth and after a while he would fill his mouth with chopped parsley; then with a fierce puff, as might see the extinction of a mammoth candle, he distributed the particles of garlicky green over the dish in question. Like his many contented customers he lived to enjoy a ripe and respectable evil-smelling old age.

GARLIC

'Garlick hath properties', wrote Thomas Nash in *The Unfortunate Traveller* (1594), 'that make a man winke, drinke and stinke.' In Nash's day, the 'stinke' was of no great importance; just another of a whole series of revolting smells two hundred years before the toothbrush, a hundred before soap, when a bath was considered eccentric, and a change of shirt made news. As personal hygiene became more generally accepted, garlic, by virtue of the 'stinke', became less and less common in this country, the aroma placing a man way down the social scale among poorman-beggarman-thief, to which must be added 'foreigner'. Now the acrid breath of garlic emanates from the best people as a status symbol of gastronomic emancipation. Enlightened young men, who in the thirties published slim leatherbound volumes of verse now run garlic and fishnet restaurants in SW3. Apart from what it does to your personal appeal, the best reason for NOT eating garlic is the fierceness of the residual patina, coating tongue and palate and tainting food and drink that follows. Of one thing there can be no doubt: meals that include dishes cooked with garlic must be most carefully considered. A dish of hot garlic bread followed by melon; an aioli of prawns before a hot house peach is not only hard on the taste-buds but a terrible waste of money, too.

A garlic press is an efficient instrument which keeps hands and working surfaces untainted while it provides you with a liquid of which you can use as little as a drop instead of as much as a slice. Used correctly your guests should look at one another and say: is there a touch of garlic in this, or is there? Used the other more popular way, it burns you down to the nostrils, gives you the devil of a thirst and throws you, by default, into the arms of your fellow diners (this is the part that Nash ingenuously referred to as 'winke').

Here are two recipes for garlic things in their starker form, though in each case the quantities can be lessened to give the dishes a semblance of delicacy.

Garlic bread

Take a small French loaf and make an incision down the long side. Into 2 oz. of butter work a clove of garlic, pressed, shape into a sausage the length of the loaf and press into the opening. Bake for 10 minutes in a hottish oven, butter side up, serve hot, provide napkins, eat with any strong soup.

Aioli

Blend the liquid from 2 pressed cloves of garlic with 2 egg yolks, a teaspoon of French mustard, a coffeespoon of five parts salt, one part black pepper, a good dessertspoon of lemon juice; stir well as you slowly add ½ pint of salad oil, giving the mixture a final fast whisk to stiffen it. Serve in avocado pears, with boiled fish, any shell fish, or small squares or corrugated brown paper; you are unlikely to be able to tell the difference.

Vegetables and Salads

The young man who chooses catering for a career is likely to spend the first year of his apprenticeship on, with, at, under, in, around and about potatoes. At the age of seventeen I knew fifty-three different ways of preparing potatoes and decided to write a definitive potato primer. At eighteen I was promoted to the sauce department and looked back upon my year's potato courtship as a juvenile folly. This is a common pattern in the hierarchy of the kitchen. It may well explain why established chefs write endlessly about the preparation of Dover soles and only fleetingly on deployments for the potato.

Some years ago, when my sepulchral voice was heard soon after the break of dawn on a BBC programme called *Hints to Housewives* I used to be asked by the producer to give recipes involving various objects which farmers were unable to sell: beetroot, turnip, mangel wurzel, that sort of delicacy . . . This was so opposed to the image of myself which I was then trying to project that in no time at all someone else was demoted to 'Hs to Hs'. I still listen to such programmes, and when I hear 'the ingredients for the next dish are: a pint of double cream, three egg yolks, a soupçon of caviare, one oyster, two turnips and a five-pound note finely chopped' I give myself a knowing look and say 'varmers be in trubble o'er turnips agin'.

A meat, a fish, even a vegetable, I feel should not only be *recognizable* after cooking; they should contribute, in cost as well as in volume, the major part of the dish which is built around it. Allow me to give you some of the more exciting ways of preparing a potato.

POTATOES

There is no classic name for a new potato boiled in its skin. You have to say, 'I want them IN their skins.' And the restaurateurs are frightened that someone will see you eating them and think the worse of them for it.

This is an appalling state of affairs. New potatoes are at their best scrubbed, boiled in salt water, served with good butter and rock salt. Yet the fear that people will think you have not bothered prevents us from presenting them like that. If no one will sponsor them – and how handsome it would be if we could NOT peel them and say 'We're having Pommes de Terre Ritz Berkeley for dinner' – I am prepared to lend my name.

New potatoes
Boil the potatoes in their skins, peel when they are just done, and slice them into a pudding basin. Get a small handful of chives and one of parsley, chop coarsely, and pound together in a mortar. For every pound of potatoes, you need ⅓ pint of double cream which you bring to the boil before adding a teaspoon of the herbs. Pour over the sliced potatoes, heat in a low oven and, if it appeals to you, sprinkle with a mixture of toasted breadcrumbs and parmesan cheese which should brown for a moment under the grill.

artichokes will be easier

Pommes Lyonnaise

Boil new potatoes in their skins until they are just cooked. Peel them and cut them into slices. Fry some thin onion rings in a pan of oil or lard, and when they are golden add the potatoes; let these colour slightly in the pan and you can serve with chopped parsley.

Potato salad

Ideally you should choose kidney-shaped new potatoes that are yellow in colour and waxy in consistency. Boil them in their skins, then peel them and slice them and mix the warm slices in a dressing of 4 parts olive oil, 1 part lemon juice, 1 part vinegar, salt and pepper. Garnish the salad with chopped spring onions and crisp streaky bacon.

For when you eventually tire of new potatoes in their skins, or when new potatoes grow up to become old, here are some other ways.

Pommes maître d'hôtel

1 lb. new potatoes, peeled and boiled and sliced and incorporated into ¼ pint of cream, a good pinch of cayenne pepper, and a tablespoon of fresh chopped parsley, serves four.

Pommes purée

are not boiled potatoes mashed with a fork, to which one adds dripping. Mashed potatoes can be so good that it is worth taking trouble, even to the extent of following this recipe.

Peel the potatoes, cut them into evenly sized pieces, and steam. When they are cooked, pass them through a sieve. To 1 lb. potatoes add 2 oz. warm melted butter, just under ¼ pint of hot milk, salt and pepper to taste, and a pinch of grated nutmeg. Blend well and serve at once. Cooked like this they are hot and delicious.

If you want to keep mashed potatoes, use a little less milk than in the recipe. Make them as above, place them in a basin, and cover the top with a thin top layer of milk and cream. Keep in the bottom of a mark 1 (275°F) oven and when needed beat in the top coat and serve.

Brown hash of potatoes

Melt 2 oz. butter and 1 tablespoon oil in a frying pan; when hot add 3 teacups of raw potato chopped small. Season well. Use wooden spoon to press down so that potatoes take up minimum space in frying pan. Grate onion on top and cover with lid or plate. Cook slowly until potatoes are soft; brown top under a hot grill.

Pommes Macaire

Ambitious cookery books tell you to use the inside of baked potatoes; this is a pointless extravagance. Steam potatoes, sieve them, add to 1 lb. potato 1½ oz. butter and season well. Shape into flat cakes, roll in flour and fry in a mixture of oil and butter until they are a good colour on each side.

Pommes Anna

These sound like a waste of time, but are delicious and look beautiful. Peel potatoes into barrel shapes and cut these into uniformly thin slices. Dry the slices. Take a round flan dish, rub with clarified butter, and place the potato slices in carefully arranged layers, adding salt, pepper and a dash of clarified butter to each layer. Cook for a minute or two on top of the stove, then cover closely with foil, and cook in a hot oven for 15 minutes; turn upside-down and cook for another 15 minutes. Turn out on to a dish and serve like a flan, cutting it in wedges.

Potato cake

Having placed a frying pan over a hot flame, grab a good-sized potato and grate it upon the half moons of a grater. You may leave the skin on, or wash it if you are fussy, and upon the same grater get to work on half a medium-sized onion. Squeeze from the mush an initial spurge of moisture – 77 per cent of water is said to make up the inside of tubers – and leaving a starchy oniony puddle on the work surface, add salt and pepper. Gather up the gratings and shape them to fit the base of your frying pan – into which, experienced campaigner that you are, you have poured a modicum of oil when the haze over it became noticeable. Now a very remarkable thing happens. The potato mixture does not cling irrevocably to the pan. It shifts easily, almost effortlessly across the greased surface, though it appreciates being shaken a little to prove this point. Add some butter or dripping to the upward-looking side and turn the mixture with a fish slice – or toss it.

The potato cake is done after 3 minutes or so on each

side, and is served in slices – or quarters or halves, depending on your popularity, guest-appeal or, let's face it, the size of the potato you selected in the first place. For Heaven's sake, when you get a new recipe try it in small quantities on yourself, your enemies or your pets and then invite people to share it with you – when you may use several potatoes and the whole onion.

As this is delicious, quick and easy without being what is called a main dish, make a main dish. I do feel that the grill of a cooker is too little used by most people. The masses employ it for the manufacture of toast and the enlightened occasionally remove the wire platform and cook assorted items that collectively hide under the name of mixed grill (though by removing the wire platform they could be summonsed under the Trades Descriptions Act). I use a grill as a short-term oven.

Pig's kidney

is a beauteous thing, God wot, as do most of us gourmets. Pierce it with a hat pin rubbed in garlic, wrap it in pig's cauling – the sort of string vest made of pork fat that you see wrapped around faggots, if you move in those circles. And then just grill away, and turn and baste and season. This will take a similar length of time as the potato – like 6 minutes – and can be done simultaneously, with an eye patch or hip bandage depending on whether you have an overhead or underplate fitting.

Now for the sauce. Boil together a sherry glass of tomato ketchup and a similar amount of strong ale and add a dessertspoon of Worcester sauce. To this you add the juices from the grill pan, salt and lemon juice and as much double cream as will turn it from a sharp liquor to the blandness you want from sauce.

PEAS

The bon viveur who gets his beef at Harrods, his Cape
Gooseberries at Jacksons and his Mont Blancs at Sagnes,
looks to his own garden for peas. Shop-bought fresh,
tinned or packeted varieties – picked and frozen in a day –
leave him cold, for even an hour between gathering and
cooking is to the pea's eternal detriment.

Peas should be boiled in a minimum of gently salted
water to which you can add mint if you like mint. They are
ready when you have eaten one and found it to be ready,
should be drained and served with enough fresh butter to
give them a shine and a thin sprinkling of castor sugar
to remove that shine.

Pea omelette

1 tablespoon freshly cooked peas, 1 of double cream, 3 eggs,
salt and pepper, blended with a fork and cooked the way
you usually cook an omelette – is an ideal first course if
you have the authority to make your guests eat as soon as
their omelette is served. If they wait until you have cooked
half a dozen or you put them in the oven until you have
cooked that many, it would be cheaper and infinitely less
trouble to give them a nice tin of spaghetti.

A dish of early summer vegetables

New carrots, scraped and sliced and washed, put in a
saucepan with 1½ oz. butter to a pound of carrots; a bare
dessertspoon sugar, a coffeespoon salt and pepper; keep
lid firmly on pan and cook on half flame for 15–20 minutes. Don't worry, they form their own liquor.

Baby beetroots, boiled, peeled and served with a sauce
of cream reduced by boiling to three-quarters, and dressed
with chopped chives.

French beans, quickly boiled, buttered and kept hot.

New potatoes, scraped, wrapped in buttered greaseproof paper and cooked 35 minutes in oven, mark 5 (375°F).

Two-portion cauliflowers, stalks indented, sparingly steamed and bathed in hollandaise sauce (page 50), might be the centre-piece.

Fritto misto

Brains. Artichoke hearts. Mushrooms. Aubergine. Cauliflower. Divide brain into 1 oz. pieces; take whole artichoke heart, mushroom caps, slices of aubergine and sprigs of cauliflower. Dust all with flour, dip in a batter made of flour and brown ale blended to the consistency of thick cream and fry in deep fat. Serve hot with a garlic-flavoured mayonnaise.

Love of animals is really one of the worst reasons for becoming a vegetarian. The death-shriek of a calf, soon to make its reappearance served with hard-boiled egg and anchovy, is only more audible, no more terrible, than the tiny scream of the severed rhubarb plant. Depriving your-

self of meat in the hope of saving the life of a quadruped is dim hope indeed! I know a woman in Muswell Hill who is a vegetarian and has four poodles to manifest her love of animals. As she gorges her tiny frame on nut cutlets and grated swede, her dogs eat tin after tin of meaty dog foods. Because of her, somewhere in the Welsh mountains a solitary sheep is shivering cold, wretched and unwanted, surplus to the nation's requirements; because of her dogs, a good old Shetland pony is sent to the knackers ready for its pressure-cooked end ... (yes, it's better because the flavour is sealed in ...). Let's face it: becoming a vegetarian is unlikely to have any real effect on the well-being of our dumb friends.

Nevertheless there is much cruelty deployed in the raising of animals whose ultimate destination is the saucepan and if your feelings are such that enjoyment of the meal is nullified by an awareness of the suffering caused to the animal ingredients, you have my sympathy; what is more, you shall have my advice:

Scrape new carrots, and new potatoes; peel some small onions, a few leeks, a savoy cabbage which you cut into quarters and a cauliflower which you treat similarly. Put all these vegetables gently into a large saucepan, cover with the minimum of salted water and simmer for half an hour, or less, using the potato as your guide to readiness.

To ½ pint of the vegetable stock, add ½ pint of single cream, 2 heaped tablespoons of plain flour and 3 oz. of butter. Whisk, or at the very least stir well, as this mixture slowly heats and thickens. Let it boil for 5 minutes, strain and give a good handful of finely chopped chives, or tarragon, or chervil if you prefer the taste.

Serve the vegetables dry on a soup plate, brushing them with a buttery pastry brush to enhance their appearance.

Serve the sauce in a soup tureen ladling generously over all but the cabbage and cauliflower which you top with some butter, blackened by fierce heat and a teaspoon of vinegar and thickened with the result of a rolling pin passed heavily over a teacupful of cornflakes. When I say the butter is blackened, perhaps I should have said coloured . . .

The streamlining of our catering industry has been responsible for the scarcity of fresh vegetables in restaurants. While time-and-motion experts, unconcerned with quality, urge the opening of ever larger tins of processed peas, even quite enlightened caterers feel that there is false economy in setting a costly man to work preparing vegetables that sell at a pittance per portion. So it's in the smaller establishment – where a cook who's not worried about time says 'I wasn't doing anything else so I got on with the carrots' – that you are most likely to get away from tin or packet: there, or at the Ritz, or at home. Here then, picked for the fresh vegetable's devotees, is as fair a selection of vegetable accompaniments to a wintery loin chop as you will get for the price.

Carrottes vichy
1 lb. carrots
1½ oz. butter
1 tablespoon soft sugar
a good pinch of salt

Top and tail the carrots, remove outer skin with a potato peeler and cut into slices the thickness of a 10p piece. Wash well, drain roughly and place in a pan with the butter, salt and sugar. Stir occasionally while butter and carrot-moisture come to the boil, then cover closely and cook on a medium-low flame for 20 minutes. Stir and reduce heat if the bottom layer begins to brown. Classically, carrottes vichy should not be coloured, but they are particularly delicious slightly glazed.

Purée de choux de bruxelles

1½ lb. sprouts
1½ oz. butter
1 tablespoon chestnut purée, tinned or tubed
top of 1 pint of milk
salt and pepper

Clean sprouts and boil until tender. Pass through sieve or liquidize, and add butter, milk, chestnut and seasoning. (This is very much tastier than it sounds.)

Parsnips au gratin

1 lb. parsnips
a cupful of white sauce
grated cheese

Clean parsnips and boil until just tender. Cut them into decent-sized dice and incorporate the pieces in the white sauce in an ovenproof dish. Sprinkle with grated cheese and cook in a hot oven for 10–15 minutes.

Broccoli

Steam your broccoli spears; serve them a little undercooked, lukewarm, with a blob of mayonnaise (Hellmann's is excellent if you don't care to make it yourself) spiced with some crushed garlic.

Red cabbage

Finely shred a medium-sized red cabbage. Take 3 oz. bacon fat and fry in this 8 oz. chopped onion and 4 oz. currants. Add the red cabbage, a large handful at a time; let it go limp in the sizzling fat before adding more. Pour into the pan ½ pint water. Season to taste and simmer for 2 hours. As the cabbage will now be blue, add vinegar to bring back the colour.

Braised onions

Peel onions, put two wooden skewers into their middle and place them in a roasting tray containing a wineglass of cider and about the same quantity of good lard or dripping. Cook in a mark 4 (350°F) oven, baste from time to time and serve when outside is brown and skewers emerge almost of their own accord. Braised onions give a lift to almost any meat dish.

Fried onion rings

Cut onions into rings, dust with flour, coat with beaten egg white, dry with another layer of flour and fry in deep fat. Restaurants who serve fried onion rings are oddly reluctant to disclose this method.

Seakale

One of our most delicate and unfortunately under produced vegetables. Clean the roots, boil them, drain well and serve with melted butter or white sauce in which cream and good butter will not be wasted.

CHICORY

Chicory can be eaten raw, or can be profitably cooked in a number of ways. Raw chicory tends to become easily discoloured unless it is kept, wrapped, in a cool place. The water content of chicory is high and when the plants are cut up they tend to 'bleed' readily. They can be chopped into rings and amalgamated with vinaigrette or mayonnaise, but the cutting and blending should be done shortly before the eating – or you'll have limp pieces swimming in a watery dressing.

Salad of chicory and orange   (for 4)

12 oz. chicory
2 oranges

salad dressing made of:
juice of half lemon
1 dessertspoon wine vinegar
bare teaspoon salt
granulated sugar
3 dessertspoons oil

Make the dressing; blend well.

Cut the rind from the oranges and with a sharp knife carve out the skinned segments (if you find this difficult cut the oranges into thin slices and quarter them). Cut the chicory into rings about ¼ inch thick. Mix and serve.

To make a mayonnaise of chicory cut the heads as for salad and incorporate into a thickish mayonnaise shortly before eating.

Chicory au gratin   (for 4)

4 large heads of chicory
2 oz. butter
2 oz. flour
½ pint milk
2 oz. grated cheddar cheese
1 oz. grated parmesan
cayenne pepper

Boil chicory in well-salted water. Drain it and arrange on a shallow greased baking dish. Sift the flour and whisk this into the milk and butter, stirring vigorously over a low flame until the sauce thickens. Add the cheddar cheese and stir until it has melted. Pour this sauce over the chicory, cover with parmesan and cook in a hot oven until the sauce is lightly browned on top.

Chicory sliced lengthwise (or left whole if the heads are small) and put in a roasting tray to accompany the last half-hour's oven-time of a joint makes a pleasant garnish for any meat.

Deep-fried chicory has its addicts too. The heads should be steamed for 15 minutes, then fried in fairly hot fat.

Braised chicory with walnuts (for 4)

4 large heads of chicory
2 oz. butter
¼ teaspoon dried basil
1 cup stock
2 teaspoons chopped walnuts
1 tablespoon butter

If the chicory is tired, remove a slice from the brown stem and place the heads in very cold water for some minutes. Dry them well, and halve the heads lengthways. Heat the butter in a large saucepan and when it has melted add the basil. Put in the chicory, salt and pepper, and brown for about 2 minutes on each side. Add stock – about a third of the cup at a time – and simmer until the chicory is tender, adding more stock as required. Finally, arrange on serving dishes and garnish with the walnuts fried in butter.

PROPERLY DRESSED

Popular literature at the turn of the century was generous in the deployment of epithets like 'dago', 'wog' and 'greasy foreigner'. As this last phrase was particularly undesirable, clean-cut Englishmen worked hard on the promotion of utterly greaseless images. Consequently, potatoes were boiled; fish steamed; meat plain roast on a rack. Never did nice people consume anything that might cause a trickle of liquid fat to run on to their chins . . . which is, of course, one of the things that makes foreigners so odious. From a gastro-social point of view we have turned full cycle: recently in a swinging bistro-type inn on the outskirts of Rotherham I heard a man say to his companion: 'There goes the sort of swine who takes no dressing on his salad.'

For myself I find naked salad of small appeal, while the best thing other people say about ungarnished leaves that taste of nothing much, tinged with slight bitterness, is 'delicate flavour'. If one were forced to select greenery to be taken neat, dandelions and watercress have a little more flavour to them than their cousins of the salad world, but why people consume these minor delicacies without dressing is as puzzling to me as why there are those who go to Chinese restaurants and order sausage and chips. The reasons would appear to be (a) lack of adventure; (b) because they disliked the sort of dressings they have tried or, (c) because they feel there is something decent and British about eating the stuff raw. These are poor reasons.

Salads require dressings and dressings should not be made by some rigorously followed recipe – but with a salad in mind; the sauce must be complementary to the leaves. It should also be remembered that, as with small children, what you are dressing requires to be well washed and meticulously dried. The ingredients are oil, acid and salt, with optional herbs and spices. The ratio is three measures of oil to one of acid and as vinegar and lemon juice cause things to dissolve, it is sensible when constructing dressings to add the oil last.

Oil is derived from olives, nuts and vegetables – or a mixture of the two latter classes. All are suitable for salads with the exception of those packed in containers marked 'for frying only'.

As olive oil is pungent and expensive it should be used only by those who care for the taste, which must be retained rather than disguised with sharp additives.

The best such dressing, ideal for the firmer types of lettuce like romaine and curly-leaved endive, is three parts olive oil to one part lemon-juice-and-wine-vinegar, plus a little salt. If you care for garlic, crush a clove on to a crust of bread and use this to wipe the inside of the salad bowl, whereafter it must be mixed and served with a minimum of delay – the longer the garlic remains the more salt is needed. There are on the market but few bad vinegars. All those that advertise are acceptable. The more expensive cider, tarragon, wine and garlic vinegars are excellent (though extravagant because you can make your own). Malt vinegar is possibly the least suitable.

The Americans have a saying that it takes four men to make a salad dressing. You need a spendthrift to lavish the oil, a miser to hoard the vinegar, an accountant to check the salt, and a madman to stir the ingredients.

Basic dressing
a good pinch of salt
a twist of fresh ground black pepper
1 tablespoon wine vinegar
3 tablespoons oil
This gives you a basis upon which to build.

For tomato salad

Peel the tomatoes, if you must, by dropping them into a pan of boiling water for 10 seconds – after which the skin comes off very easily. Slice them and to the basic dressing add:

another pinch of salt
a level teaspoon granulated sugar
chopped sweet basil

For cucumber salad

Peel and slice the cucumber, add salt and squeeze the slices gently between two plates. Pour off the resultant liquid and put the slices into the basic dressing to which you add:

another tablespoon oil
1 teaspoon lemon juice
chopped chives

For watercress salad

Pluck the cress to remove the thick stalks, wash, drain and to the basic dressing add:

½ teaspoon French mustard
1 small fresh peeled chopped pear

For chicory salad

The important thing is not to cut the chicory until the last moment. When the time comes, slice it and dress it and mix it and eat it within the course of half an hour at most. To the basic dressing add:

another pinch of salt
1 teaspoon lemon juice
the peeled chopped segments of an orange

For a salad of French beans

Boil the French beans until they are just tender, remove them from the water and while they are still lukewarm, dress with the basic dressing, to which you add:

1 teaspoon of castor sugar
1 dessertspoon of finely chopped onion
some chopped parsley

For cauliflower salad

Cut away most of the stalk of the cauliflower, and boil until just tender in well-salted water, covering the cauliflower with a crust of bread, unless of course you like the smell. Drain, cool, divide into portions.

Put the basic dressing into a liquidizer and add:

1 whole egg
1 teaspoon grated onion
1 dessertspoon tomato purée

Pour this over the cauliflower and decorate with sprigs of fresh dill.

For coleslaw

You need a very firm white cabbage. Cut it in half, remove the stalk and cut very thinly with a sharp knife. Liquidize the basic dressing with:

1 egg
1 dessertspoon sugar
1 teaspoon lemon juice
1 sherry glass orange juice

Mix in the shredded cabbage and add a handful of sultanas and a tablespoon of finely sliced onion.

SOMETHING SPECIAL FOR THE SALAD

One of the problems of having learnt to cook professionally – as opposed to picking it up from Mum, Aunt Sadie or a crash course at Rent-a-Gourmet – is that one has the steady conviction that one knows it all. The other day a house guest asked if I would like her to make the salad dressing. I smiled indulgently, spooned another quenelle of lobster into the simmering pan of *Entre deux Mers* and bade her go ahead.

The good lady went to work . . . and 15 minutes later came up with vinaigrette, French dressing or whatever you care to call it, and then wanted it to stand for 30 minutes. I was naturally too polite to say that she had done it in 14½ minutes over par . . . until I tasted the salad and realized that she was right and I wrong and were it not for her radical husband and my reputation I would have asked for the recipe on the spot. A week or two later, reading in the *Guardian* that her man was addressing a flush of Young Liberals in the barricaded library of a provincial university, I telephoned and said, 'About this salad dressing now . . .'

And she said: 'I stir.'

I told her I had noticed, and wondered what it was she had stirred.

Well, a coffeespoon each of salt and French mustard – La Favorite, or a similar yellow, as opposed to brown, mustard; a teaspoon of sugar, and freshly ground black pepper to taste. Add a tablespoon of wine vinegar and stir for at least 5 minutes before pouring on 3 tablespoons of best olive oil, either chopped mint or tarragon and both chopped parsley and some chopped chives.

Leave the dressing to stand for half an hour and put in the lettuce a minute or two before it is to be eaten. Turn it comprehensively in the dressing and, if you care for garlic, see that the salad bowl has been rubbed with a clove thereof. This recipe may supersede any previous salad dressing recipes I have given.

Caesar salad   (for 6)

salt and 1 clove garlic
1 teaspoon dry English mustard
1 tablespoon lemon juice

dash of Tabasco
3 tablespoons oil
2 heads of romaine or cos, etc.
1 tablespoon grated parmesan cheese
1 small tin anchovy fillets
1 beaten egg
½ cup of small squares of white bread

Take a wooden salad bowl, sprinkle the bottom with salt and rub the garlic into this until it disintegrates. Add mustard, lemon juice and Tabasco and stir until the salt is dissolved. Then add the pieces of washed, dried lettuce and give them a gentle, initial mix in the dressing. On to this sprinkle the parmesan cheese, add to it the anchovy fillets drained of oil, making sure that you remove such bones as anchovy canners leave in the tins, and then pour the egg over the salad. Mix again. Just before serving, add the cubes of bread fried in very hot olive oil, drained and salted. Remix and serve.

Salad of haricot beans

Buy dried white haricot beans, soak them overnight, boil in stock flavoured with bacon rind until beans are just cooked; when lukewarm drain and mix them in a dressing of three parts olive oil to one part wine vinegar; add small cubes of garlic sausage, finely cut slices of raw onion and chopped parsley. Serve cold.

Eggs

On a chalkwhite plate you lie
With loathing in your yellow eye
Swimming in sickly fat
Ugh

So wrote my brother Lucian before he gave up poetry and concentrated on painting at the age of 12. It sums up a general antipathy to the egg that has done little to help the work of the Egg Marketing Board. This is sad. For an egg, a good fresh egg, even an egg kept in a cool place for up to a week, is something that a cook cannot do without.

An egg elevated to haute cuisine is known as *un oeuf*. An egg can be taken to weigh 2 oz., which is a useful thing to remember in cake-making when it is necessary to match the weight of eggs with sugar, flour or fat. A fresh egg should sink in cold water.

An egg consists of a shell, which has little culinary worth; a yolk, which is useful for thickening; and albumen, or white which can be beaten and used for lightening. Practise separating yolk from white. The simplest way is to break the egg over a bowl and pass the yolk from half-shell to half-shell, letting the white run off into

167

the bowl. Or break the egg into the palm of your hand, tilt your hand forward and let the white run through your fingers. A little white left with the yolk does not harm: any impurity at all in the white will prevent you from beating it to a snow.

THE YOLK

The yolk of 1 egg will thicken about ⅓ pint of liquid. Remember that when eggs are thus used in soups or sauces the liquid must not be allowed to boil again or the eggs will curdle; it should be brought to the required temperature in a double boiler, or pudding basin placed in simmering water.

Two egg yolks whisked into ⅛ pint of single cream will turn a pint of thin broth into a soup of immaculate richness. Pour the boiling soup over the eggs, rather than vice-versa.

Mayonnaise

Take 1 egg yolk, a coffeespoon of lemon juice and a pinch of salt. Drip a coffeecup of oil drop by drop into this mixture, beating as you do so. The result is a mayonnaise.

Hollandaise Custard (for sauce recipe see page 50)

Take 1 egg yolk and 1 dessertspoon of castor sugar. Add 1½ coffee cups of milk. Whisk well and pour into a pudding basin. Stand this in a baking tray of hot water and put into a slow oven mark 2 (310°F) – for about an hour. The result is called custard.

There is basically nothing difficult about any of these operations and in every case if you increased the ratio of egg to liquid it would be impossible to go wrong provided you did not overheat the dish. Thus a hollandaise made

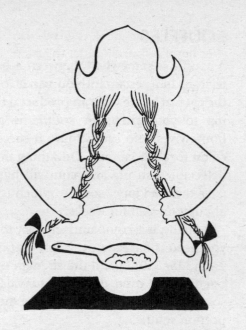

with 4 egg yolks and 6 oz. of butter cannot fail though it may become so thick that it will need a few drops of white wine to make it less pudding-like in texture. On the other hand it will be no better a sauce than the hollandaise sauce made with 2 egg yolks. It will just be more expensive.

THE WHITE

This sort of cooking tends to leave you with a lot of egg whites. Store these whites in a refrigerator, but bring them back to room temperature before you beat them.

If you like meringues, a surplus of albumen presents no problem. If you don't, stiffly beaten egg white can be used in mayonnaise and hollandaise to give a creamier texture. Omelettes and scrambled eggs made with extra whites are excellent. Soufflés invariably call for more white than yolk and there is a confection which has its addicts called soufflé surprise (page 174).

SOUFFLÉS

A soufflé is somewhere between a party piece and a confection. In a restaurant you use it to gauge the quality of the chef; at home you can produce a soufflé instead of talking to your guests. A soufflé is a prestige dish, and housewives who can achieve it successfully receive much credit for their labours. Odd thing that. Give your guests a delectable fish pie and you will hardly get a thank-you. Give them a kipper soufflé, which is foul, and they'll talk about your skill for weeks.

Actually, it is comparatively easy to make a soufflé; what you need is a steady oven, pre-warmed and kept at mark 2–3 (325–350°F) and the strength of mind to desist from opening the oven door at intervals trying to watch the soufflé rise. This is how you make the basic one-pint, four-portion soufflé:

1. Prepare a smooth, thick, white sauce from 2 oz. butter, 2 oz. flour, ⅔ pint milk, and let it cool.
2. Add seasoning and 4 well-beaten egg yolks.
3. Add up to 8 oz. chopped, sieved, grated or flaked fish, flesh, fowl or cheese.
4. Beat stiffly 5 egg whites and fold them into this mixture.
5. Lightly butter a soufflé dish and shake some grated parmesan cheese or paprika over the buttered surface.
6. Fill the dish three-quarters full with the soufflé mixture.
7. Cook for 25 to 30 minutes in a mark 2–3 oven (325–350°F).

Stages 1, 2, 3 and 5 can be completed in the morning, leaving only the beating of the egg whites, assembly, and cooking, for the evening.

Contrary to its cartoon image, a properly cooked soufflé is a hardy confection and will not collapse as someone opens the window or strikes a match. To ensure that it is ready for the table, open the oven door and shake the dish gently; the top should move softly in sympathy with the shaking, rather than tremble dangerously in fear of it. (The trembling soufflé needs a few more minutes.)

There are two kinds of soufflés: those that are held together by egg yolks cooked in a double boiler; those that are bound by flour cooked in butter. What they have in common is that they both need heatproof moulds, generously rubbed with butter, the savoury one sprinkled with cheese, the sweet one with castor sugar; this allows the bottom crust to be easily disengaged from its housing. As it is desirable to have the soufflé rise over the rim of the dish and stay there, it is not at all a bad idea to get a piece of greaseproof paper and treat it similarly, i.e. rub with butter and dust with sugar or cheese; you tie this round the dish to make a sort of collar.

The important thing to remember is that it is the guests and not the soufflés that must do the waiting. Count on half an hour, which is roughly the time it takes to eat two courses, inspect after 25 minutes and, if done, turn down oven and tell your guests to get a move on.

As a first course:

Oeuf mollet en soufflé

soufflé mixture
1 very softly poached egg per person
These should be made in individual soufflé moulds. To your white sauce add a good pinch of cayenne and 3 oz. parmesan cheese. Mix well.

Put 2 tablespoons of the mixture at the bottom of the mould, add the poached egg and top up with more mixture to three-quarters of the way up. Cook for 20 minutes on mark 2 (325°F).

As a main dish – for four:

171

Shrimp or lobster soufflé

⅔ pint well-seasoned white sauce
8 oz. peeled shrimps or lobster meat, liquidized or sieved
2 anchovy fillets sieved with a teaspoon of anchovy oil
4 eggs

Chicken soufflé

⅔ pint well-seasoned white sauce
6 oz. finely minced breast of chicken
2 oz. sliced mushrooms simmered in butter, and minced
1 coffeespoon Worcester sauce
5 eggs

Cheese soufflé

3 level tablespoons of plain flour or
 1 oz. if you have no tablespoons
4 ditto of butter . . . say 1¼ oz.
⅓ pint of hot milk
2 oz. parmesan cheese
2 oz. grated Gruyère cheese
4 whole eggs, and 2 egg whites
½ teaspoon salt
some pepper
a little nutmeg

Dissolve the butter in a pan, add the flour and cook this until the roux (which is the official name for flour cooked in butter) is done – that is, looks like sand, and as you have stirred it while it cooked, the roux is completely white. Remove pan from flame and add the hot milk; replace on a small flame and whisk as the mixture thickens. Let it boil, stirring until the sauce is smooth and thick. Now remove pan from flame once more, let it cool for a minute or two and beat in the 4 egg yolks, whisking well.

The egg whites and cheese come next. Egg whites are best beaten at room temperature so if you have the kinky habit of keeping eggs in the refrigerator, let them out some time before use. If you beat them with a hand whisk they froth up better than they do with a rotary – but it is asking a bit much. What you really need are 6 stiffly beaten egg whites.

Fold about half of them into the mixture, using a spatula and a lazy circular movement; then add all but 1 tablespoon of cheese, stir some more and put in the rest of the egg whites. As soon as the mixture is smooth and of one colour, pour it into the mould, pass a spatula over the top to remove peaks and sprinkle on it the final crumbs of cheese. Put this into a mark 6 (400°F) oven which you reduce to mark 5 (375°F) after the first flourish of heat.

If there is any justice in this world the soufflé should have risen from three-quarters of the way up the dish to a couple of inches over it after 25 minutes. Usually, when the soufflé has risen the inside is exactly as beautiful as it should be . . . then you should become rich and famous and have no trouble at all in finding a desirable husband/lover and be able to give dinner parties for people who need not even be amusing.

A sweet:

Soufflé au Grand Marnier

2 oz. butter
2 oz. flour
⅔ pint milk
3 oz. sugar
grated rind of 1 lemon
4 egg yolks
3 tablespoons Grand Marnier
5 egg whites
4 oz. strawberries
2 tablespoons brandy

Make your basic white sauce with flour, butter and milk;

when smooth and thick, add sugar and lemon rind. Cool, add beaten yolks and Grand Marnier and fold in stiffly beaten egg whites. Lightly butter a soufflé dish and put in a thin layer of sliced strawberries marinaded in sugar and brandy. Add the mixture so as to three-quarters fill the dish and cook for 25 to 30 minutes, by which time it should be puffed and golden. Sprinkle with icing sugar and, if you wish, set alight with a little warmed Grand Marnier.

Or, for four:

Soufflé surprise

8 sponge fingers, moistened with brandy
a family block of ice cream
4 egg whites
3 egg yolks
2½ oz. castor sugar
glacé cherries

Line a fireproof dish with sponge fingers, which act as insulation.

Beat the egg whites until stiff, add sugar and egg yolks and beat until stiff once more. Feed this mixture into a piping bag with a star nozzle.

Cut the ice cream into four portions and lay these on to the sponge fingers. Cover the dish with piped egg mixture. Sprinkle with castor sugar.

Bake in the top of a very hot mark 8 (450°F) oven for 4 minutes, turning the dish at half time so that the egg mixture colours evenly all over. Decorate the peaks of egg mixture with some glacé cherries.

Now all you have to do is seize a good big spoon and enjoy yourself.

Egg mousse

The best egg mousse I have ever eaten was served to me at the White Hart in Hamstead Marshall near Newbury.

Being loath to ask how it was made I produced one of similar allure in what is loosely called the privacy of my own kitchen.

6 hard-boiled eggs, whites finely chopped, yolks sieved
¼ pint water
1 envelope gelatine } *simmered together*
muslin bag of dill seeds }

A mayonnaise made with 2 egg yolks, ½ pint olive oil, 1 teaspoon lemon juice, 1 teaspoon cider vinegar, ⅛ pint double cream, whipped until fairly stiff.

Pour the simmered dill-flavoured gelatine over the hard-boiled eggs that have been treated as described. Mix this into the mayonnaise to which cream is added, blend, garnish with sizeable sprigs of parsley rough chopped on a board wiped with a clove of garlic, and set in a cool place.

OMELETTES

I am bored by kitchen fetishes, but it is not a bad idea to earmark one special wooden spoon for stirring coffee, to reserve one container for heating up petfood, and to keep a pan exclusively for making omelettes. The omelette pan is included in this list because an omelette is cooked by being manipulated across the hot buttered base of a pan, which is less easy if the bottom is scratched by fork or palette knife. One myth about omelettes is that they should be 'as light as a feather', but such a dish, whatever it may be, has none of the qualities required of an omelette. Another myth is that people are 'born omelette-makers'. Not true: absolutely anyone with a good, solid frying pan and enough eggs for practice can become competent.

For each omelette you make you need 3 eggs, 1 tablespoon of cold water, some salt and pepper, a warm plate and someone sitting down, forked raised, ready to eat it.

To make a plain omelette

Put the eggs, water and seasoning into a bowl and beat with a fork. Place the pan, which should be heavy and could be iron, on a high flame and leave it there. By the time you are ready to make your omelette the pan should be hot enough to complete the whole cooking process without having to be replaced on the flame. Into the hot pan toss a dessertspoon of butter, and shake it so that the whole of the bottom of the pan glistens; immediately pour in the egg mixture. Hold the pan in your left hand and rock it backwards and forwards while with a wooden fork – or even a metal one if you are careful – you loosen from the side and bottom of the pan whatever has settled there. When the omelette has cooked, tilt the pan away from you, fold the mixture into the far curve of the pan and turn it out on a plate.

To make a filled omelette

The safer way is to make a slit in the top of the cooked omelette and insert hot asparagus tips, creamed haddock or whatever. The second method is to add the cooked ingredients to the egg mixture, and this is really the better way. There are no problems when you put in bacon or mushrooms but in the case of grated cheese or wet fillings such as tomato, the pieces are more liable to stick to the bottom of the pan and spoil the appearance of the finished product.

Omelette fines herbes

If you have fresh herbs, take parsley, chives, tarragon and chervil and add a mixed tablespoon per omelette. If you cook this beautifully you have got yourself, as Americans tend to say, a dish.

The trouble about omelettes is that an omelette is an omelette is an omelette. As with people's cooking which so often has no more prominent taste that that borrowed from the contents of the fourth herb jar from the left, omelettes have become technically perfect, boring in all other respects. For a rethink omelette, try this. Beat with a fork:

3 whole eggs

2 tablespoons dry sherry

1 tablespoon chopped walnuts

1 tablespoon crumbled gorgonzola cheese

Make your omelette by getting the pan very hot, adding ½ oz. of butter in four small pieces, and the moment this has dissolved add the egg mixture, stirring with a wooden spatula and then tilting the pan away from you to let the contents assume the correct shape. Slit the top with a knife, sprinkle the crumbled gorgonzola cheese into the aperture and add a little more butter to the pan before gently turning the omelette to seize up the opening. This serves one human being and can be adapted, or religiously repeated, depending on the taste of the said being.

Poach perfect

A poached egg can be anything from an egg lodged on a bed of creamed smoked haddock to one resting beneath a cloak of truffled Bayonne ham dressed with Béarnaise sauce. The temperature of the finished article is all-important; you need a hot serving dish, a freshly poached egg, a bubbling sauce and the ability to do a fast assembly job.

A poached egg is not – must never again be – an egg dropped into a poacher and boiled to distraction. The best way of poaching an egg is to get a pan of boiling water, add a few drops of vinegar and stir the water around with a fork to make a whirlpool. Drop the egg into this and give it about 2 minutes before lifting it out with an egg slice, a spoon with holes or a tea-sieve. Let it swim in a basin of lukewarm water and trim off such straggly pieces of white as resulted from your lack of dexterity in projecting the egg from the ladle. Drain, place immediately on, say, a hot purée of French beans, cover with hot hollandaise sauce and decorate with an asparagus tip sizzled in butter.

Here is another happy setting for an egg. Take:

8 oz. Jerusalem artichokes
4 poached eggs
half a cucumber
2½ oz. butter
¼ pint double cream

Simmer the artichokes in well-seasoned stock until they are tender and pass them through a sieve, blending with 1 oz. of butter. Now shred the half-cucumber on the half moons of a grater, dust the strips with seasoned flour and fry gently in 1½ oz. butter, but do not allow them to brown. When the cucumber loses its resilience – about 2 or 3 minutes – add the cream and cook gently until the mixture thickens.

Lay the poached eggs on the purée of artichokes, cover with a spoonful of cucumber-cream sauce, glaze momentarily under the grill, then decorate with paprika.

Poached eggs en matelote

Reduce ½ pint of red wine by boiling it for 5 minutes with a sprig of rosemary, 6 crushed peppercorns and some celery salt. Add 1 oz. of flour rubbed into 1 oz. of butter and stir while the sauce thickens. Gently poach 4 eggs and place them on pieces of bread rubbed with garlic and fried in oil, cover with sauce, strained through a sieve.

Oeufs en cocotte à la crême

is perhaps the perfect egg dish, and one of the true tests of a chef's ability. *Michelin* inspectors are said to use this as a preliminary test in newly opened establishments. You require individual cocottes, which are mini pudding basins made of ovenproof glass or china. Give these bowls a minute in a warm oven, paint them with butter and break an egg into each. Bake the cocottes for 4½–5 minutes in the top of a mark 6 (400°F) oven. In the meantime put some double cream into a pan, bring it to the boil and reduce it by about a quarter. When the eggs are cooked – the white just set, the yolk entirely creamy and the whole thing perfectly hot – season with salt and top each with a tablespoon of the cream. Add a few grains of cayenne pepper and serve at once.

Fruits

When the manufacturers of tinned foods make their final journey to the Great Canneries, they will have much to answer for in respect of fruit salad. Their excuse – shortly before they are condemned – will be that only a limited selection of fruit can be left in syrup for any length of time. It's a fair excuse. However, the average housewife seldom keeps her fresh fruit salad that long, so we may forget about the half-pear swimming beside the maraschino cherry by courtesy of the Metal Box Company.

Winter fruit salad
small fresh pineapple
12 glacé cherries
2 tablespoons sugar
1 miniature bottle Grand Marnier (which may be left out for tee-total children and used in the adult portion of whipped cream)
2 Cox's apples
2 oranges
half a small melon
2 bananas
2 oz. sugar
1 lemon

Peel, core and chop the pineapple and quarter the glacé cherries. Mix them together, cover them with sugar and add liqueur. Leave this for at least 2 hours, stirring occasionally. This is the basis of your fruit salad. The other ingredients can then be added and the salad left for an hour and a half without deterioration. *Apples:* peel, quarter and chop. *Oranges:* peel, and cut clean segments from the skin with a sharp knife. If the segments are large, halve them. *Melon:* cut into slices, remove the ripe flesh from the outer skin and chop this into pieces roughly the same size as the apple pieces. *Bananas:* peel and cut into thin rounds. Mix the apple, orange, melon and bananas with the matured pineapple and cherries and add a syrup made by boiling together for 3 minutes 2 oz. sugar and a wineglass of water and a lemon cut into slices. Sieve the syrup over the salad, mix and leave to cool.

If I have been unkind to fruit tinners, I should like to put on record that much of their produce is desirable – though none so perfect that a little enterprise will not make it more so. Take

Figs Maria

1 tin figs
¼ pint sour cream
2 tablespoons Tia Maria liqueur
1 tablespoonful of grated plain chocolate

Drain the figs. Mix the sour cream and Tia Maria; place the figs on a serving dish and cover them with the liqueured cream. Dust with grated chocolate. If you like cold rice pudding, use it as a base; alternatively serve on a figleaf – or even in a figleaf.

Green figs in Pernod and double cream

The first item comes in a tin, the other two in bottles. There's nothing very complicated about this confection but it's very very good. The ratio: for each fig, 1 teaspoon Pernod, 3 tablespoons fig syrup, and double cream according to your budget.

Grapefruit

Oranges and lemons now come in handy plastic containers and the bustle of life has even made us buy grapefruit in tins. Segments in thin syrup (which restaurants call cocktail because they add one cherry) were probably the reason for our *au pair* straightening out the mother-of-pearl grapefruit knife with a hammer, one cold, wet, Suffolk Sunday afternoon. When you buy fresh grapefruit, roll them to your ear like a cigar, listening for squelch instead of dry crackle.

Having selected them, cut your plump grapefruits in halves, free the segments from the pith and place them, round side down, in an oven tray. On to each half heap a tablespoonful of brown sugar, a hazelnut of butter and a liqueur glass of brandy, rum or Grand Marnier. Give them 20 minutes in a slow oven (mark 3/325°F), then stand them on the bottom shelf on the lowest oven register until you need them, basting them in their liquor every now and then.

Orange salad

At the end of a meal, provide oranges, peeled regardless of cost so that neither pith nor skin remains, then thinly sliced and laid in a glass bowl and sprinkled with sugar and Curaçao (or port). Build up until the fruit bowl is full or you run out of orange slices. Spoon the liquor over the fruit every now and then. Naturally you will serve these cold, in glasses 'frosted' by wiping the rim with a slice of lemon and then drying the lemon with castor sugar.

Salad of pears

Cut pears into quarters, peel them and remove cores. Sprinkle with castor sugar and a little cinnamon, baste now and then with the liquid formed and serve from the coldest part of the refrigerator.

APPLES

A small caterer whose chef married his waitress and emigrated to the Isle of Wight asked me what he should do now. I told him to put a basket of apples and a mountain of Lancashire cheese on each table and sit himself behind the cash desk. My friend spurned my advice. Yet I meant what I said. We are in the era of gimmicky restaurants; all pancakes in one, nothing but pizzas in another, and fish-and-chipperies galore. Appleterias may well be next.

You can do many congenial things with apples: flans and fritters, pies and puddings, apple charlottes and apple dumplings. Coleridge, indeed, held that a man who refuses apple dumplings cannot have a pure mind. While this may be going a bit far, it does seem an excellent opportunity to give you the recipe.

Apple dumplings (for 4)

8 oz. self-raising flour
½ teaspoon salt
4 oz. chopped suet
¼ pint of water

Sieve the flour and salt, add suet and mix. Now pour in the water and stir with a knife until you have a dough. Turn this out on a floured board and knead lightly. Let it rest a few minutes as you peel and core 4 medium-sized eating apples and prepare

1½ oz. butter
2 oz. brown sugar

grated rind of a lemon
1 level coffeespoon cinnamon
1 liqueur glass brandy

Mix butter, sugar, lemon, cinnamon and brandy in a warm basin; roll into sausage shapes the size of the apple cores and insert into the apples. Divide the pastry into four, roll out each piece, place apple in centre, paint perimeter of pastry with top of the milk and enclose the fruit, sealing the top by pressing. Wrap each dumpling tightly in aluminium foil and cook on a baking sheet for 40 minutes in the middle of a mark 4 (350°F) oven. Remove the foil, put the dumplings on a dish and sprinkle with castor sugar.

What Coleridge didn't mention was the waistlines of those who didn't refuse dumplings. Weight-conscious people used to peel the suet crust from the apples and feed it to the dogs. Then came

Baked apples

Take 4 medium-sized, firm eating apples, wipe and core them and put them in a baking tray with ¼ pint cider, 1 oz. butter, 3 oz. brown sugar. Cook 25–60 minutes (depending on the type of apple) in a mark 3½ (335°F) oven, basting every 10 minutes. Serve with double cream. If you don't like the apple skins try

Pommes balbec

Take some fine eating apples; core them, peel them and cut them into quarters. Clarify some unsalted butter (page 17), heat this in a frying pan and put in the quarters one by one, turning them so that they are lightly browned on each side. Take care, or the cooked quarters may break.

When they are well cooked – 3 or 4 minutes – sprinkle a spoonful or two of sugar into the pan, pour in a glass of Calvados (or other liqueur), set it alight and serve at once with a bowlful of iced whipped cream.

And if you have a glut of apples and don't care for jar upon jar of apple sauce make some

Apple butter

3 quarts sweet cider
8 lb. apples
1–1½ lb. brown sugar
2 teaspoons ground cinnamon
½ teaspoon ground cloves
½ teaspoon salt

Boil the cider in a stainless steel or enamel pan until it is reduced by half – a process which should take 25–30 minutes. Core and quarter the apples, cut them in ½-inch slices, add to the reduced cider and cook over a low heat until they are tender. When this is done pass the mixture through a sieve and return to the pan, adding sugar, salt and spices. Cook over a low heat, stirring almost constantly until the mixture thickens; pour at once into sterile jars, cover with waxed paper and seal in the normal manner. Apple butter is an ideal filling for pancakes and a useful standby.

. . . and when you become deeply applomanic, you can use the apple butter to spread between slices of apple loaf and make an apple sandwich.

Apple loaf

requires a preheated mark 4 (350°F) oven and a loaf tin. Also:

1 lb. plain flour
1 teaspoon baking powder
½ teaspoon soda
1 teaspoon salt
4 oz. butter
6 oz. sugar
2 eggs
1 breakfast cup unpeeled grated apple and juice
4 oz. grated cheddar cheese – the stronger the better
2 oz. chopped nuts

Sift flour, baking powder, soda and salt into a basin. Take another basin, cream butter, add sugar and work until the mixture is frothy; add eggs one by one and keep mixing. Then put in apples, cheese and nuts and mix again. Add the flour etc. to the batter, mixing only until all the flour is damp, and then turn into a well-buttered loaf tin, pushing the batter well up in the corners, leaving the centre slightly concave. Bake for an hour.

Apple charlotte

Butter a pie dish. Fill it with layers of cubes of rindless buttered bread, peeled, cored, chopped apple, grated lemon peel mixed with three times its volume of castor sugar. Put alternate layers of bread, apple and sweet lemon peel, moisten with melted apple jelly or marmalade, cover with foil and bake in a mark 6 (400°F) oven for 45 minutes. Turn out, sprinkle with sugar and serve with cream.

Apple fritters (see page 300)

RHUBARB

Rhubarb fool

Simmer 2 lb. of rhubarb with 1 tablespoonful of water until soft; drain, and beat into this sufficient white sugar to attain the stiffness you require. Add 3 egg yolks and 3 small sponge cakes, liquidize or pass through a sieve and allow to set in a cool place.

Rhubarb and ginger crumble

Clean 1 lb. rhubarb, cut into 1-inch lengths and put into the bottom of an oven dish with 3 tablespoonsful of water and 2 of granulated sugar; add a few slices of preserved or crystallized ginger.

Make a crumble by sieving 6 oz. flour and 3 oz. sugar. Rub in 4 oz. butter and when the mixture is the consistency of sand, grate into it the rind of a lemon. Sprinkle this mixture over the rhubarb and bake in a mark 5 (375°F) oven for 30 minutes. If the top is not by then the colour of light mahogany, sprinkle onto it some castor sugar and glaze under a hot grill.

Locket's raspberries

Put into the bottom of a sweet bowl a small tin of raspberries, drained. Spoon onto this ¼ pint double cream stiffly whipped with 2 tablespoons of top of the milk and 1 tablespoon castor sugar. Spread the cream evenly with a knife and sprinkle over it a layer of demerara sugar. Now get a poker or some other piece of metal, heat it over a fierce flame and press it gently on the top layer of brown sugar to caramelize it.

STRAWBERRIES

The season is a many splendoured thing. Whether you use the word in respect of a strawberry, a débutante or a broodmare, there is in each instance the promise of plenty, the probability of infinite disappointment.

Ideally, strawberries should be washed and eaten – actually picked, washed and eaten – within 20 minutes; dredged with castor sugar which has housed a vanilla pod, sprinkled with optional liqueur and accompanied by whipped cream that could be lightened with a stiffly beaten white of egg. Château d'Yquem, or other expensive, cloying, chateau-bottled, white Bordeaux that you might have found undrinkably sweet at room temperature with the fishcakes, make an incomparable accompaniment to strawberries. Serve the wine abundantly over-iced, in sherry glasses.

The trouble with strawberries is that you think about them affectionately for ten months of the year and you then get a glut. 'Ah, strawberries!' tends to become – 'Oh dear, strawberries!' and finally, 'Not strawberries *again*!'

If they are absolutely perfect, but expensive, make

Strawberry romanoff
1 lb. prepared strawberries
juice of 1 sweet orange
1 miniature bottle Grand Marnier
3 tablespoons castor sugar
¼ pint double cream
⅛ pint single cream
1 tablespoon top of the milk
1 egg white stiffly beaten
sugar to taste

Cut strawberries in half and marinade them in orange, sugar and liqueur. Place in the refrigerator for at least an hour, and serve very cold under extravagant quantities of whipped cream (made by beating the milk and cream until fairly stiff, adding sugar, then folding in the egg white).

If they are perfect and cheap, make

Strawberry preserve

Preserved strawberries, like preserved peaches, undergo a chemical change in their consistency: the more liquid the preserving liquor, the mushier they become. The best way is probably to use

to every 1 lb. strawberries
1¼ lb. castor sugar
1 pint redcurrant juice – made by boiling 1 lb. redcurrants
and 1 pint water, reducing and sieving
(or ¼ pint Ribena with ¾ pint water)

Clean and rinse the strawberries, and sprinkle over them half the sugar, shaking them so that the sugar is equally distributed around the fruit. Let them stand in a cool place for a day. Add the remainder of the sugar to the redcurrant juice and boil until it forms a thin syrup; put into this the sugared strawberries and simmer until the liquid is jellied. The test for this is to pour a coffeespoonful into a saucer, let it cool for a moment, then tilt the saucer. The liquid should form a skin which wrinkles; if it drops off, it needs to be boiled some more.

If strawberries are very ripe (but before they have turned to shades of brown or green) make a

Strawberry pulp

3 cups strawberries
4 cups sugar
2 cups water
juice of one lemon

Boil up sugar and water to 240°F; failing a sugar thermometer, this is the temperature at which syrup boils in large gobstopper-sized bubbles. Allow to cool a little, add lemon juice and strawberries rubbed through a sieve. Simmer, remove the scum, and pour into glass jars to cool. This pulp can be frozen, with or without added cream, to make strawberry ice, or used as a basis for strawberry milkshakes. It is also an ideal foundation for

Strawberry mousse (for 4)

½ lb. strawberry pulp
3 eggs
1 miniature bottle Framboise

Put strawberry pulp into a basin over a pan of boiling water, add egg yolks and liqueur and whisk until the mixture thickens. Remove bowl from pan and when lukewarm fold in stiffly beaten whites of eggs. Allow the mousse to set in the coldest part of your refrigerator.

Strawberries that are midway between excellent and suitability for pulp can be used to make

A filling for flans and tarts

1 lb. strawberries, rinsed, dried and sliced
1 rounded dessertspoon cornflour
⅓ pint water
2–3 tablespoons sugar

Gently boil water, sugar and cornflour and, when smooth and thick, add sliced strawberries and, optionally, a miniature bottle of Cherry Brandy. Simmer for 3–4 minutes. To give your flan or tart a sheen when it cools and sets, use this mixture as a filling when still warm.

Strawberry water ice

2 lb. fresh strawberries, 8 oz. sugar, 1 tablespoon lemon juice, 2 tablespoons orange juice, ¼ pint water. Boil the

sugar and water together on a good flame for 5 minutes. Liquidize the cleaned strawberries and sieve result (if liquidizer-less, just sieve). Add the lemon and orange juice and when the syrup is cold add this to the strawberry pulp. Mix well, and freeze in the ice-making trays of a refrigerator. This is enough for about six people.

If a meal cries out for a savoury rather than a sweet, you could try strawberries and pepper: a man sitting opposite me on an Air France flight did, with audible enjoyment.

For those prepared to devote an hour or two to making a really noble confection, there is

Rice romanoff
½ lb. long-grained rice
3 pints water
½ pint double cream
2 tablespoons Grand Marnier
2 tablespoons sugar
2 oz. peeled almonds
1 oz. sugar
¾ oz. butter
1 lb. of macaroons cut up and soaked in liqueur

For the strawberry sauce:
1 packet frozen strawberries
2 tablespoons sugar
3 tablespoons water
1 liqueur glass brandy

Boil the rice in lightly salted water for 20 minutes, when it should be entirely tender. Drain well and wash out the starch in hot water. Whip the cream, sugar and Grand Marnier and stir into the rice. Put the sugar and butter into a pan with a teaspoon of water – turn up flame and when the mixture reaches a light mahogany colour, put in the almonds. Turn off flame and stir well. Let the candied almonds cool, then chop them and incorporate into the creamed rice.

Take a very beautiful sweet-bowl, put in one-third of the rice as a bottom layer and cover with a layer of macaroons softened in liqueur, another layer of rice, another of macaroons, repeating the process once more. Chill the bowl for several hours and decorate portions with strawberry sauce made by passing the frozen strawberries through a sieve and adding this pulp to the sugar, water and brandy in a pan. Let it boil for a minute or two and then cool well, before serving.

If you should have some Kilner jars or similar receptacles, it seems to me that if there is a void in the range of our swinging food industry it is in the provision of high quality fruit in liqueur.

Peaches in brandy

The peaches have to be good – the myth that substandard food can be bottled or pickled is totally unfounded on fact. Wash the fruit, rub off the fuzz, do not peel them (the most cunning way to peel peaches when you need to is to rub them all over with the back of a knife and then simply lift off the skin), prick them with a fork and prepare your syrup: 1¼ pints of water to 1 lb. of sugar. Boil till the syrup is smooth, allow the peaches 5–6 minutes in this to make them tender and then pack them gently into your jars. Fill two-thirds of the way up with syrup, and when this has cooled top up with brandy and seal tightly. It is a mistake to eat these until they have been in the jar for about a month.

Sweet Talk

Sweets and puddings have suffered most grievously from the disappearance of underpaid donkey workers in the kitchen. Nevertheless, if you choose your menu wisely, you can produce excellent dishes without too much hard labour. In 5 minutes you can make what is perhaps the fastest haute cuisine sweet:

Zabaglione

which is also a useful word for crossword puzzles. This was a sweet they used to make in front of people in restaurants – until they found that three or four minutes of continued beating was not only uncompulsive viewing but also rather noisy. It is good, when not eaten too often. For each person provide

1 egg yolk
1 half eggshell of sugar
1 half eggshell of water
1 half eggshell of sherry, Madeira or Marsala

Marsala is the classic stuff, but most reinforced wines will do very well. Put all the ingredients into the top of a double boiler, or a pudding basin suspended in water, and whisk away while the water boils and the zabaglione thickens. Pour it then into champagne glasses and eat with a spoon. Failure to whisk and cook the mixture until it is really thick will give you glasses containing a bottom layer of brown liquid bearing a quantity of froth. The finished product should be uniformly light yellow in colour and the consistency of lightly whipped cream. Eat it fairly soon, as the froth disintegrates. If you have undercooked it, don't try to recook it because it won't work.

The separated egg whites will keep almost indefinitely in the refrigerator – or in winter – in contrast to the life of barley an hour for the yolk, before it congeals beyond redemption. Meringues therefore are best as a byproduct of anything that requires only the yolk.

Meringues

When you have collected 6 whites, beat them until they are well risen and stiff and add to them ½ lb. castor sugar and a bare teaspoonful of salt. Blend the mixture and pipe it or spoon it on to a buttered, floured baking tray. Halfway up an open oven turned up to full is an alternative to the bottom of the oven on a low regulo like ½. They cannot do with less than 1½ hours but their readiness is easily discernible to the touch. A ready meringue is dry and crisp; one not yet with it, soft and sticky.

A quick sweet for four requiring both the yolk and the white of the egg is a

Sweet omelette   (for 4)

½ oz. butter
1 tablespoon vegetable oil
5 eggs
3 half eggshells filled with sugar
2 tablespoons Tiptree's Little Scarlet strawberry jam
2 tablespoons brandy or liqueur

Separate the egg whites from the yolks; beat the whites

194

until they are fairly stiff, and the yolks until they froth lightly. Join together; add sugar, and mix well. Heat the brandy in a saucepan, ignite it and when the flame dies add the jam and allow to simmer. Dissolve oil and butter in a frying pan. When hot, add the egg mixture, shaking it if you are an expert, otherwise folding it into itself with a wooden spatula. When the omelette is cooked – though still moist – pour the strawberry liqueur into the centre, fold over, sprinkle with sugar and hold momentarily under the grill.

Not so quick but definitely delicious is an

Orange soufflé

For better or for worse the success of a soufflé is measured by the height to which the crust has risen above its housing . . . and the length of time it stays up. I was immensely impressed by an orange soufflé served in Portugal. The inside of the orange had been scooped out, the segments blended with stiffly beaten egg white, 1 yolk and castor sugar and given a very short sojourn in a very hot oven. The orange arrived with twice its height in soufflé mixture towering above it . . . and people oohed and aaahed and no one realized that this was exactly the height of mixture the chef had piped into the scooped-out orange before dusting it with icing sugar and colouring it a little in the aforesaid hot oven.

MOUSSE

Mousses come hot or cold. They can be fashioned of any number of different things – fish, fowl, flesh, fruit or fondant (the basis of confectionery) – and have, as common factors, no more than the presence of eggs, cream or gelatine as a setting agent. The remark 'I like mousse' is about as profound as 'I like books'. To order a savoury mousse in a restaurant you don't know is to court disaster, for mousses, like curries, *can* be the end of the line for left-overs. This is not so in the case of sweet mousses, of which the classic example is

Chocolate mousse

4 oz. bar of plain (or bitter, if you prefer it) chocolate
1 tablespoon sweet sherry
1 tablespoon strong black coffee (instant is as good as fresh)
3 large eggs

Break up the chocolate and melt it in the coffee and sherry over a low flame. Stir until it is smoothly blended. Next, separate the eggs and add the yolks to the melted chocolate; keep stirring until the mixture is of a uniform consistency. Remove from the flame. Now whisk the egg whites until they are stiff, and with a wooden spoon fold them into the lukewarm mixture until the whole mousse is smooth and frothy. This can now be set in a dish in the refrigerator, or poured into individual glass bowls containing – if there is cause for special celebration – some pieces of macaroon that have been soaked in brandy for an hour or two. It serves four people.

Frozen apricot mousse

4 oz. dried apricots, cooked and sweetened
3 eggs
2 oz. sugar
¼ pint double cream
⅛ pint single cream

Beat the eggs until they are frothy; add the sugar gradually and combine with the sieved or liquidized apricots. Now whip the single and double cream together until fairly stiff, and fold this into the mixture. Put the mousse into the freezing compartment of the refrigerator – in the ice trays if necessary – until it is firmly set. After this it can be stored in the main part of the refrigerator until it is needed.

ICE CREAM

The making of ice cream, which involves mixing the ingredients as they freeze, is not for the modern household and makes us dependent on the manufactured article. If you have read the right books, you will know that long, long ago in the coldest of winters, our ancestors would hook their flints into the floating blocks of river ice and drag them into cold dark caves. Here, it is said, the ice was stored and used for the manufacture of monolithic sorbets cultured, one supposes, on floor and ceiling and marketed as stalagmites and stalactites. This is almost certainly untrue. What does appear to be factual is that ice cream was originally made from fresh fruit, cane sugar and cream. It was then found that millions of people could not tell the difference if it was made from pulped apples, glucose and milk powder. The present stuff, which is admittedly getting better, is a sort of compromise between the original and the economical. But whatever you buy can be improved.

Even so, there is really no excuse for buying a slab of ivory ice cream, cutting it into hunks and serving it to your guests on a plate, with a smile; not even to please the man who invented vanilla essence. A vanilla family block – presumably sponsored by the Family Planning Association – was never really intended to be taken neat. Ice cream, like the rest of us, reaches a point of no return, and the makers' warning not to attempt to refreeze it once it has melted is superfluous advice to anyone who has seen the thin, gently fermenting liquid swimming around at the bottom of a broken-down refrigerator.

For *mixing*, use ice cream of the consistency at which an average four-year-old can put a finger right through it with only a little effort; mix into it strong black coffee, a teaspoon per two portions with a few drops of Tia Maria liqueur. Alternately some coarsely grated Suchard Bittra chocolate and chopped burnt almonds, or a mixture of lemon, orange and grapefruit peel finely grated and mixed with castor sugar. In each case whip in the addition with a fork and serve immediately. When people say how splendid . . . what is it? – you can say with a fair degree of truth that you made it yourself, using the word made in its secondary sense, as in 'you made my evening' when addressing a mortal.

Ice cream as *filling* should be as soft as hard porridge or advertising margarine. An inexpensive cherry cake, cut horizontally into layers, each layer spread thickly with ice cream and the reconstituted cake cut into slices, does much for cake and ice cream. If you use it in a hot sweet, the ice should of course be very cold to resist the warmth of the oven. Use an earthenware rather than a metal dish, give it an insulating layer of cake crumbs, sponge fingers, sugar-puffs if you like, place the ice cream on this, portion by portion, and cover it with the result of 3 stiffly whisked egg whites to which you have added 1 egg yolk, some sugar and the grated rind of a lemon. Sprinkle with icing sugar, place in the top of the hottest oven for barely 2 minutes and then colour under a hot grill.

For *covering*, get the ice cream as hard as you can. Pour on a hot chocolate sauce made with chocolate powder, the juice from a tin of pears, a little butter and cornflour for thickening (you've got to stir all the time while this one comes to the boil).

Further in the hot sauce line, 3 tablespoons of sugar, 1 of golden syrup and ¼ oz. of butter heated till it is light brown and will go brittle if dropped into cold water gives you a crisp layer of toffee when poured over the ice cream, while an extra ¾ oz. of butter in the same mixture, cooked for a little longer, will give you a softer, fudgier sauce only to be attempted if your teeth are your own.

I remember that in my youth we had an ice cream machine: an inner container was filled with cream and eggs and sugar; the surrounding jacket contained crushed ice. You turned a handle for an hour or two, opened up, and hey presto, it was every bit as good as the stop-me-and-buy-one stuff that came on tricycles.

Commercially, I suppose, ingredients should be mixed while they freeze; in the home one can achieve excellent results with a little imagination and a workable freeze compartment of a refrigerator.

Creams are the easiest: use ½ pint of double and ¼ pint of single cream as base, whisk it until it is pleasantly thick, sweeten it, add such liqueur as you care for, and for your next step you can decide whether to make any or all of the following.

Blackcurrant ice cream

The cream will have to be a little thicker – more double, less single – and you add this to 3 tablespoons of Ribena and 1 teaspoon of sloe gin.

Chocolate crème de menthe

Use good plain chocolate grated on the half moons of a grater, say 2 oz. Add a miniature bottle of crème de menthe and a tablespoon of very strong coffee and blend with the cream.

Cassata

Almost anything goes. Line a freezing tray with thin slices of sponge cake; buy a slab of vanilla ice cream and mix into this some crystallized pineapple cut into strips, crystallized cherries, halved slices of preserved ginger and a few raisins that have spent an hour in a glass of brandy. Blend well, cover with another slice of sponge cake, freeze hard and serve in slices.

Melon sorbet

One of the best ices I have ever had was a melon sorbet which was sold in a cafe on the harbour at St Tropez. Liquidize or sieve a peeled, cleaned Charentais melon; add to it a similar quantity of beaten egg whites to which you allow a level teaspoon of icing sugar per egg, blend and freeze.

Lemon ice cream

Prepare
  grated rind of one lemon
  juice of half a lemon
  grated rind of half a grapefruit
  1 heaped tablespoon sugar
  1 optional tablespoon liqueur
Stir this together and blend into plain vanilla ice cream just before bringing it to the table.

Crème caramel

should be the most subtle of sweets – a distant relative of the artificially yellowed, fiercely glazed and oversweetened things that glare at you from the lower shelves of London sweet trolleys. For six portions, take that number of moulds (or coffee cups will do very well).

Place 4 eggs in a pudding basin, whisk well, add 4 oz. of sugar, whisk again and pour on 1 pint of milk. Whisk until the sugar has dissolved. Taste the mixture and if you like it sweeter, then make it sweeter. Into a small saucepan, over a high flame, pour a large spoonful of golden syrup and add a similar quantity of granulated sugar. Stir until it darkens from the colour of honey to that of light mahogany, and pour sufficient of this into cups or moulds to cover the bottom thereof. Rewhisk the egg milk mixture and pour onto the caramel to within ¼ inch of the top.

Stand the moulds or cups in a baking tray into which you have poured a pint of water and cook for about an hour in a cool (mark 2/300°F) oven. If you are not sure whether they are cooked, take them out after an hour, tilt them away from you and examine your shoes; if they are splodged with milk and egg, cook for a little longer. The sweet is best swerve cool in the container in which it has been cooked, with a topping of cream. Do not freeze it.

Crème brûlée

Take ½ pint milk, ½ pint cream, 1 oz. sugar and grated rind of half a lemon. Pour this mixture into a basin containing 1 whole egg beaten with 4 egg yolks and beat well. Add one bayleaf. Decant into oven dish set in a roasting tray half filled with water and bake in mark 2 (300°F) oven until set (about 1¼ hours). Allow to cool, cover with 6 oz. demerara sugar and place under a very hot grill until the caramel is brown. Tilt the dish to get an even glaze.

Crème frite

1 pint milk
4 oz. vanilla-flavoured sugar

2 oz. plain flour
1 egg
6 egg yolks
pinch of salt

Take the milk and bring it slowly to the boil. Mix the other ingredients in a bowl and add the boiling milk ladle by ladle, beating as you do so. Hold the bowl over a pan of boiling water and beat as it thickens. When it is the consistency of thick porridge, pour it on a greased board or tray and let it get cold. You will find that it spreads slowly and then stops spreading to remain about ½ inch thick. When it is quite cold, cut it into oblong shapes, coat them lightly with beaten egg and breadcrumbs and fry in hot clarified butter (page 17) until they are crisp on the outside.

Crêpes Suzette

I care little for waiters who cook at me in restaurants. The motivation for serving food by which you can read lies somewhere between the desire to be seen doing something special for a customer, and the normal process of ensuring that what you are serving is properly hot. In the days when kitchens were far removed from restaurants this had some point. It now has none.

The spirit lamp performs a dual function in a restaurant; the first, to which I take no exception if the job is discreetly done, is to reheat dishes and ensure that plates are properly hot. The second, which I resent, is the full production number. You sit in a corner telling your bird that it was the unique look of truth and innocence that caused you to phone her and not her flatmate (who was out), when a waiter muttering what sounds like some liturgical incantation spoils the intimate moment of magic by setting fire to his cooking brandy.

On a more cheerful note, crêpes Suzette as they are

made in some restaurants – precooked in the kitchen and reheated in the buttery goo when their time comes – have much to recommend them. Both sauce and pancakes can be made in advance, and the heating/assembly job requires no more than a couple of minutes' absence from the table – a pause that is amply rewarded by the triumphant illuminated return.

But, at its best, it is a freshly made thin sweet pancake of high quality, dressed with a hot sauce fashioned of butter, orange and liqueurs. A pancake, any pancake, is made of starch, liquid and egg. The best pancakes are made with plain flour, milk and 2 egg yolks for every white. Sugar is put into the mixture before cooking, as is melted butter and flavouring. To make about a dozen thin pancakes in a 5-inch pan, take

4 oz. plain flour
1 oz. sugar
1 whole egg
1 egg yolk
½ oz. butter
1 dessertspoon orange juice
½ pint and 2 tablespoons milk

Sieve the flour and sugar into a bowl, make a well and put into it the whole egg, the extra yolk, the orange juice and the butter melted over a low flame. Blend lightly with a wooden spoon, add ½ pint milk as you stir and when all the ingredients are mixed, beat with a rotary whisk until the mixture is smooth. Let it rest for half an hour if you can spare the time; the mixture will thicken slightly. Before use, add the 2 tablespoons of milk and rewhisk.

Pancakes are best made in small frying pans, ideally ones that have few deep scratches in the base. The pan should be very hot with a shimmering, no more, of cooking oil; a pastry brush is useful for putting this on. Pancakes are not fried in fat; the fat is there to stop them sticking – and to this end the mixture already contains butter.

A pancake should be very thin. So it is important not to have the pan so hot that all the mixture sets on contact. Let the film of oil begin to smoke, remove the pan from the flame for 15 seconds and then pour a large tablespoonful into the tilted pan, moving it about so that the whole of the base is covered. You may well find that a tablespoon is not quite enough and it is useful to get a small ladle that will take exactly the quantity required for your pan.

There is nothing clever – or difficult – about tossing a pancake; most chefs use a palette knife. Ease the edge of the pancake from the pan and turn it as you like after about 20 seconds. Give the second side the same time and remember that it is the first side that has the pattern; whether you roll it or fold it, that should be on view.

For the sauce:
  1½ oz. butter
  2 tablespoons orange juice
  1 tablespoon lemon juice
  2 oz. sugar
  1 miniature bottle orange Curaçao
  1 tablespoon brandy

Melt the butter, sugar and fruit juice in a large frying pan and when the mixture begins to thicken turn down the flame and add the liqueur. Put the pancakes into the pan. Turn them over and fold them into four. When all have been folded in this way, turn them again, add the brandy, light it and bring to the table at once.

Bread-and-butter pudding

In moments of considerable strain I tend to take to bread-and-butter pudding. There is something about the blandness of soggy bread, the crispness of the golden outer crust and the unadulterated pleasure of a lightly set custard that makes the world seem a better place in which to live.

Cooks, on the whole, are sweet-makers or non-sweet-makers. The former, flexing their cool fingers at the cake-mix, overpower their guests with butter cream and fondant in yet another creation that failed to win last month's recipe competition in Ladies' Home Journal. The latter have learned to make zabaglione and pancakes – as I have taught myself to play the Blue Danube, by numbers: 2, 2, 4, 6, 6, 66, 66 . . . Both factions feel that bread-and-butter pudding is a nursery dish of small merit; this is so swinishly unfair an evaluation that I shall go to some lengths to prove otherwise.

For five portions – that is to say, to suit a dinner party of eight at which three people are on a diet – make 6 generous butter sandwiches. Press together firmly, take off the rinds and cut each double slice into ½-inch cubes. Sprinkle half of these into a pie dish of a size for this amount of bread to occupy about a third. Now wash 3 oz. of sultanas, heat them in a sherry glass of sweet white vermouth and add half of these to the dish. Next take ½ lb. of Tiptree's Little Scarlet strawberry jam, dilute with a coffeecupful of boiling water and spoon half the resultant syrup evenly onto the dish. If you have followed these instructions as diligently as you ought, there will now be in your kitchen some more bread, alcoholic currants and liquid jam. With these make another layer.

In a pudding basin, well whisk 4 whole eggs, add 3 oz. of castor sugar and after a while pour in 1 pint of milk. Keep whisking until all is yellow and rich and slightly frothy . . . and then pour onto the top layer in the pie dish. Next, butter 3 slices of bread lightly on both sides, take off the rinds, square off and cut diagonally into quarters. These steam-baked isosceles triangles are then secured, long side down, in the soggy top of the pudding, so that the twelve protruding apexes make a handsome pattern. Now, or an hour before the dish is required, put it in the middle of a cool (mark 2/325°F) oven, and if the top triangles become brown rather than golden, lower the dish and paint the bread with a little melted butter.

Irrespective of the problems of this world it would be a mistake to produce such a pudding more than once a fortnight and as, by and large, one eats sweet courses more frequently than that, this may be a good time to examine an alternative or two.

Candied bread   (for 4)

4 slices crustless bread
1 oz. butter

1 tablespoon oil
3 rounded tablespoons sugar
1 tablespoon lemon juice

Melt butter and oil in a frying pan, add sugar and lemon juice and cook until the mixture begins to caramelize and turns a light brown. Then put in the bread, cut into halves or quarters or fingers. Turn after half a minute, baste, and after a minute or so take from the pan and serve as you would fritters . . . on a heated, sugared plate.

Tipsy cake

This is really no more than a Victorian name for an alcoholic trifle. Get some pieces of old sponge cake – or similar confection – moisten it well with a mixture of half sweet sherry and half brandy and stick into the sodden cake some slivers of sweet almonds, stirred into a mixture of sugar and butter brought to the light brown caramel stage. Cover the cake with custard made by whisking 3 whole eggs into ½ pint of milk and cooking this mixture, suitably sweetened, in the top of a double boiler until thick. Garnish with whipped cream and raspberries.

CAKES

The natural cook – she who potters around the kitchen and produces exciting soups, impeccable stews and acceptable sauces – fails when it comes to cakes. For there is no such person as a 'natural cake-maker'. There is no short cut to weighing the ingredients, mixing them properly and cooking them at the right temperature for the right length of time. For the cake-maker, scales, patience, cool fingers and the ability to curb the spirit of adventure are absolutely essential. But making a cake according to instructions is not unlike going to a race meeting and backing odds-on favourites for a place: the exercise is invariably rewarding

and permanently unexciting. However, what dampens the ardour of many a pastry-cook is not so much lack of excitement as the fact that the results of her labours will be less succulent and more expensive than cakes bought from run-of-the-mill bakers and grocers. This is the result of choosing the wrong recipe; it is no easier to make a bad cake than a good one. Here is a good cake which will be appreciated by all who do not dislike the taste of almonds.

Franzipan cake

Stage 1 – sweet short pastry:
  2 oz. castor sugar
  4 oz. butter
  8 oz. plain flour
  1 small egg – beaten
Blend the butter and sugar for about a minute, no more,

and then incorporate the beaten egg; fold in sieved flour until it is completely mixed and work the mixture until the pastry is of a uniform texture. Roll it out on a floured board to the thickness of a 10p piece and use it to line a shallow 8-inch cake tin. (There will be some pastry over, which can be used for jam tarts, fruit flans, etc.; exact quantities to line an 8-inch cake dish would entail fractions of ounces and teaspoon measures of beaten egg.) Pat the pastry against the sides of the tin and trim the edges to level with the sides.

Stage 2. Sprinkle 2 oz. of cake crumbs or sweet biscuit crumbs evenly on the pastry base.

Stage 3. Open a tin of stoned Morello cherries, drain them well in a sieve and arrange them in a loose single layer on the cake crumbs.

Stage 4 – franzipan:
  2 oz. butter
  2 oz. castor sugar
  1 egg
  1 oz. plain flour
  3 oz. ground almonds
Cream the butter and sugar, blend in the egg and fold in the almonds and flour. Heap this on the cherries in the cake tray, smoothing off the top level with the sides. Decorate the top with several thin strips of sweet short pastry. Bake in the middle of a mark 4 (350°F) oven for 30–40 minutes. A few minutes after you take the cake from the oven you can remove it from the tray and let it breathe on a wire tray.

Stage 5 – glazing: take 2 tablespoons of apricot jam and 1 dessertspoon of water, boil, and sieve into a bowl. With a pastry brush give the top of the cake two coats of this syrup.

Stage 6 – icing can be applied within 5 minutes or so of the apricot glaze. To make it, take 4 rounded tablespoons of sieved icing sugar (a rolling pin is useful for decomposing lumps which tend to form), 1 tablespoon of water flavoured with lemon juice.

Mix the sugar and water and bring almost to boiling point, when the icing becomes opaque. Give the cake top two thin coats.

Ambrosia cake

12 oz. flour
3 teaspoons baking powder
½ teaspoon salt
4 oz. butter
8 oz. castor sugar
3 eggs
⅓ pint milk

Sift flour, baking powder and salt into basin. Cream butter, add it to the sugar and beat until light and fluffy. Then add the eggs one by one and the milk, beating all the time. Add the creamy mixture to the dry ingredients, mixing no more than is absolutely necessary to blend properly. *Do not beat.* Pour into two greased 9-inch layer-cake tins and bake for 35 minutes in preheated mark 4 (350°F) oven.

Filling:
2 oz. sugar
2 dessertspoons cornflour
3 tablespoons plain flour
3 lightly beaten egg yolks
just under ½ pint milk
¼ pint double cream

miniature bottle Tia Maria
2 bananas

Mix sugar, flours and beaten egg yolks in the top of a double boiler and gradually pour on simmering milk as you whisk the mixture. Let this cook as you whisk until the mixture is thick and smooth. Strain into a basin, let it cool and add Tia Maria and the cream, well whipped.

When the cake is cool, cut a thin slice from one cake layer and spread the flattened surface with the filling; garnish with thin slices of banana. Top with the second layer and dust the whole cake with icing sugar.

Brandy snaps

are confusing names for confections which tend to be soggy and contain no brandy. And yet, it was not always so. Nor, if you read on, need it continue thus.

The ingredients are:

2 oz. butter
2 oz. castor sugar
4 oz. golden syrup
1 level teaspoon ground ginger
grated rind of half a lemon
fractionally less than 2 oz. plain flour

(It is important to use plain flour in brandy snaps if you want to succeed.)

Melt butter, sugar and golden syrup (which you weigh by dusting the scales with flour and pouring on syrup so that it skids off without the use of a Squeegee) until blended. Sieve flour and ginger into the mixture and add the lemon rind. Blend well.

Take a couple of baking sheets, grease them and put rounded teaspoons of the stuff sufficiently far apart to allow the quail's-egg-shaped dollops of snap-batter to become free-standing, elegantly golden circles – 4 inches in diameter. This spreading/colouring process tends to take

211

just over 10 minutes in a mark 4 (350°F) oven . . . and if all brandy snaps are to be of an even hue, change the trays over at half time – like top tray to bottom, bottom to top. When the time is up, leave the trays on the kitchen table for 2 minutes, at which point gently prise the snaps from the baking sheets with a palette knife and roll them around your forefinger . . . or a greased handle of a wooden spoon, which is the mode Beetonesque. Unless you are very quick – or until you are very quick – you might do better to put the trays into the oven at 3-minute intervals so that the brandy snap that is ideally tacky 2 minutes after leaving the oven does not become brittle when you finally get round to rolling it. The best brandy snap is served within an hour of construction, filled with very cold whipped cream flavoured with brandy.

There are many who will look at this recipe and say 'too rich' or 'who is going to eat all that at the end of a meal?' Well now. If you are going to present a super pudding, let it be the focal point. Serve a cup of iced consommé, a suggestion of salmon trout in champagne sauce and then three or four filled brandy snaps. The joy of a brandy snap is that it can also be filled with whipped cream flavoured with liqueur to provide an entirely sophisticated accompaniment to nursery puddings.

Hazelnut yeast cakes (Stollen)

are made with yeast, baked in a slow oven, brushed with melted butter and dredged with castor sugar. The Germans call them *Stollen*. Marie Antoinette clearly had them in mind when she told her starving people to eat cake. If you make one, and have the strength of mind to let it get cold, cut it in slices, spread it with unsalted butter and your teatime existence will take on a new dimension.

If you are going to go to the trouble of baking – which entails weighing and measuring, mixing and rolling and kneading, not to mention preparing the oven to a set temperature – you might just as well be adventurous and bake something really delicious, like this hazelnut yeast cake . . . or *Stolle* if you like.

For the dough:
  6¼ oz. sifted plain flour
  ⅔ oz. yeast (or ⅓ oz. dried yeast) (page 233)
  1 oz. warm milk
  1 oz. castor sugar
  3 oz. soft butter
  pinch of salt

Mix yeast and 1 oz. warm water, add a level dessertspoon of plain flour, stir until smooth and let this 'ferment' stand for 15 minutes in a warm place to become smooth and sticky. Then mix together all the ingredients and work them thoroughly into a uniformly coloured, homogeneous ball. Place it in a bowl and set it in a warm place – such as on the stove when the oven is preheating. Cover with a cloth and leave it for an hour.

For the filling:
  3½ oz. ground roasted hazelnuts
  4 oz. sugar
  2 oz. sponge cake or sweet biscuit crumbs
  1 small egg

Buy peeled hazelnuts and roast them in a tray in a medium oven for about 20 minutes. Crush them to an oily crumble with a rolling pin. Add sugar, cake crumbs, 1 oz. water and egg and mix well.

When the dough has risen, roll it out on a floured surface to make a strip as wide as your baking tin is long – which should be about 8 inches – and as long as possible, say 20 inches. On to this dough spread the filling to within ½ inch of the edges. Roll the dough from both ends towards the middle. Place it in the well-buttered bread tin (8 × 3 × 3 inches is about the right size) and leave it, covered, in a warm place so that the yeast can rise again.

Then bake for 1¼ hours in a mark 2 (300°F) oven. Remove from the tin and let it cool and then brush with melted unsalted butter and roll in castor sugar.

Pastry and Bread

SHORTCRUST PASTRY

I approve of people who enter kitchens with a spirit of adventure. I am in favour of those who read cookery books as if they were novels, put them down, and decide to go it alone. Unfortunately, when it comes to making pastry the improvising all-action culinary whizz-kid gets scant reward for his enterprise. The reason for this is that unless luck shines on his countenance the way luck never shone on mine, chancing his arm with flour, fat and liquid provides an end-product that is inferior to that achieved by those who religiously follow the well-documented paths of the basic recipes.

What is known in England as having 'light' or 'cool' fingers is called *tour de main* in France. It means quite simply, the ability to make good pastry. There was a time when this was considered a gift of nature with which one was born; it is now generally recognized that making pastry is something that can be learnt. The woman who has *tour de main* rubs fat into flour with her fingertips and naturally desists from then rubbing her fingers together and brushing the strips of pastry back into the bowl. (If you have not got *tour de main* you will just have to remember not to do this sort of thing.)

When you knead pastry, they used to tell housewives, 'do this for just the right length of time'. It is now agreed that pastry should be kneaded for no longer than is necessary to blend the ingredients and free the pastry from cracks.

When you roll out the pastry, use as little flour as will efficiently stop it from sticking to the board or rolling pin – and sieve this flour. When you roll pastry, do so lightly and firmly; there is no advantage in rolling first one side, then the other. If it begins to stick, lift the pastry on the rolling pin, dust with a little more flour, then roll some more.

The Victorian lady – if she cooked at all – would make shortcrust pastry and submit it to her betters. If they shook their heads and pronounced failure, she would give up making shortcrust pastry. Research into the subject has shown us the various reasons for failure. If pastry is hard – there is too much water, too little fat, or it has been overworked, perhaps with hot heavy fingers. If the pastry is too crumbly, the opposite reasons apply: too little water, too much fat, possibly the use of self-raising instead of plain flour. If it blisters in baking – the fat has not been rubbed into the flour sufficiently. If it shrinks, it has been over-rolled. If it is speckled, the sugar grains were not dissolved (this cannot happen if you use icing sugar), and if you use the same oven for meat or anything that generates steam, your results are unlikely to be crisp and good; if you are a compulsive oven-door opener and slammer, you'll be no luckier. False colourings indicate wrong oven temperature; if the oven is too hot, or the pastry placed on too high a shelf, it will blacken before it is cooked.

When they stopped making activated pies (the word pie came into use as a result of a fifteenth-century practical joke in which live magpies fluttered from the cut pastry with heaven knows what ill effects from their droppings), the marriage of fruit and pastry became less complicated and in time gave way to the open pie – or flan. This is a shortcrust base, filled with fruit; theoretically a perfect confection – but for the danger that the moisture of the filling will make the pastry sodden. There are two ways of avoiding this: baking 'blind', which means pre-baking the flan case independently of the filling; or insulation – painting the uncooked pastry with syrup or egg yolk.

I make a treacle tart of quality. It is known as *my* treacle tart. But it is the filling and not the pastry that is personal to me. The tart is shortcrust and, loath as I have always been to accord credit where it is due, shortcrust pastry comes straight out of the book. There is no alternative to weighing and sifting and blending . . . though I have given you roughly the reasons why one does what, and the consequences of not doing so.

Treacle tart

Shortcrust pastry: you need 7 oz. of flour . . . plain flour, for once, though it is only just worth going out to buy it if you only have self-raising around.

> 3 oz. of butter – or margarine or fat if you care for that sort
>   of thing
> ½ teaspoon salt
> 3 tablespoons water

Sift the flour and salt into a basin. This aerates it and removes lumps. Warm the butter to get it to the consistency you would expect on a reasonable summer's day and with your fingertips, rub this into the flour so that the end product is like soft breadcrumbs in appearance. (If the butter is too cold you get tough isolationist worms instead of soft companionable crumbs.) When that is done, lift the mixture and let it run through your hands into the bowl.

This ensures lumplessness and aerates some more.

Now add water. Once the liquid is in the mixture it must be handled as little and also as gently as possible, otherwise the pastry could become hard and tough. Cut the water into the pastry with a knife and when it begins to cling together scoop it up in your cool hands, knead it gently on a sparsely floured board and then let it rest for 20 minutes or so in a cloth, in a cool place. It is now ready to be shaped and cooked.

With your palms press the ball into a shape to which you can get a rolling pin, sprinkle the surface and pin with a minimum of flour and roll it to the required vital statistics with quick, light strokes all executed in the same direction. Pick up the pastry on the rolling pin, remove the surplus flour with a brush and drape it over the tart case. Release a little pastry into the edges and roll the pin over the rim to cut off the surplus. Now press the pastry into the corners and pinch it against the sides.

This is the basic tart. If you are going to make a fruit or jam tart, you can add a well-beaten egg instead of water. If you want a sweet tart case you can add 1 oz. of sugar to the beaten egg. Contrary to public opinion this basic and unsensational shape tastes exactly as good as it would if you scalloped the edges, used trendy knives to serrate the sides or decorated the whole shooting match with pastry leaves. What *is* useful is to brush any part of the pastry that is going to be exposed with top-of-the-milk – or cream if you are rich; the burning point of cream is lower than that of pastry so you obtain a pretty, brown finish as a bonus issue.

The filling: you need 2½ oz. of soft breadcrumbs . . . which you obtain in a liquidizer or by being very patient and crumbling away at not very fresh slices of crustless bread – white or brown but nothing kinky like granary or fruit;

6 oz. of golden syrup. You weigh golden syrup by pouring it on the already weighed breadcrumbs and remembering that $2\frac{1}{2} + 6 = 8\frac{1}{2}$; then sliding all into a pan or bowl; 1 dessertspoon of lemon juice and two pieces of crystallized or preserved ginger, finely cut. Mix well, pour into the pastry case and cook for 30 minutes in a mark 5 (375°F) oven. Give the treacle about 15 minutes in which to set and ideally eat it lukewarm with cold double cream.

Flan pastry

sufficient to line a 9-inch case
    8 oz. plain flour
    4 oz. soft butter
    a pinch of salt
    1 oz. icing sugar
    1 egg yolk whisked with
        1 tablespoon water

Sieve the flour, salt and sugar into a bowl. Add the butter and rub it into the flour lightly with your fingertips. When it is the consistency of breadcrumbs, add egg and water, cut into the mixture with a knife until it begins to cling together and then press it into a ball. Put this on a floured surface, knead gently and roll out to make a circle 2 inches bigger than your flan ring. Pick up the pastry on the rolling pin, transfer it on to a buttered flan ring and ease it into place by pressing lightly with your fingers. Cut off the surplus pastry by rolling across the flan ring with a rolling pin.

Apple flan   (for 6)
    shortcrust flan pastry (above)
    1 lb. peeled apples
    2 oz. butter
    2 oz. sugar
    3 tablespoons cider

3 tablespoons apricot jam

1 tablespoon Kirsch

2 apples for decoration

Put the apples, butter, cider and sugar into a pan. Simmer until the fruit is soft, then sieve or liquidize. Heat the apricot jam and Kirsch and sieve. Line a flan ring with pastry, paint the base and sides with some of the dissolved jam and let this cool. Add the sieved apple. Core but do not peel the decorating apples, and cut them into slices just under ¼ inch thick. Arrange them on the sieved apple.

Bake on a baking tray for 20 minutes at mark 5 (375°F) then reduce heat and give a further 25 minutes at mark 2 (300°F). Slide the flan on to a wire tray – you may have to turn flan upside down on to a covering plate, then reverse it on to the wire. Reheat the apricot jam and with a pastry brush gently glaze the apple rings.

Apple flan 2

pastry as before

1 wineglass cider

1¼ lb. peeled cored apples cut into segments

1 egg yolk beaten with a teaspoon of water

sugar for dredging

2 oz. butter

2 oz. sugar

Make the pastry and line the flan ring as before. Then line the flan with foil or greaseproof paper and fill with dried beans. Cook on a baking sheet for 15 minutes in a mark 5 (375°F) oven. Remove foil and beans, paint the base very lightly with the egg yolk and bake for another 20 minutes.

In the meantime, bring cider, butter and sugar to the boil, put in the apple segments and let them simmer until almost soft (about 2–3 minutes), stirring gently. Turn off the heat and let them cool a little in the liquor. When the pastry is cooked, let it breathe on a wire tray; then fill with apple segments, reduce the apple liquor to make a glaze, dredge with sugar and brown slightly for a minute or two in the top of a hot oven. Flambé the flan with Calvados and serve with whipped cream – if you can't leave well alone.

PUFF PASTRY

The principle of making puff – or flaky – pastry is much simpler than its successful execution: using four parts of flour to three of fat, you make 'poor pastry' (pastry short on fat) with flour, water and a quarter of the fat. You then dot the remaining fat on the pastry and by folding, rolling, refolding and rerolling the pastry (remembering to press down the sides to seal in the air), end up with around one thousand layers of pastry, separated by fat – hence *'mille feuilles'*.

In practice it is easy to go wrong. If you lose count and fold too many times or too few, the operation is ruined. The water must be very cold: the pastry has to rest and be chilled. The rolling should be light, the oven steadily hot . . . If you are determined to try your hand as a pastry-cook there are other books which tell you pretty well everything about pastry-making. If you are less keen to see whether you have cool fingers, you can now buy flaky pastry of acceptable quality in most supermarkets – though perhaps the fat used makes it more suitable for savoury than sweet.

For the following recipes the common factors are flaky pastry – home-made or commercial – a beaten egg yolk, a pastry brush, a rolling pin, and a little plain flour with which to dust the working surface.

Ham croissant
4 oz. of finely chopped lean ham mixed with 1 egg yolk
Roll out the pastry to the thickness of a 5p piece and cut out a 4-inch square. Cut this square into two triangles.

Now put a teaspoon of the filling 1 inch from the base of one triangle. Point the triangle towards you; hold the apex in one hand and fold the pastry over the ham mixture with the other, rolling the pastry towards you as you pull. You are left with sausage shapes that are thick in the middle and taper towards the ends. Brush these with beaten egg, join the two thin ends and press them together. Seal the join at the thickest part of the croissant with a small, thin triangle of puff pastry, which must also be brushed with egg. Bake for 15—18 minutes in a mark 7 (425°F) oven – and there's your croissant.

Cheese straws (page 14)

Anchovy straws (page 323)

Cuttings of puff pastry are useful for *en croute* dishes – such as a well-seasoned fillet steak baked in pastry. Seal the

steak before wrapping in pastry crust by giving it 20 seconds on each side in sizzling butter. If you want a well-done steak, you have to cook it before wrapping it in pastry.

BREAD

Our daily bread, like our daily beer, is becoming increasingly standardized – a state of affairs one can either accept or challenge. If you do tire of the steam-baked, pre-cut, hygienically wrapped, untouched-by-human-hand loaves, it is not very much trouble to bake your own. You will need yeast – not medicinal yeast, as it is not activated, and not brewers' yeast, because the results it gives are unpredictable. Get fresh yeast. It will keep for about a week in a cool place; it will last a month in an airtight box in a refrigerator, and you can store it in a deep freeze for a year. Otherwise, buy dried yeast. This comes in airtight packs and is usually satisfactory; use exactly half quantities of dried to fresh – thus in a recipe calling for 2 oz. of yeast, you require 1 oz. of dried yeast.

To get some variation into your bread you will also need wholemeal flour. If you want to start on a career of breadmaking begin with a quick wholemeal loaf. Take two flowerpots with a 5-inch diameter and 'season' them by grating the inside and giving them a few spells in the oven when you are roasting or baking something else.

Two flowerpot loaves
   8 oz. plain white flour
   8 oz. wholemeal flour
   2 level teaspoons salt
   2 level teaspoons sugar
   1 oz. yeast
   3 dessertspoons cracked wheat or crushed cornflakes
   a bare ½ pint warm water

You cannot sift wholemeal flour, and provided you buy a decent-quality plain flour there is no need to sift that. Weigh out the flour and put it in a basin; add salt and sugar; gauge level teaspoons by filling a teaspoon and levelling it off with a knife.

If you have *fresh* yeast, put 1 oz. into a basin, add the warm water and stir with a wooden spoon or fork for 30 seconds until dissolved. If you use *dried* yeast, put ½ oz. into a basin, add one of the teaspoons of sugar to the yeast, top up with the warm water and let this stand for about 10 minutes, when the yeast will have dissolved. In either case, add yeast and water to the seasoned flour in one swoop and mix with a wooden spoon until the dough leaves the side of the bowl. Gather it up, put it on a very lightly floured board and knead it for 3 to 4 minutes (the greater the proportion of white flour in the dough, the longer you will have to knead it). You now have a smooth-backed hedgehog of dough sufficient to make two flowerpot loaves.

Grease well the insides of the flowerpots with lard or cooking fat and sprinkle with some cracked wheat or crushed cornflakes. Cut the dough in half – each half should weigh 13½ oz. – and shape these roughly to fit the flowerpots. Sprinkle the wide end with wheat or crushed cornflakes and feed them into the pots.

The dough now has to rise; ideally it should do this at room temperature, covered with a polythene bag so that you can see what is going on. The average time for this is an hour. You can give it half an hour in a warm place, but the rise you get will be a light, loose, quick one and the bread will be the poorer for it. You can let it rise in a cool room, for about two hours, or even in a refrigerator overnight. The important thing is that the 13½ oz. of dough in a standard 5-inch diameter flowerpot must rise until the centre of the bulge is ½ inch above the rim of the pot. It is then ready to be baked for 30–40 minutes in the middle of a pre-warmed mark 8 (450°F) oven.

If you like your bread extra crisp, take it out of the flowerpot and bake it for the final 5 minutes on the rails of the oven-shelf. On the other hand, if you like it soft, flour the dough well before you put it into the flowerpot, and omit the cracked wheat or the crushed cornflakes.

One of the earlier shaggy dog stories concerned a man who went to infinite trouble to drag an uncooperative horse up to the second floor of his house, push it into the bathroom, topple it into the bath and shoot it. He did this so that when his know-all wife returned from the hairdresser, went upstairs to powder her nose and reappeared on the landing screaming 'there's a dead horse in the bath' he would be able to look up and say, 'Yes dear, I know.' In matters culinary it is not essential to go to quite such lengths to amaze people; for instance when the good ladies from the Women's Institute ask you whether you indulge in baking bread, you might look them in the eye and say, 'Actually I do . . . without yeast . . . in a frying pan.'

Quick yeastless bread
Baking bread in a frying pan in 35 minutes – and obtaining a result of such excellence that you may never return to the supermarket and fumble with wrapped loaves inscribed 'Happy Tuesday' – cannot be bad.

You need:

1 lb. of flour . . . any flour

1 level teaspoon each bicarbonate of soda, cream of tartar and salt

2 oz. of soft butter

½ pint of plain yoghurt or sour milk

Sieve dry ingredients into a bowl, rub in the butter, add yoghurt, mix to a dough and shape this into a flying saucer to fit the largest frying pan you have – 12 inches in diameter would be most suitable.

Rub the pan with a little fat or dripping and introduce the dough. Put it on a medium heat and cook it for about half an hour, cutting it into quarters and turning the quarters from time to time. Cooking time is just under half an hour . . . and you test the bread by sticking a knife into it and seeing whether it emerges stickily (not done) or cleanly. As the chances of someone living in a bedsitter having a 12-inch pan are remote, let me add that smaller pans can be used, albeit with smaller quantities of dough and an end-product of less bread.

One of the good things about this basic mixture . . . 1 lb. of flour, ½ pint liquid, teaspoon each salt, bicarb. and tartar, with optional fat . . . is that you can use it for any quick bread and by changing the flour you can achieve wholemeal, brown or whatever. Try using half wholemeal flour, half white; the same process but for fat, which you melt and pour into the dough after you have added the yoghurt. Put it into a greased baking tin, allow 25 minutes in a mark 6 (400°F) oven and the result will be incredibly acceptable; when the initial tension has gone, you may even paint the name of your loved one on top of the uncooked loaf with cream or egg yolk to give that personalized touch which is currently so fashionable.

The one difference between yeastless and yeast bread is that the former should not be eaten until it is cool, so, if your ambition is to mix, bake and consume within 45 minutes I am not at all sure that I can help.

Breakfast

FIRST THING IN THE MORNING, WEEKDAY STYLE

Unlike the population of the farmyard who are denied food for some days before slaughter the condemned human is fed right up to the off; moreover rumour has it that he is allowed to choose his last meal. Due to a reluctance to gossip on the part of the prison cook, and an impossibility to do so on the part of his clients, it is difficult to prove this point. What we do know is that the law dispenses capital punishment in the early hours of the morning; that breakfast is traditionally the prisoner's last meal and that breakfast is a notoriously difficult meal to serve with a flourish.

If I were to be hanged I should certainly elect to go in the late evening after dinner, for mornings find me with gummed eye and tainted palate, belching reminiscently with but small appetite for more than a cleansing cup of hot liquid. This may not be the lot of us all and if there are those who break their fast heartily then it would be wrong to do nothing for them; some – like the prisoner – eat because they have had an insubstantial evening meal;

227

others because they like to go to work on a full stomach. Whatever the reason no one deserves to be sent to face the day on what British Rail call a 'full breakfast' – an enormous, ill-assorted meal that lurches towards you as you imperceptibly approach your destination on square wheels.

Let us start at the beginning. First, the acidity of the unfed body should be countered on awakening with a cup of hot liquid, tea, coffee, milk and honey, what you will. After this any natural exuberance can be regulated with a glance at the *Financial Times*, then brush your teeth, and on to the serious problem of eating.

The general belief, and it may be true, is that the palate must be reawakened each morning, startled back to life with differing tastes, consistencies and temperatures. Fiercely we ram down hot water in the tea, iced milk in the cereal; honey on toast heralds kippers dripping butter; bacon meets marmalade, grapefruit joins with smoked haddock, there are stewed prunes and gentleman's relish; all have their claims to the breakfast table and make the diet of a cannibal modest and restrained by comparison.

If you value your gourmet, here is a gentle and abundant breakfast that will send him, and his innards, contentedly to work:

Tea or coffee, freshly made and kept decently hot.
Fresh croissants with unsalted butter and black cherry jam.
Brown toast, hot buttered, with poached eggs (eggs that are broken into a soup ladle, spilt carefully into boiling water to which a drop of vinegar is added and boiled for one minute before they are removed with a tea sieve).
Bradenham ham.
Fresh peaches.

snap
popple
crack

If only a dozen families living within a half-mile radius of a baker ordered fresh croissants every morning, it would be worth his while to deliver them daily for breakfast, through the letter box if you are asleep.

PS – Lock up the dog.

BREAKFASTING AT WEEKENDS

If I had to leave England, I think I would miss very much this convivial country-house breakfast scene: the sideboard sporting black Bradenham ham and smoked ox-tongue; the platoon of silver chafing dishes containing kippers, haddock, eggs, sausages, bacon, kidneys, cutlets and grilled tomatoes. What makes the prospect even more distressing is that, whether I stay in England or die in some foreign hell-hole tomorrow morning, I shall have missed all this anyway – because the circumference of *my* social world does not extend to the chafing-dish set.

Nevertheless one speculates about it. 'Breakfast any time between 9 a.m. and cocktails,' says your host on a Saturday evening as he kicks the last magnum of Krug under the davenport. After dispensing early morning cups of tea, his staff furiously set about ironing the Sunday papers (a little-advertised job that must have increased alarmingly in this colour magazine era). Then, as promised, the dishes chafe away on the sideboard from 9 a.m.

How – my informants are never able to tell me – are the eggs by 11.15? And is the bacon going to get more delicious? My only eligible chafing-dish acquaintance thought for a while when I asked him and said: 'Let me see . . . if you are down late . . . well, the devilled pheasant survives terribly well.'

Such guests as brave C. Freud hospitality find nary a glimmer of a chafing dish, but the idea of a rich breakfast is engaging enough to emulate. A moment's thought will tell you that substituting aluminium foil for silver, a low oven for a spirit-lamp, is an infinitely more effective way of going about making one. What makes that even more attractive for the hostess bent on breakfast entertaining is that nearly all of the breakfast can be prepared in advance.

For preparation you need a roll of foil, salt and pepper, a bowl of melted butter and a pastry brush.

Bacon: remove rind. Spread out on foil. Do not cover, but bend up edges of foil to prevent bacon fat dripping down.

Mushrooms: cut off stalks (breakfast mushrooms should be sizeable and black and uncultivated). Brush foil with butter, lay on mushrooms – white side up – brush tops with more butter, season well and fold foil closely.

Sausages: prick the skins and put the sausages in cold water; bring to the boil. Now place them in an open oven-proof dish and brush them with fat.

Tomatoes: run a sharp knife round the circumference of each tomato and brush the whole with butter. Season with salt and a pinch of basil and wrap them in a piece of foil, making sure you do not crush the fruit too close together in the parcelling process.

Eggs: brush individual ramekins (small moulds) with butter, break in an egg – making sure the yolk remains intact – and add a dessertspoon of cream and a pinch of salt. Wrap each ramekin tightly in the foil.

Thus prepared, the ingredients can be left on oven trays in the evening to be introduced into a mark 3 (325°F) oven for 25 minutes. This, I have found, is the most satisfactory overall temperature and time. It is perfect for mushrooms and tomatoes; it would not be long enough for the bacon – which has to produce its own fat and then cook in it – if the foil were closed, and would be too long for the eggs were they not especially tightly wrapped. There is no norm for chipolatas, but the treatment suited the ones that I used.

Supplementary breakfast dishes

Kedgeree: classically this is a sort of mash on a rice foundation with additives. It consists of cooked rice, béchamel sauce or cream sauce, flakes of cooked fish, cooked, sliced mushrooms, warmed together and served with a flourish, and possibly some grated cheese. It should stop recipients from hogging too many of the eggs (page 80).

Smokies: smokies, baby haddock, are one of the features of that excellent eating-house, The Bell at Aston Clinton, which, as the *Guide Michelin* would say, is 'worth a detour'. At The Bell, where the smokies are sent direct from Arbroath by a Mr O'Cargill, they take the meat from the bone in strips. To about 2½ oz. of fish placed in individual well-buttered fire-proof cocottes they add:

1 tablespoon cream
1 tablespoon white wine
1 tablespoon peeled chopped tomato
1 tablespoon grated cheese

This is mixed and cooked under a hot grill for a few minutes. But if you take finnan haddock and use the top of a hot oven, the main difference between your result and The Bell's would be the atmosphere.

A BREAKFAST PARTY

To be cook-host at a breakfast party demands some thought and planning.

Orange juice

1 tin orange juice
1 fresh orange, pressed
A coffeespoonful of water boiled for 3 minutes with
 2 heaped tablespoons sugar, 6 lumps of ice

Liquidize and strain into glasses whose rims have been wiped with lemon and dried in castor sugar.

Cereal

Kelloggs Frosties. I stumbled on these when I found that the single packet of Frosties in the jumbo-breakfast-assortment disappeared as predictably as the All Bran remained in the larder. Into a cereal bowl strew a thin layer of Frosties. A layer of fresh pear, peeled, cored and thinly sliced and then another layer of cereal. Sprinkle with demerara sugar and serve with very cold Jersey milk. Porridge – in the absence of minced Harris tweed – is an alternative for addicts and Scotophiles.

Toast

This has to be made and eaten – in that order, preferably – without much delay. An electric toaster on the dining table may be the answer. Otherwise, rolls sprinkled with water and baked on a rack in a mark 6 (400°F) oven for a few minutes give the impression that you have just returned from the baker. Toast Melba is made by toasting thin-cut slices of bread on both sides; remove the crust, slip a sharp knife between the two toasted sides and dry off the inner layers of bread under a not very hot grill. Butter should be unsalted and marmalade must be purchased with discrimination. There is a feeling that only cads or Frenchmen eat jam for breakfast. I agree.

Coffee

Use the best and most expensive instant brand. If you take cream and sugar in your coffee, use any other decent make. If you are among the one per cent of the population who can tell the difference between instant and fresh coffee, make fresh coffee – but don't talk about it; coffee snobs are even greater bores than wine snobs.

Then – and here is the master stroke – announce an interval during which the children can play in the garden, on the tenement staircase, or Ring-A-Roses in the throne room – and you return to the kitchen.

Eggs and bacon

Scramble eggs very slowly and turn them on to diamond-shaped pieces of fried bread with accompanying rashers of crisp, streaky bacon.

Upmarketing

I reckon that a well-designed kitchen should not only have the standard spice shelf, refrigerator, liquidizer and rubbish-bin. Somewhere, tucked unobtrusively in a corner, there ought to be the space for an emergency larder which should be able to cater for three eventualities.

Firstly, disenchantment by people who have been fed ... like children who were less than enthusiastic about the pheasant kedgeree; unexpected vegetarians, followers of McRobiot, and other kinks. For them there should be unequivocal goodies: Heinz tomato soup. Salted almonds. Boxes of fudge. Packets of Jaffa Cakes. Slabs of Cadbury's fruit and nut. Crunchie bars. San Pellegrino orangeade. Tins of Chivers' raspberries. Peppermint Matchmakers.

The second shelf of the larder should house foodstuffs designed to upgrade meals ... to be used for such eventualities as rich uncles dropping in or the discovery that the man you thought was just another of your daughter's boyfriends is also Parliamentary Secretary to the Department of the Environment dealing with the proposed demolition of your house. On this shelf you'll need cream to enrich a dismal soup; artichoke hearts to be drained and halved and browned in butter with garlic and

lemon juice as a companion to steaks and chops; asparagus tips and chanterelles (a fungus that resists the process of canning better than mushrooms) or mushrooms; jars of cod's roe and boxes of St Ivel cream cheese to whip together with chopped chives, black pepper and French mustard – as a canapé spread; tins of lobster bisque and turtle soup; real *pâté de foie gras*; Stilton cheese in stone jars; Bath Oliver biscuits, and good cheese biscuits in airtight boxes; a duck in Curaçao; bottles of fruit in brandy; Escoffier Sauce Robert, and Sauce Cumberland; miniatures of liqueur; ginger in tins or jars to be chilled in the refrigerator and topped with cream as an alternative to the tapioca and prunes we would have had otherwise; Tiptree's Little Scarlet strawberry jam, to put inside pancakes or dissolve in an equal quantity of Chateau d'Yquem to make a quick sauce for a dull ice cream. Items all that can elevate to a three-course feast the cheese and biscuits you were intending to munch. Grilled lamb cutlets will shine under a Cumberland sauce. Open the tin of duck and slice the breast across slivers of toast for a starter.

The final part of the store should cater for the occasions when you bring home half a dozen people – at least two of whom, you were pretty certain, were taking you out to a meal. This section of provisions must be long-lasting on the basis that it may never happen. What you do is think of a staggeringly simple, totally delicious menu which is based entirely on tins. (We work on the assumption that you always have butter, cream and one or two other essentials of the good life in your refrigerator.)

A sample menu might be:

Vichyssoise

Ham in champagne
New potatoes
Petits pois

White peaches *flambés*

First course. For this you need a tin of vichyssoise. Some cream. Ice cubes. A liquidizer. And if you should have any chives, spring onions or onions that sprout, this is a distinct advantage. Empty the tin of soup into the liquidizer, add half the volume of soup in cream and quarter the volume in ice cubes. Whizz until the clonking noise stops which denotes that the ice has been pulverized and serve with a topping of chopped oniony greenery and a bowl of Maldon salt.

Main dish. Open the tins of ham, new potatoes and peas. Slice the new potatoes into a pan in which ¼ pint of cream (it can be tinned cream) has come to the boil in the company of a good pinch of cayenne pepper. Prepare to serve this liberally sprinkled with parsley chopped on a board wiped with a crushed clove of garlic.

Drain the peas and toss them in a frying pan with a knob of butter and a dessertspoon of sugar.

Slice the ham and warm it at the top of a medium oven in a dish containing a quarter-bottle of champagne. Just like that.

The pudding. Drain the white peaches; put into a large frying pan 2 oz. butter, 2 rounded dessertspoons sugar, 1 dessertspoon lemon juice and stir as the mixture begins to colour. Turn down the flame and put in the peach halves; baste them with the caramel in the pan, add a miniature bottle of brandy or *eau de vie*, incline the pan towards the gas to ignite the contents and serve, flaming.

When the time comes to replenish that compartment of your emergency store, think of another menu and purchase accordingly.

LATE NIGHT LARDER

If I were asked to select the perfect hostess, I should not go for her who steams cauliflower to perfection, pours over it toasted breadcrumbs fried in black butter and garnishes the dish with sieved hard-boiled egg and chopped chives ... though she would receive a mention. With a little training, anyone can achieve a series of well-cooked courses. What separates The Woman from twitty ladies is an ability to cater for impromptu, unexpected snacks; as a judge, I should, like an unplacated trufflehound, make a beeline for storeroom and refrigerator and award marks for what I found therein.

The late night snack scene is not unfamiliar: one returns from dinner parties, backgammon contests or blue films, pads into the kitchen, a light coating of froth upon the tongue while taste buds holler out for satisfaction. (Was that a drool you heard behind you?) Open the door of the fridge; now what will it be? Thin-cut slices of Hungarian salami cunningly arranged on wholemeal bread, buttered to a fault, spiked with peppercorns? A julienne of blanched celeriac in lemon mayonnaise? Whipped cream tinged with Tia Maria liqueur spooned over a purée of sweet chestnuts upon a bed of crushed meringue? Or a peach, liquidized (quietly so as not to wake the lodger) and added to a quarter-bottle of cold champagne?

The eyes focus to take in the full horror of the situation. At eye level there are ice cubes and an economy packet of frozen Brussels sprouts. Down a bit and you find the standard half-squeezed tube of tomato paste; the remains of last night's ravioli set grimly in a Tupperware dish. Dripping marked 'fish' and dripping unmarked – which has been there for some time in case it is fish.

There is also a packet of margarine which you had intended to try in case you really could not tell the difference – but never had the courage.

Below, in a drawer marked 'Crispator', a lettuce languishes greenly, stretching a browning leaf towards three tomatoes in that uneasy stage when they cease to be useful for salads and are not yet bad enough for stews. To the right, in a cavity fashioned inside the door, a row of uncontroversial eggs stands at attention like pale-faced conscripts.

This display merits barely two out of ten. There has got to be cream and mushrooms and melon – Ogen or Charentais; Petit Suisse cream cheese in a wooden box – or if times are bad, Philadelphia in silver foil. Avocado pears should lie around, soft to the point where they yield to the touch without spewing forth their interior; cut them in half and fill the cavity with lemon juice and sugar. Strips of underdone beef, thin-cut rings of raw onion, slivers of apple and celery, all dressed in a light mayonnaise – Hellmann's if you cannot make it yourself; and smoked ham – Parma or Bayonne or Lachschinken, which is German.

Chocolate mousses are obtainable at supermarkets or can be made according to the recipe on page 196; they need cream in inverse ratio to their quality. If your refrigerator has enough stars to take ice cream, store ice cream. The best simple sauce is made by dissolving a Mars bar and pouring it over the cold unwrapped slab; you could even add a few drops of liqueur – Tia Maria is eminently suitable – to make it taste positively plutocratic. And if you have a liquidizer, whizz the contents of a small tin of asparagus tips, heat, add half a cup of milk and a spoonful of a product called Precis. This is a roux – flour cooked in butter, gently seasoned and containing whatever keeps it in prime condition. The result is a memorable cream of asparagus soup made in 4 minutes.

If you are still hungry, there should have been kidneys and bacon, and while the livers of broilers are not likely to be chosen as manna of the decade, there is much to commend livers of capons and ducks. Cut these into slices, dust with seasoned flour, simmer in butter containing a coffee-spoon of grated onion, and when the blood oozes into the juice, add a spoonful of double cream and a shake of cayenne pepper. Pile the mixture on to a piece of toast, and if you want to impress someone or take longer time, sprinkle with grated cheese and colour under a hot grill.

Scrambled eggs should not be ignored as a midnight snack. Cut a kidney into small pieces, fry these in butter and scramble around the hot, cooked kidney two eggs blended with a spoonful of cream and salt and pepper. You scramble eggs over the lowest heat, gently moving the mixture that has set at the base of the pan, so that more liquid can receive the benefit of the heat.

All in Good Time

PRIOR PLANNING FOR PARTY FOOD

'Congealed fat is pretty much the same irrespective of the delicacy around which it congeals.' This came from a man who had been invited to a dinner party of some pretension – at which the hostess cooked and the guests had to wait until they, and finally she, had been served before eating commenced.

After a sharp pang of pity for the unappreciated hostess, one finishes up squarely in sympathy with the ungrateful guest. From a guest's point of view, there is really no reason why a hostess should *not* spend the entire evening among her pots and pans. It is, however, generally accepted that the hostess/cook must not only be permanently in evidence, but must also at all times look cool and collected, if possible giving the impression that she has someone else in the kitchen doing the work. She can achieve this either by *having* someone else in the kitchen or by very careful planning. Restaurants employ faceless men to cook – or possibly recook precooked food – to your command. As you eat, they work. They are always a course ahead of you. They poach fish as you sip soup, and grill the meat while you eat your mushroomed mullet. Frankly there is no need to keep your guests waiting; no need to spend long minutes carving (however expertly) thin slices of meat off a joint and then piling on the procrastinating agony by spooning three of French beans next to two of sautée potatoes, adding a gulp of gravy and then rushing out to the kitchen to fetch the forgotten horseradish cream.

If you must invite more people than can casually help themselves to your good food and you don't want the trouble, expense and potential dishonesty of the casual waiter then you must plan your menu accordingly. The cook who plans to eat with her guests must not try to emulate the food of smart restaurants. This cuts out the soufflé, grill, pancakes type of meal, but still leaves an enormous choice of desirable dishes.

FIRST COURSES

These can be divided into those you prepare in advance – like peeled prawns, blended with equal parts of chopped

hard-boiled egg and mayonnaise, seasoned with salt, lemon juice and chopped chives, and filled into scooped-out tomatoes; and those that boil while the guests are gathering and are ready when you sit down to dine. These can be corn on the cob – 25 minutes and lots of butter (page 27) – or artichokes, 40 minutes. For an artichoke dip, brown 4 oz. of cheap butter in a pan, add a teaspoon of vinegar and a Weetabix, broken up with a rolling-pin.

There are also first courses that you can cook in the afternoon and warm up, such as:

Watercress soup (for 4)

   1 lb. new potatoes
   1 bunch watercress
   2 tablespoons flour
   2 oz. butter
   1 grated onion (medium sized)
   1 quart stock or water

Melt butter in pan; add grated onion, potatoes (peeled and sliced), watercress (finely chopped). Cook with lid on for 5 minutes, stirring now and then. Add flour and seasoning, and when flour is cooked, but not brown, add stock. Stir as it comes to the boil and simmer for 30 minutes. Strain and ladle onto soup plates containing a spoonful of double cream.

With soup, you can work out how long it takes for the required quantity to reach boiling point on an arranged low gas or electricity setting. You then leave your guests only long enough to light the flame or turn on the electricity under the pan. You return, and the requisite number of minutes later you can mumble, casually: 'Shall we go and eat something?'

Or you can use individual soup bowls – marmites they are called – with two handles and a decent-fitting lid which will keep the contents hot while you call your guests. If you have a fetish about serving soup which is too hot to drink you can put the marmites into the oven – that is what the dishes are made for – and if the oven is engaged in roasting, give the soup a topping of grated cheese to justify the excessive heat.

SECOND COURSES

If you must have them, these should be assembly jobs. For example

Poached eggs Arnold Bennett

Eggs can be lightly poached in the afternoon and kept in cold water; smoked haddock is simmered in milk, flaked and buttered; mornay sauce – a white sauce flavoured with a little mustard in which grated cheese is dissolved – keeps for days. Grate a little more cheese to add as the top dressing.

While husbands bring in the soup-plates, quick wives put individual dishes of egg balanced on haddock, covered in mornay sauce sprinkled with cheese into the middle of a medium oven, or lower down if it is too hot, and turn on the grill ready for colouring.

MAIN COURSES

Avoid grills. Favour casseroles. Serve large fowls and roast joints only if there is an efficient carver in the family. Crown of lamb is ideal as it needs a separator rather than a carver (page 120).

Small birds are fine, from expensive partridge to plebeian pigeon or blackcock. Butchers will prepare them for you so that they need only to be stuffed with seasoned butter and dressed with a rasher of streaky bacon to protect the lean breast. Cook in a hot oven for 20 minutes or more depending on age and size of bird, and your palate. Gauge when to put them into the oven so that they will emerge on cue.

Gravy-to-be – to accompany the pigeon or partridge, or crown of lamb – can be made in the morning. A tablespoon of flour; coffeecup of milk and of Guinness; spoonful of redcurrant jelly. Salt and pepper. Pour into the juices of the oven dish as you lift the birds. Cook for a minute and sieve into sauce boat. Sauces, jellies and relishes deserve individual bowls or one bowl or jug for every two guests; this is a very small expenditure towards the greater appreciation of hot fresh food on your guests' plates.

New potatoes, peeled and buttered, can rewarm in a closed dish in the bottom of the oven in 10 minutes. Or peel and slice them into a rich, well-seasoned béchamel sauce. Have chopped parsley ready to decorate. Mashed potatoes need the protection of a thin film of cream or milk to stop the top forming a crust. Keep these in your plate-warming compartment (the oven will be too hot) and whisk in cream before serving.

Cook green vegetables in advance. Leave them in a colander and suspend it in a pan of boiling water (turned on as you serve the soup) for a few minutes before you need them. Have melted butter and a paintbrush to revive anything that looks tired. Peas can be filled into large scooped-out tomatoes or halves of aubergine; beans topped, tailed and tied into bundles with fine string before they are boiled. If your knives are sharp your guests can cut the string with a minimum of discomfort. Broad beans can be mounted on thin skewers, boiled and served 'en brochette' with a shine of butter.

SWEET

For a sweet, prepare a crème caramel (page 200) which you can serve that evening with cream and frozen strawberries thawed in cherry brandy. Or you can make almost any ice palatable by adding

Chocolate sauce
½ oz. butter
2 oz. chocolate powder
2 oz. sugar
¼ pint milk

Boil until thick then leave and reheat before using. If you overcook this it will in the fullness of time become fudge, toffee, caramel and finally charcoal, after which it would be a mistake to keep the saucepan.

SAVOURY

A hot sweet is just showing off. But a hot savoury is a splendid idea. Here is

Croque Monsieur   (for 6)
Cut 8 thin slices off a white loaf. Make two 4-decker cheese sandwiches – 3 slices of cheese between 4 slices of bread – well buttered. Cut off the crusts and then cut vertically down to make inch-wide, 4-deck strips. Coat these in flour, beaten egg and breadcrumbs and fry them in medium hot fat during the afternoon. Then leave them to drain off.

As you bring in the sweet, turn on the heat under a frying pan half filled with oil. As you clear away, dip the strips for 1 minute. Drain and serve.

Buy a decent cheese (as opposed to an indecent one) and give him the company of radishes and celery.

Finally, take half an ounce of coarse-ground coffee and put it on the metal plate under the grill. As the aroma of the toasting beans reaches your guests, pour near-boiling water on to an adequate quantity of any good brand of instant coffee, and bring it to your guests with double cream and candied sugar.

A SPLENDIDLY UNDEMANDING DINNER PARTY

Imagine yourself in the kitchen of a well-organized cook/hostess on the afternoon of a dinner party for four people. The menu is:

Bisque de crevette
Oeuf poché Florentine
Roast guineafowl
Gravy
Buttered potatoes
Garden peas
Salad
Syllabub
Coffee

Nothing she will have to do to complete the meal will take her from her guests for more than a minute or two or – if she takes some care – harm her party dress.

Bisque de crevette

1 pint peeled shrimps
1 large onion
1 tablespoon tomato purée
3 oz. butter
1½ oz. flour
1½ pints water
1 soup cube

Grate onion, let it simmer in the butter and add the shrimps, tomato purée and seasoning. Cook with the lid on, medium flame, for 10 minutes, stirring from time to time. Add flour, let it cook on a good flame and then lower heat; add water and soup cube and stir as it comes to the boil. Simmer for 45 minutes and pass what you can through a sieve.

Oeuf poché Florentine

4 poached eggs
8 oz. buttered spinach
½ pint mornay sauce
grated parmesan cheese

Poach eggs gently in water containing a dash of vinegar; extract, trim and store in clean water. Cook (or defrost) the spinach and toss in the melted butter. Heat ½ pint of milk and 1½ oz. of butter and 2 oz. of grated cheese on a low flame and beat in 3 tablespoons of plain flour. Whisk the mixture as it comes slowly to the boil; let it bubble gently for 5 minutes and strain into a pudding basin and back into a clean pan.

To assemble: place the egg on buttered spinach, cover with warm sauce and sprinkle with parmesan.

Roast guineafowl

Inside each bird place 1 oz. of well-seasoned butter.

Into a sherry glass of red wine put a dessertspoonful each of salt and French mustard and paint the outside of the birds before protecting the breasts with streaky bacon. Roast for 35 to 50 minutes depending on size and your own preference.

Gravy mixture

1 small grated onion
2 dessertspoons plain flour
1 bottle brown ale
1 teaspoon marmalade

Salad dressing

1 level teaspoon mild mustard
juice of a lemon
1 tablespoon vinegar
salt and pepper
3 tablespoons oil
1 dessertspoon chopped chives

Syllabub

Grate the rind from one lemon and half a grapefruit. Add the juice of the lemon and 3 oz. castor sugar, blend well and beat in ½ pint double cream and ¼ pint single cream until the mixture thickens.

Put in individual dishes and store in the coldest part of the refrigerator.

Half an hour before dinner, turn the oven to no. 6 setting – 425°F.

Twenty minutes before dinner put the birds in the oven.

Ten minutes before dinner (or work out the time more exactly by timing an equivalent volume of soup from cold to hot) put soup pan on a low flame and place mornay saucepan in the bottom of the oven.

Two minutes before dinner, announce dinner and go into the kitchen. Assemble the eggs and put them in the oven. Pour the soup over a tablespoonful of cream in each bowl. If you feel rich add a teaspoonful of brandy per bowl.

As you bring back the soup bowls, take the eggs from the oven. Put the potatoes in the oven. Take the guineafowl from the oven dish and store on a serving dish in the plate-warmer. Pour the gravy mixture into the juices of the guineafowl pan and replace at the top of the oven. Light the gas under the hot salted water pan (for peas) and pour the dressing on the salad. Bring the eggs into the dining-room.

As you take out the egg plates, plunge the pea-sieve into boiling water. Arrange guineafowl on dish. Strain gravy into sauce-boat. Take the potatoes from the oven. Drain peas and brush with butter and sprinkle with sugar.

As you take out meat plates, light the gas under the coffee and bring in the syllabub.

MEAL FOR SIX PREPARED TWO DAYS AHEAD

Today's hostess with the mostest is the one who can cook her Sunday meal on Friday afternoon – then go away for the weekend. Within 15 minutes of coming home she is ready to feed her guests. This quarter of an hour is devoted to turning on the oven and an optional dusting of the dining-table, laid on the Friday.

Soused herrings
Danish bread and butter

Stuffed fillets of pork
Red cabbage
Salad of French beans

Apple and mincemeat crumble
Cream

Boursin à l'ail et fines herbes
Biscuits
Butter

Soused herrings

6 herrings

Marinade:
½ bottle dry white wine
¼ bottle cider vinegar
1 large onion, finely sliced
1 carrot, sliced
12 peppercorns
4 cloves
a bayleaf
a sprig of thyme
1 crushed clove garlic
1 envelope gelatine
salt

Simmer the marinade until the slices of carrot are cooked.
Pour this over the 6 herrings, cleaned and boned and split
open. Give them 10 minutes on the lowest of flames, in a
tightly covered saucepan, shaking it from time to time.
Then let them cool and set in the liquor. Cover the dish
and keep it in the larder, and take the herrings from their
marinade only when it is time to serve them.

Danish bread is hard and long and brown and keeps well for a week or more. Cut it thin and butter it generously.

Stuffed fillets of pork

6 small pork fillets or 3 large ones

Stuffing:
  4 oz. minced kidney
  1 tablespoon brandy
  2 oz. soft white breadcrumbs
  salt and pepper
Mix these ingredients together.

Seasoned flour:
  2 tablespoons flour
  1 dessertspoon garlic salt
  1 coffeespoon ground black pepper
  1 coffeespoon paprika

For cooking the fillet:
  2 oz. butter
  2 oz. grated onion
  8 oz. button mushrooms
  ¼ pint cider
  ¼ pint double cream
Butchers sell pork fillets, which are long and tender and pink and generally have attached to them a few ounces of skirting, a little fat and some tough skin, all of which you must remove. (Keep the trimmings to mince and make a terrine.)

You are now left with an outsized sausage shape. Make an incision lengthwise, open out the meat and make two more long incisions halfway between centre and outside so that your sausage becomes a rectangle. Spread this with the kidney stuffing, roll up to its original shape and tie

251

firmly in three or four places. Roll the fillets in the seasoned flour.

Melt the butter in a frying pan. Gently brown the outsides of the fillets and add onion and sliced mushrooms to the pan. Let this cook gently for a minute or two, add cider and cream, bring to the boil and decant into a casserole or oven dish. Cover and cook for 45 minutes on mark 4 (325°F).

When it is cooked, remove it from the oven; keep the casserole in a cool place and reclaim by letting it have 20–25 minutes in a medium oven – or the bottom of a hot oven.

Red cabbage

1 medium-sized red cabbage, shredded finely
4 oz. pork fat or dripping
8 oz. onion – sliced
4 oz. currants
salt and pepper and a tablespoon or more of vinegar

Melt the fat, fry the onion on a medium flame and then add the cabbage. Do this a handful at a time, mixing the shredded cabbage into the oniony fat and cooking with the lid on the pan until the cabbage loses resilience and allows you pot room to add more. When all the cabbage is in the saucepan let it cook with the lid on over a low flame for 15 minutes; press down, and add just enough water to come up to the level of the cabbage. Add currants, salt and pepper and let it cook slowly either in a covered pan or in a casserole dish in a mark 4 (350°F) oven.

Allow an hour and a half and when it is cooked add vinegar, mix well and check seasoning.

Salad of French beans

large tin haricots verts, drained
French dressing, which you surely make in a large bottle
  once a month. Failing that:

4 tablespoons olive oil
1 dessertspoon tarragon vinegar
1 dessertspoon lemon juice
1 coffeespoon salt
1 coffeespoon sugar
1 coffeespoon French mustard

Blend well before pouring it over the beans.

Apple and mincemeat crumble

8 oz. mincemeat
8 oz. sieved cooked apple
1 tablespoon brandy

Crumble:
8 oz. self-raising flour
4 oz. butter
6 oz. sugar
grated peel of 1 lemon

Mix the mincemeat, apple and brandy and leave in an ovenproof dish. Rub the butter into the flour, add the sugar and lemon peel and store in the refrigerator. No harm will come to it for 4 or 5 days.

To assemble, pour the crumble on to the apple-and-mincemeat and bake for 40 minutes in a hot mark 7 (425°F) oven.

SUPPERTIME IS ANYTIME

If you are bringing guests back, it is a relief to both guests and hostess to know that you have already done your homework on the evening meal. Don't ask people back for dinner and look inscrutable when you open the oven door and say 'You'll never guess'. Because they will guess. They will guess it's a stew even if you call it a casserole, a blanquette, or a little thing I ran up earlier this evening. One can smell stew from three doors down the road . . . and stew does not get better with time; it gets distinctly worse. And it is heavy.

A lovely supper to come home to would be:

Boiled ham

freshly cut and gently warmed up in champagne (if the guests can't see the bottle, use any dry sparkling wine). Soak the ham for 2 days – not 1 – and change the water every 12 hours. Then bring it to simmering point and never let the water do more than shiver around the ham. Allow 30 minutes to the pound and when it is cooked pour off half the water, top up with boiling water and let it cool in this liquor.

Cumberland sauce

which you can make the day before (page 127).

Pease pudding

is one of the few vegetable accompaniments that actually improves each time it is warmed up. Soak dried peas in water overnight (1 lb. makes 6 good servings). Simmer until tender in water containing bacon rinds. Strain. Liquidize (or sieve) when hot – with 1 cup of single cream to 4 cups of cooked dried peas. Season with celery salt and coarsely crushed black pepper.

Warm it by putting pease pudding little by little into a pan containing milk and quite a lot of butter, brought to boiling point.

Cauliflower salad

Separate the cauliflower into individual stems and simmer them in salted water until they are just tender (cover the water in the pan with a crust of bread to kill the smell). Strain and sprinkle with lemon juice to preserve the white-ness. Leave in a cool place.

For the dressing:
  1 dessertspoon lemon juice
  1 dessertspoon wine vinegar
  2 tablespoons oil
  1 teaspoon castor sugar
  half a coffeespoon salt
  ground white pepper

You can make and blend the dressing before you leave. Also prepare a level dessertspoon of chopped parsley – you wash parsley, chop it, put it in a cloth, squeeze out the water and store the dry parsley in a cool place. Hard boil an egg and pass it through a sieve. Mix the cauliflower and the dressing just before the meal; garnish with parsley and egg.

If you really want to do no more upon coming home than push a saucepan on the stove and you do not begrudge time spent on preparation, then you can lay the table before you leave and put on to it:

A bowl of beautifully cooked cold rice, to which you have added currants simmered in wine, and a tinned red pimento, chopped up.

A bowl of mango chutney.

A bowl of hard-boiled eggs, halved and dressed with a sauce produced by boiling together ¼ pint double cream, a liqueur glass of sweet sherry and 1 dessertspoon of curry powder.

A bowl of sliced peeled tomatoes, sprinkled with salt, sugar and oil. (You peel tomatoes by suspending them in boiling water for 10 seconds, making token incisions and lifting off the skin.)

A bowl of sliced shallots, dressed in tarragon vinegar.

A bowl of slices of orange.

A bowl of drained sweetcorn, dressed in a garlicky mayonnaise. (Incorporate this at the last moment as however well you drain the corn it will continue to lose liquid into the mayonnaise.)

A bowl of chilli sauce . . . which need be no more than your best classic brown sauce in which you have simmered half a dozen chilli peppers and added a sizeable dash of Tabasco.

Naturally that morning you have been working on the preparation of your curry.

Curry (for 6)

3 rounded tablespoons of curry powder
3 lb. of boned shoulder of lamb
3 oz. butter
6 oz. finely chopped onion
2 oz. finely chopped preserved or crystallized ginger
½ teaspoon dried mint
½ teaspoon sugar
½ coffeespoon freshly ground black pepper
2 teaspoons salt
¼ pint milk (poured over 2 oz. dried coconut, left to stand for 20 minutes and strained)
4 oz. grated coconut
¼ pint of lemon juice
¼ pint of double cream

Melt 1½ oz. butter and in it fry the onions until they are transparent. Remove the onion with a slotted spoon, add the rest of the butter and in it brown the lamb, cut into small pieces. Return the onion to the pan and add ginger, sugar, pepper, salt, curry powder and mint. Mix well, place lid on pan, and let this cook gently for 10 minutes.

Add half the coconut milk, stir as the mixture comes to the boil and let it simmer with the lid on for an hour.

Add the rest of the coconut milk and the grated coconut, and stir in the lemon juice. Let this come to the boil and blend with the other ingredients before adding double

cream. Let this simmer for about 15 minutes or until the lamb is very tender.

Warm up in an oven dish in a medium oven – or slowly in a pan on top of the stove.

LUNCH OF THE WEEK

As I said to Mrs Probert-Dalrymple . . . Sunday lunch only requires an oven in good working order and an immaculate sense of timing. She gave her famous Mona Lisa/battery-hen smile and, thus encouraged, I continued: Take a simple meal for six, I said:

Anchoyade

Beetroot soup

Roast brisket of beef
Gravy
Horseradish cream

Baked potatoes
Broad beans

Pineapple and ginger crumble

Anchoyade

1 tin anchovy fillets
1 dessertspoon grated onion
1 dessertspoon sieved hard-boiled egg
cayenne pepper

Lift the anchovies out of their oil and pass them through a sieve. Add onion and egg, season with cayenne pepper and spread this mixture on 2 fairly thick slices of bread. Cut the slices into 6 fingers each, put them on a well-oiled roasting-tray, brush them with oil from the anchovy tin and bake in the top of the oven for 15 minutes.

Beetroot soup

1 large beetroot, preferably uncooked
1 medium-sized onion
1 level teaspoon celery salt
1½ oz. butter
1 oz. flour
2 chicken stock cubes
1½ pints water
¼ pint sour cream
salt and pepper

Chop the onion, chop or grate the beetroot and simmer them in the butter for 10 to 15 minutes with a lid on the pan. Season with celery salt, add flour, let it cook but not brown, and then add the water and soup cubes. Let the soup boil gently for 30 minutes. Liquidize or pass through a sieve, and let a spoonful of cold sour cream float upon each bowl of hot red soup.

258

Brisket of beef

This is reasonably cheap . . . even the butcher whom I no longer patronize for reasons of economy sells it thus. Contrary to belief, butchers are absolutely delighted to sell unfashionable low-priced joints and will score briskets for you as they do legs of pork. A whole brisket weighs 10–11 lb. and costs as much as a plump duckling. If your family is small, get half a brisket.

Make a solution of:
- *1 tablespoon black treacle or*
- *1 tablespoon of golden syrup mixed with 1 teaspoon of gravy browning*
- *1 dessertspoon salt*
- *1 tablespoon wine vinegar*

Heat the mixture a little so that it will blend well, and using a pastry brush paint the outside of the brisket with the mixture, paying particular attention to the scored side.

The meat should be started off for 20 minutes in a pre-heated oven on mark 7 (425°F). Then roast for 4–5 hours on mark 3 (325°F). If the outside gets too crisp, protect it with foil, which must be removed for the last half-hour of cooking.

Gravy

Mix:
- *1 level teaspoon plain flour*
- *1 level dessertspoon blackcurrant jelly*
- *1 teaspoon vinegar*
- *1 teaspoon tomato ketchup*
- *1 pint water*
- *salt and pepper*

When the meat emerges from the oven pan, pour off most of the fat and put into the roasting tray the above mixture. Stir to dissolve all the deposits, let the gravy come slowly to the boil and strain before serving. There will be meat left over for stewing or braising.

Baked potatoes
Scrub the potatoes, place them on a baking sheet spread with a thin layer of cooking salt and give them 2½–3 hours in the oven . . . more if they are very large. Cut them in half, scoop out the potato, mix it with cream and butter if you like and spoon it back into the potato cases. Decorate with chives.

Horseradish cream
Grate fresh horseradish into a bowl. Beat up equal quantities of single cream and double cream – say, 2 tablespoons of each – and add some of the white of an egg, stiffly beaten. Fold in the horseradish.

Pineapple crumble
1 small Cape pineapple or a tin of pineapple chunks –
  drained
3 pieces of preserved or crystallized ginger
6 oz. flour
4½ oz. butter
3 oz. sugar
quite a lot of cream

Take the pieces of pineapple, and if your guests are adult, add to them a miniature bottle of Curaçao and the ginger thinly sliced. Put these in an ovenproof bowl and cover with the crumble: flour, into which you have rubbed the butter . . . before you added the sugar.

If you are to have lunch at 1 p.m. on Sunday
On Saturday evening you make the soup; the gravy mixture; the anchoyade; the crumble mixture; and if the

pineapple is fresh, cut it into chunks and sprinkle with sugar and liqueur. You might also scrub potatoes and prepare a baking sheet, and give the brisket a brisk half-hour in a mark 7 (425°F) oven . . . it can cool while you sleep.

On Sunday turn oven on mark 3 (325°F) at 8.30 a.m. Put in the meat when the oven is properly hot.

Put a tray of potatoes in the top of oven at 10.30 a.m. and if the meat looks like getting too dark, cover it.

At 12.45 remove meat from the tin and keep it in a warm place. Pour off the surplus fat, pour in gravy mixture, stir well and put in bottom oven shelf. Turn oven up to mark 5 (375°F). Spread thick slices of bread with anchoyade mixture and put them on a baking sheet in the top of the oven. Put the soup on a low flame. Boil the cream, add the drained broad beans and leave them in a covered oven dish in the bottom of the oven.

When the anchoyade is done (after 15 minutes' baking), put the assembled pineapple crumble into the top shelf of the oven.

Croûtons, Crackling and Custard

We have a house rule about Sunday lunch; all may eat what they like and leave what they do not like . . . provided they don't talk about it. So silence reigns at the Freud board – though I have noticed of late that the dog and the cat are putting on weight while my children, with the exception of Emma, are getting thinner.

As head of a democratic outfit I asked my children to pick a representative to discuss meals in general and Sunday lunch in particular. By way of hors d'oeuvres, I asked the spokesman whether the Sunday rule was still to their liking. He replied that it was the consensus of opinion that if I actually wanted them to eat more and leave less, I should cook for children rather than for adults.

Take meat for a start, he said. I pointed out that we usually took soup for a start but he brushed logic aside and asked whether I had ever bothered to look and see how much meat they actually consumed . . . except Emma, of course. He elaborated. When we had pork they all had the crackling of which there was never enough. If we had chicken only Emma ate the meat. They had the crisp skin and wishbones. And potatoes should be chips; other families had chips. What was so special about us anyway?

Then custard. All right, Emma eats custard, the rest of them liked custard skin, so why couldn't I make less custard and more custard skin? And on the subject of puddings and cheeses did I notice that the Gruyère didn't have as many holes in it as it used to. And you all like the holes? It turned out that they did, except Emma who preferred the cheese.

Thinking about the conversation, their argument made reasonable sense. In this day and age you can get all the vitamins you need via a couple of pills and the argument for a balanced diet, a sufficiency of greens, steamed fish and protein-rich foods no longer applies. The following menu may not be everyone's ideal composition, but it is what sociologists call children-orientated and was received with complete approval by five children whom the *Good Food Guide* would call a discriminating clientèle.

First course: slices of orange that have swum in a weak Pimm's No. 1.

Second course: croûtons – cubes of crustless white bread fried in bacon fat, drained and gently salted. Soup spoils these.

Third course: pork crackling, bread sauce (page 310), Yorkshire pudding. Even if butchers do not actually give you the skin from a belly of pork, they are damned pleased when someone asks for it. The price is not prohibitive. Ask for the skin to be scored; dissolve a level teaspoon of salt in a tablespoon of oil and rub this into the scored skin. Leave it overnight and roast for about 40 minutes in a mark 6 (400°F) oven, basting now and then, turning the dish around and upping the temperature of the oven for the final 10 minutes if the crackling is not, by then, all it should be.

Yorkshire pudding

3 oz. self-raising flour
a pinch of Bird's Golden Raising Agent
a coffeespoon of salt
1 egg, milk

Sieve flour and salt into a basin, add egg yolk and enough milk to make a fairly thick mixture; fold well-beaten egg white and pour into a frying pan containing very hot oil or dripping. If you are clever turn the 'pudding' with two fish slices. If timid, set the top side under a red hot grill before turning.

Fourth course: custard skin and hot chocolate sauce (page 245). Make custard in the usual way, i.e. the way it tells you on the tin. Pour this into a shallow roasting dish. It is not essential to pour the sauce over the custard skin.

BACK TO SCHOOL

By the day my last child has gone back to school, the garlic, the curry powder and the cooking brandy have come back, out of their summer holiday storage. We can eat mushrooms again and sprinkle cheese over things in the kitchen where the dish is hot, instead of having to strew it surreptitiously on some plates . . . not on others.

The farewell dinner, by request, was fillets of plaice, fried in a batter made of milk and self-raising flour, served in selected pages of favourite comics followed by

Banana milkshake

⅔ of a banana
2 tablespoons sugar
2 lumps ice
just under ½ pint milk

Whizz on 'full' for 25 seconds in the liquidizer. Then lemon pancakes, then fingers of toast, spread with sandwich spread and peanut butter.

Tonight we shall have the antidote.

Game soup

made of every sort of forbidden fruit: what was left of a partridge I ran over on the way to Lowestoft; the heel of a bottle of port; the carcass of a pigeon I had (surreptitiously) for breakfast; a washed-out jar of patum peperium; a great handful of parsley stalks and a rather smaller one of lemon thyme. Put in twice as much water as you want soup – boiling will reduce; sieving will make presentable; cornflour will thicken. Then taste and season alternately until you are happy, or there is no soup left, or both. A burnt onion will provide colour if you are inclined to worry about that sort of thing.

As a second course, a quiet pint of Burgundy, to which nothing is really more complementary than another quiet pint, though

Chicken livers

soaked overnight in white wine and garlic (crushed), rolled into a protection of streaky bacon and fried in olive oil, make a pleasing break between bottles.

We shall finish with cheese, something really unspeakable about which the children would never stop talking; a cheese with the power of Tilsiter or a very creamy gorgonzola, bulging from its protective wrapping; the sort of cheese that you could never mislay. After that coffee and more coffee, and then the sad thought of all the quiet meals to come.

DO'S AND DON'TS AT A CHILDREN'S PARTY

A children's party is potentially a many-splendoured thing – and likely to be more so if you remember that it is first and foremost a party, and only incidentally for children. You need a cake. It's not very important what is in the cake, though sponge is more suitable than heavy fruit, because few children will eat much of it. But it has got to look absolutely smashing. Children don't deeply care whether or not you have baked it yourself, so if you are not an adept cake-maker, go and buy one, as ornately garnished as you like, and then buy some

> candles
> glacé cherries
> candied pineapple
> angelica
> a Mars bar

Cut the Mars bar into thin slices and garnish some more.

The cake

The following cake, when we were in our cake-making era, was highly successful, much appreciated and little trouble.

> 8 egg whites
> 12 oz. castor sugar
> ½ pint double cream
> 2 oz. grated plain chocolate
> 2 oz. chopped roasted almonds (roasted in a lightly buttered tin for 20 minutes in the top of a mark 2/300°F oven)
> ½ teaspoon instant coffee
> 1 oz. halved, blanched almonds for decoration

Beat 6 of the egg whites with a couple of pinches of salt until the mixture is stiff and dry. Then fold in 12 oz. of sugar. (90 per cent of meringue failures can be attributed directly to the absence of an electric beater or weakness of

266

the elbows.) On two pieces of lightly buttered greaseproof paper, draw 8-inch diameter circles and pipe half the meringue mixture over each circle (it will probably expand to 9-inch diameter). Place the meringued sheets on baking sheets and cook for 2 hours in a mark 1 (275°F) oven, interchanging the position of the two sheets after an hour. Remove the greaseproof paper and let the meringue halves cool. (If you can buy sheets of rice paper, you can save yourself this trouble.)

Gently whip the double cream, blend in the remaining egg whites, stiffly beaten, and add to this cream the grated chocolate, chopped roasted almonds and instant coffee. Mix well and use the cream as a filling between the meringue halves, and as a topping, which you decorate with the almonds, angelica, glacé cherries, etc.

It would be pointless to overwrite recipes for a score of assorted goodies because children of different ages, nurtured in different dining-rooms, appreciate different things. We have had success with a fish and chip party – using comics instead of newspapers for the wrapping. Make your batter as you will; the important thing is the freshness of the fish and the quality and cleanliness of the fat. Cut your chips into any shape you fancy; thin if you like them crisp; thick and cook them slowly if you like them pale and floury. The inexcusable thing, it seems to me, is to embarrass an honest plate of fish and chips with pretentious courses before and after.

Our children and their friends love potato crisps, sausages and sausage rolls, pasties and cheese straws and filled savoury vol-au-vents as long as they are of a size that can be eaten in a maximum of two bites. They also suffer from a major hang-up on flavoured potato crisps. Our local grocer sells these, subheaded 'salt 'n' vinegar', 'beef 'n' onion', 'chicken', etc. Frankly I am astonished at the

manufacturers' lack of enterprise. As people are daily conforming less, there must be a fortune to be made in a really way-out range of new flavours. Gooseberry and newt springs to mind, possibly as the brand leader. But lentil and ferret; turtle and grape; loganberry and gherkin . . . I simply do not believe that they have all been tried and rejected. I think they have just not bothered to research the market.

We have failed with a do-it-yourself party, mostly I think because children want to sit down and eat, then get up and play; the provision of buttered slices of French bread and a battery of jams and pastes and spreads that had seemed such a good idea had to be cleared away almost untouched.

Drink depends on available manpower: if you have little help, the answer is a large jug of fruit squash with lots of ice. If you have helpers, you can offer assorted bottles of Coca-Cola, lemonade, ginger beer and – if you can get it – Vittel Framboise, which is the best soft drink I know; straws are essential. If you own a liquidizer and have a full-time dispenser, provide milkshakes to order.

If there is not room to seat everyone at the table, patissiers' white cardboard boxes filled with food to be eaten on the floor have worked well.

Guests' initials baked in gingerbread (very little ginger) are easy to make and much appreciated.

One final word of advice: take the telephone numbers of the visiting children. You will then avoid our recent predicament of being stuck until 7.30 p.m. with an anonymous, bilious five-year-old whose parents – who can blame them? – had forgotten about her.

A MENU FOR A TEENAGE PARTY

'Butter,' said my sixteen-year-old daughter. 'Lots and lots of lovely butter.'

Her friends – when asked what they would most like to eat at a teenage party – said respectively:

'Mustard pickles.'

'Anything that you can eat without a knife and fork.'

'Salted almonds.'

'Enough.'

On reflection they all agreed that a party consisting of nothing but a sufficiency of their chosen ingredients would make pretty unsatisfactory fare, and the following teenage party menu is published with their approval.

Garlic bread and Maldon salt

To make this satisfactorily you need French bread, preferably what the French call a 'flute'. Slice the loaf at ½-inch intervals, stopping when you get to the bottom crust so that the loaf keeps its shape; place it on a sheet of kitchen foil. For 12 inches of French bread, you need

5 oz. butter

2 medium-sized cloves of garlic

a tablespoon of chopped basil

Melt the butter, add finely chopped garlic and the basil and pour this evenly over the bread so that the garlicky herbaceous butter sinks into the incisions.

Wrap the loaf firmly in foil, let it cook for 15 minutes in the middle of a mark 3 (325°F) oven, whereafter unwrap the loaf and leave the bread lying on the open foil in the top of the oven to crisp for 5 minutes.

Maldon salt, or sea salt, also known as rock salt, can be bought at health food stores and most supermarkets. If no one has yet given you a saltmill for Christmas, serve it just as it is, in crystals.

Rice salads

To make a rice salad it is essential to use long-grain rice. Count on 5 portions to 1 lb. of rice:

2 tablespoons olive oil
1 tablespoons rosemary
2 tablespoon chopped onions
1 lb. rice
water – twice the volume of 1 lb. of rice
a soup cube
salt and white pepper

Simmer the onion in oil until translucent, add the rosemary and rice and let this cook until each grain of rice is shining with oil. Increase flame, add the two bowls of water, salt, pepper and soup cube and stir diligently until the water comes to the boil. Cover closely and reduce heat to give a very gentle simmer.

Let this cook *without stirring* for 20–25 minutes, when all the water will have been taken up by the rice and the surface of the rice pitted with small suction holes. Let it rest for some time with the lid on so that the rice dries out thoroughly. Then pour into a bowl and let it cool. This is the foundation to make steak and pimento rice salad.

Steak and pimento rice salad

For each person you need:

3 oz. of the rice, cooked

2 oz. strips of fillet steak – or skirting

1 oz. chopped sweet pepper

Simmer the sweet pepper in a half-oil half-butter mixture until it is entirely tender, lift out the pieces, heat up the fat and in this fry the meat cut into small strips and well seasoned with garlic, salt and paprika. For a minute or two, no more. Add sweet pepper, meat and juices in the pan to the rice, check seasoning and add lemon juice, Tabasco or Dijon mustard to make it more piquant. To make a

Fish and egg rice salad

you add.

half a roughly chopped hard-boiled egg

*2 oz. of steamed flaked fillet of cod or fresh haddock to the
   3 oz. of rice per person*

season with lemon juice, double cream and herbs

In either case serve grated cheese for those that care to sprinkle it over their rice salads, and a battery of sauces, pickles, chutneys and relishes.

Rashers of crisp streaky bacon

There is absolutely no reason why grocers – even super-markets – should not cut the rind from bacon before machine cutting it. Ask them to do this and cut for you 1 lb. streaky bacon on 2½ to 3, which gives a thin slice. Ask them to give you the rind – for which you will have to pay: it helps to flavour soup. Arrange the bacon on a baking sheet at the top of a mark 5 (375°F) oven. Turn over the rashers and pour off the fat after 10 minutes and give them a few minutes on the other side so they are as crisp as you would have them be.

Sweets

These have to be absolutely super or nonexistent. The best way out is to buy a sufficiency of Cox's apples, which are now considered old-fashioned but to my taste are still the most desirable – and a lot of crumbly Lancashire or Double Gloucester cheese.

Going away soup . . .

which should be dark and strong and very hot and lace-able with sherry or madeira unless you believe that children should wait until they are sixteen before they start on the demon drink . . . in which case you are unlikely still to be reading what I write.

For 20 people:
  some veal bones
  1 lb. shin of beef
  3 sets chicken necks and giblets
  1 lb. onions
  1 lb. leeks
  1 lb. potatoes
  4 oz. butter
  4 tablespoons oil
  2 tablespoons sugar
  ½ lb. carrots
  a fistful of assorted herbs
  6 oz. plain flour
  salt and pepper
  7 pints of water

Roast the veal bones in the top of a very hot oven for 20 minutes. Clean and chop the onion, leeks, potatoes, carrots and meat and cook in oil and butter over a good flame, stirring from time to time. Add sugar and let the mixture brown a little.

Now add the flour and let this take up the moisture and

brown – but not burn. Add the water, a pint or two at a time, letting it boil before you add more. Then add herbs and seasoning and veal bones, and let the soup simmer for at least 2 hours.

Strain and serve and, if you like it darker, add gravy browning . . . or make this yourself. It needs no more than sugar, a strong saucepan, courage and the ability to put up with the smell.

Wooing
Food

When I was ten years old and banished to a coeducational school in Devon I knew a girl who would do anything for a Crunchie bar. As one gets older the mechanics of wooing perforce become more complex, more subtle and more expensive. Consequently my suggestions for a meal for swinging lovers – or for lovers about to embark on a career of swinging – will cost more than the twopenny chocolate-coated honeycomb that used to stand me in such good stead.

I have no great faith in the advertised aphrodisiac qualities of certain foodstuffs, because given the right atmosphere you can become very passionate on sago pudding – just as you can remain frigid to a degree on a diet of peppercorns. In spite of this it is sensible to remember that such foods as shellfish, ginger and oysters have a reputation on which all sorts of unEnglish behaviour can be blamed. For myself I think oysters are much overrated as a sexual stimulant. The last time I went to Wheeler's and ordered half a dozen Whitstables only four of them worked.

But it is possible to achieve one's amorous ends by choosing the right food and the right drink and presenting it to the right person in the right way at the right time; and St Valentine's Day is traditionally that right time.

There is one danger: when all is so carefully planned, Eros is inclined to strike before the fish course. This is a terrible waste of underdone beef, passion-fruit ice cream, mint tea *et al*. So here is a menu for a simple meal which can be cooked on a gas ring erected by the side of the bed, though it may be advisable to do the overture with

Oyster patties
made with tinned oysters and fashioned in puff pastry. Paint them with cream to get a pretty colour, and bake

them for 15–20 minutes in a mark 6 (400°F) oven. As an accompaniment serve Black Velvet – half non-vintage champagne, half Guinness – in large and beautiful glasses at cooler-than-room temperature. The room should be warm.

Ginger omelette

1 tablespoon single cream
4 eggs, pinch of ground ginger
1 oz. crystallized ginger cut into strips
½ oz. butter

Mix eggs, cream and ginger and beat with a fork. Get a frying pan, ideally a nonstick pan, very hot, put in the butter, let it skid across the pan and immediately pour in the omelette mixture. Shake the pan over the flame so that the egg mixture gains a number of skins through contact with the base, then incline the pan away from you and let the omelette form a crescent shape in the far curve. Decant the omelette on to a heated plate and serve with two forks.

Steak au poivre

Ask your butcher to cut you two 6 oz. fillet steaks. Turn them a few times in a saucer of oil – and salt gently. Distribute about three dozen crushed black peppercorns around each steak. Cook them for 2 minutes on each side in a pan containing 1 oz. butter and 1 tablespoon of oil heated to the point at which the butter has stopped sizzling.

Caesar salad

The best type of lettuce for this is romaine – but cos or endive will do well; the important thing is the dressing.

1 egg, 3 tablespoons olive oil
1 tablespoon lemon juice
1 large clove garlic, crushed
1 rounded tablespoon parmesan cheese

Mix the dressing well in a salad bowl, add lettuce and turn the leaves until they lose some of their rigidity (what the French call *fatigué la salade*). When the steaks come out of the pan put into the hot fat half a teacup of small cubes of bread; fry them until they are brown, drain them, salt them and add these to the salad. Some time later you may like to wipe the frying pan on the pillowcase and produce

White peaches in Curaçao

Lift four half-peaches from a tin, and introduce them to the pan in which is melted ½ oz. of butter and a rounded dessertspoon of sugar. Heat the peaches and add 2 liqueur glasses of Curaçao; ignite and serve by their own light.

As Ovid wrote: 'Women can always be caught; that is the first rule of the game.' If all goes well, Grapenuts and cream, toast and ginger marmalade, and some good hot strong coffee should be the next kitchen chore for you.

A VALENTINE'S FEAST FOR MORE THAN TWO

Pâté à poivre

8 oz. minced pork
8 oz. minced veal
6 oz. minced liver
3 oz. roughly chopped streaky bacon
4 oz. grated onion (1 medium onion)
2 eggs
2 level teaspoons coarse-ground black pepper
1 level teaspoon salt
1 small crushed clove of garlic for the sake of togetherness
½ oz. powdered gelatine
3 tablespoons brandy

Reserve gelatine and brandy and mix the other ingredients in a basin, putting the mixture into a lightly buttered dish.

Cook for 1 hour 20 minutes in the middle of a mark 5 (375°F) oven. You will then notice that the pâté has risen in the middle (this is because of the eggs). Take a saucer and press down the pâté – pouring off the juices as they appear. Keep pressing down until the pâté is flat. Put the juices from the pâté into a pan, skim off excess fat and add gelatine. When this has dissolved, remove the pan from the flame, add the brandy and pour gently over the pâté. Let it cool and serve in thick slices; it will keep for days in a cool place.

Stuffed lamb's hearts

Lamb's hearts are too easily dismissed as being the sort of thing other people eat – but they are excellent value, with a surprising amount of good, entirely tender meat. For each person take one lamb's heart. With a sharp knife cut from the open end such gristle as protrudes. Open up the two small compartments of the heart to make one, dredge with flour, salt and paprika and fry gently on all sides in a butter/oil mixture. Then stuff the hearts as follows:

For six hearts:
  2 oz. white breadcrumbs
  1 oz. finely chopped onion
  2 oz. minced kidneys
  1 beaten egg
  1 dessertspoon mixed herbs (sage on its own is dull stuff)
  salt and pepper

For the sauce:
  1 tablespoon redcurrant jelly
  1 tablespoon port

Heat the oil and butter in roasting tin in a mark 5 (375°F) oven for 5 minutes; put into it the hearts, stuffing-side down, and cook, basting fairly frequently, for 50 minutes.

For the sauce, take up the juices in the pan with a table-spoonful of redcurrant jelly and one of port and skim off excess fat. Thicken with double cream or not and serve with the very best mashed potatoes.

Valentine's cake
A cake for eight – or a main dish for four hungry, sweet-toothed lovers.

1 lb. ginger nut biscuits
1 pint strong black coffee (instant will do very well)
1 miniature bottle Crème de Cacao liqueur
½ pint double cream
2 egg whites
2 oz. sugar
3 or 4 pieces of stem ginger

Bring the coffee to the boil, and drop into it one by one the ginger nuts, fishing them out with a slatted spoon the moment they are submerged. Place the biscuits on a piece of foil (it is essential that the coffee is very hot and the biscuits have only a bare second's baptism). When all the biscuits are thus dunked, sprinkle each with the liqueur.

Now whisk the egg whites until they are stiff, add sugar and beat some more. Beat the double cream with 3 table-spoons of top of the milk and 1 dessertspoon of syrup from the preserved ginger. When it is thick, fold in the egg whites and blend with a wooden spoon.

Arrange one-third of the biscuits in a circle or oval – as you desire. Spread on each ¼ inch of whipped cream and cover with another layer of biscuits. Add cream to these and cover with the last layer. Decorate with whipped cream and adorn the top with thinly sliced ginger and Mars bars.

All on a Winter's Night . . .

The advent of television brought about a radical change in our eating habits; fried nasties called TV snacks took the place of such carefully matured delicacies as Philadelphia Hotpot. Pre-cooked hamburgerettes attained the popularity vote over portmanteau steak, also called a carpetbagger (a thick wad of tender sirloin, stuffed with peppered oysters, sewn up, and carefully fried in butter).

Some time ago I chastised my daughter for wasting a whole evening watching ITV. After a decorous pause for tears she retorted that I had wasted a similar period of time contemplating the log fire. This, although I had some difficulty in explaining it to my child, is a ridiculous argument. My evening was spent nobly, altruistically, unselfishly; hers basely, derivatively, commercially. She drank an unspeakable bottle of mud-coloured fizz, I mulled from time to time a pint of burgundy with a red hot poker: cinnamon stick, sugar lump and cloves sewn into a muslin bag dangled in the wine and were withdrawn. Why, there was no comparison. On reflection, what I really tried to convey to my daughter was that a log fire is not only attractive and instructive to watch but that it is altogether a more complete, a more composite companion than an idiot-box for a cold evening.

Take one log fire on any winter's night; add to it man's natural reluctance to move from the chair in front of the hearth. To make this a success, a certain amount of preparation or a willing slave is needed.

For wine, use up the cheap bottles of red that we will charitably suppose you were given for Christmas. No one actually buys cheap wine (I quote my wine merchant). Draw the cork before you move it to the heat, or it will decork itself. Sweeten or not as you desire. No matter what you do, for some strange reason nasty wine is more drinkable hot than cold.

For the menu, start with corn on the cob, obtainable frozen, in packets. Skewer this, and roast it until the kernels are just beginning to colour. Then brush generously with butter. Next, a quiet white marshmallow, toasted at the end of a fork. A crumpet lightly spread with anchovy butter for a fish course. A few chestnuts, roasted in the embers – as an apéritif for the main course of prunes, properly soaked in water, then tightly wrapped in streaky bacon and skewered alternately with pieces of brown bread to take up the melting bacon fat.

Another marshmallow, a pink one, and as the comforting words of the epilogue fade into the middle distance from the next room, some more burgundy. Then, as it is unlikely you've taken much exercise during the evening, a glass of what my youngest son called Uncle Seltzer.

GUY FAWKES NIGHT

There is an old Austrian saying that 'trees should grow in the neighours' garden'. I feel rather like that about Guy Fawkes Night parties, for celebrations involving different generations are always potentially disastrous. But just as someone has to grow trees, so some people must give Bonfire Night beanos. Here is some gustatory wisdom. If it is your turn, meet your guests with

Mulled wine

You can always cool it down with water for those who like it cooler. The point about any hot wine mixture is that the wine itself must never come to the boil. For one quart of mulled wine:

1 teaspoon ground cloves
1 teaspoon ground nutmeg
2 teaspoons ground cinnamon
half chopped orange
half chopped lemon
5 oz. sugar
1 pint of water

Bring all the ingredients to the boil and simmer for at least an hour. Strain through a muslin cloth and add the resultant syrup – it should be, or should be made up to, two-thirds of a pint – to a bottle of inexpensive but unvinegary red wine. (While mulled claret sounds better, mulled burgundy is really the better drink. Somehow cheap burgundy is always more acceptable than the cheap wines that come from Bordeaux.) Heat to just below boiling point.

The wineless mulling-syrup keeps almost indefinitely, and if you care for the finished article you can bottle a gallon of syrup at a time and summon up mulled wine at 5 minutes' notice throughout the winter.

The Guy Fawkes food problem is affected by the sheer timelessness of the occasion and is best solved by hot dishes that can be eaten cold, or cold dishes that retain their freshness and a modicum of their beauty.

For hot dishes try: pot-roast sirloin of beef with whipped cream horseradish sauce. Ratatouille.

Pot-roast

This requires courage and a stout saucepan. Buy a decent piece of sirloin, boned and tightly rolled, and rub the outside with the contents of a tablespoonful of olive oil saturated with two parts salt and one part black pepper. Put the meat into the hot, dry saucepan set on a medium flame on top of the stove. Turn the joint to seal the outside and then put on the lid. Roast for no more than 10 minutes to the pound, turning the meat at half-time. When it is cooked, turn off the flame, leave on the lid and let it form a mahogany-coloured gravy, which you then pour over exquisitely pink, tender slices of beef, fringed by a dark outer crust. If you like meat well done, pot-roasting is a wasteful and laborious way of overcooking it.

Horseradish sauce

Use fresh horseradish if you can find any; if not, tins of dehydrated horseradish powder are better than those bottles of coarsely grated stuff. Then beat ⅛ pint of double cream into a similar quantity of single cream and add 2 dessertspoons of finely grated fresh horseradish or a soupspoon of revived horseradish powder; season with salt and lemon juice.

Ratatouille (for 12)

1½ lb. sliced onions
1½ lb. green peppers, chopped
1½ lb. aubergines, peeled and sliced
1½ lb. courgettes, peeled and sliced
1 large tin peeled tomatoes
3 cloves of garlic, crushed
½ pint of olive oil
salt, pepper, ½ pint dry white wine

Heat the olive oil in a large pan and cook the onions until they are transparent. Add peppers and cook until they lose their resistance. Then add aubergines, courgettes, garlic and seasoning, stirring as they stew gently in the oil. After 10 minutes of this, empty the saucepan into a large casserole dish, add roughly chopped tomatoes and wine and cook in a slow oven for 40 minutes, covering with paper or foil to prevent the formation of a crust. Add more water if it becomes too dry.

For cold dishes try:

Mayonnaise of tinned sweetcorn and chopped tinned pimento.

Salad of watercress and sliced hard-boiled eggs (page 317).

Crème caramel (page 200).

Meringues (page 194).

Stilton cheese and Bath Oliver biscuits or, if you feel unrich, cream cheese and Ritz biscuits.

GIVE THE WIFE A BREAK . . .

There should come an evening when a husband tells his wife to stay where she is – in front of book, fire or the television set – while he goes to the kitchen to cook a meal. ('Don't make it a fry up,' said my wife. 'I don't care how little I eat as long as I don't have to go and wash dirty pans afterwards.') Certain stocks will have to be purchased and preparations made for such a gesture, because it is point-less to whisper 'I'll do it' into a fond feminine ear and return with a warmed-up tin of rice-pudding when *she* had cold lamb, green tomato chutney and red tomato salad ready and waiting. ('I'll settle for mashed bananas and castor sugar and double cream – with disposable plates,' said my wife.)

You might start the feast with an

Avocado pear

To be ripe the pear must be yielding to the touch; don't believe greengrocers who say that a hard fruit will be per-fect tomorrow. Don't cut it until it is ready to be eaten. Remove the stone and fill the cavity that is left with
(1) lemon juice and a dessertspoon of granulated sugar.
(2) Some peeled prawns out of jar, tin or frozen packet gently thawed, and served in a sauce made of 1 tablespoon salad cream, 1 of tomato ketchup, as much Worcester sauce up to a coffeespoon as you care for and a hard-boiled egg passed through a sieve.
Or (3) a few radishes, chopped into thin slices in a sauce made of 1 dessertspoon of oil, 1 teaspoon of vinegar, a good pinch of salt and a sprinkling of sugar.

An alternative is

Smoked salmon

Good delicatessen shops sell best Scotch smoked salmon sliced and ready to serve. Serve it with brown bread and butter and eat a mouthful or two before you baste it with lemon juice and pepper although that is currently the thing to do.

But these are assembly jobs for the tired, the rich and the disinterested husbands. For the poorer, the more devoted, and the more enterprising there is nothing for it but off to the kitchen and up with the flame. ('For heaven's sake,' said my wife, 'tell them to put on an apron.')

Cucumber soup (for 2)

1 medium onion, grated
½ cucumber peeled and sliced
2 tablespoons flour
1 soup cube
¾ pint water
2 tablespoons cream
1 oz. butter
1 tablespoon oil
salt and white pepper

Heat oil and butter in a pan and when it begins to sizzle, add onion and cucumber, salt and pepper. Turn flame to low, put on lid and allow it to simmer for 5 minutes. Now remove lid, increase heat, add flour and cook – but do not

brown. Remove pan from flame as you add half the water; stir, replace and let it come to the boil slowly, still stirring. When the mixture thickens, add the rest of the water and the soup cube, stir as it regains the boil and let it simmer, with the lid on, for 20 minutes. Liquidize before serving if you don't care for tender cubes of cucumber lounging in your soup. Serve in bowls, adding a spoonful of cream to each bowl.

Kidney risotto (for 2)

1 onion, peeled and chopped
1 sweet pepper (pips removed), chopped
4 lamb kidneys or 6 oz. ox kidney – thinly sliced
1 teacup Patna rice (not pudding rice)
2 teacups water
½ chicken soup cube
1 bayleaf
salt and pepper
3 tablespoons oil
1 tablespoon flour, 1 teaspoon salt, some black pepper – in a bowl

In a heavy pan, with a lid, heat oil and fry the onions and sweet peppers until the onions are golden and the peppers lose their resilience. Roll the kidney slices in the flour-salt-pepper bowl and add to the pan, stirring until the kidneys begin to blend. Add the rice and bayleaf, mix well, raise the heat and add the water and soup cube, stirring now and then until the mixture comes to the boil. If you don't stir, the rice will clot and cook in great stuck-together clusters. When the liquid starts bubbling, lower the heat so that it just maintains a steady simmer when a lid is firmly covering the saucepan. Do not stir again. Cook for 25 minutes, by which time the water will have been taken up by the rice and the grains will be tender. Taste a grain for peace of mind. Serve with grated cheese.

Reform lamb cutlets

4 lamb cutlets
1 egg
breadcrumbs
1 oz. butter
3 tablespoons oil
1 dessertspoon flour, 1 dessertspoon dry English mustard,
*   1 teaspoon salt – mixed*
Worcester sauce and 1 oz. butter
3 tablespoons sour cream
1 egg
black pepper

Beat your lamb cutlets with a rolling pin so that they become thinner and bigger. (Butchers will do this for unaggressive husbands.) Sprinkle the cutlets with the flour-mustard-salt mixture on both sides.

Now break an egg into a bowl, add a tablespoon of water, a pinch of salt and a good shake of black pepper, beat with a whisk and place the coated cutlets into this; wash one at a time before drying them in a soup-plate filled with toasted breadcrumbs, patting the crumbs firmly into position on them. Now heat the oil and butter in a pan and when they are hot, but not smoking, put in the cutlets. They will need 3 to 4 minutes on each side – a little less if you like them pink. Turn them frequently to make sure the coating does not burn before the meat is cooked (if this looks like happening the heat is excessive).

For the sauce, strain the fat remaining in the frying pan through a sieve into a small saucepan. Turn up the flame, add a little more butter, the sour cream and a dash or two of Worcester sauce and put a spoonful over each cutlet. The plates must be hot or the sauce will congeal. If you store cutlets in the oven, leave the oven door open; if you do not, the coating will become soggy.

Apple crumble
(for 2)

4 small apples (about 1 lb.) peeled, cored and sliced
1 heaped tablespoon mincemeat
1 heaped tablespoon brown sugar
2 tablespoons water
3 oz. flour
2 oz. butter
1½ oz. sugar
the grated peel of 1 lemon

Take an oven dish and put into it the apple, mincemeat, brown sugar and water. Sieve the plain flour into a bowl; add butter and rub together until the mixture has the consistency of sand; then add the sugar and lemon peel, mix with a spoon and spread over the apple-mincemeat mixture. Cook at the top of a mark 5 (375°F) oven for 30 minutes, when the crumble should be honey-coloured. Serve with double cream.

Banana flambé
(for 2)

3 bananas halved lengthways
1 oz. butter
1 oz. sugar
juice of an orange
juice of half a lemon
1 liqueur glass of brandy
1 liqueur glass of Tia Maria

Melt butter and sugar in a frying pan, add orange and lemon juice and let it simmer to make a syrup. Now add the bananas, turn up the flame a little and let them cook, shaking the pan to prevent them from sticking and turning them over now and then. Do this for about 3 minutes. Shortly before serving, add brandy and Tia Maria; let them warm for a moment in the juices of the pan and ignite with a match – or do so by tilting the pan towards the fire if you use gas. Serve on hot plates.

Cheese ramekins (for 2)

  1 egg
  1 breakfast cup milk (just under ½ pint)
  1 oz. grated Cheddar or Lancashire cheese
  ½ oz. grated parmesan
  1 coffeespoon paprika
  2 tablespoons cream
  cayenne pepper

Break the egg into a bowl and whisk well. Add milk, cheese and paprika, whisk until smooth and pour the mixture into individual fireproof moulds. Stand these in a roasting tin half filled with hot water. Cook two-thirds of the way down in a mark 2 (300°F) oven until set, which should take 60–90 minutes. Cool, turn out of moulds and serve with a topping of a spoonful of cream and a shake of cayenne pepper.

('And do let him put the coffee in a vacuum flask and serve it out of paper cups,' said my wife.)

VIEWING FOOD

When commercial television first reared its ugly break, the provision market became temporarily flooded with goodies sold as 'television snacks'. If one now hears little of television snacks, it is because so many people watch the commercials and retire during the actual programmes. However, for the odd compulsive transmission here is a balanced diet – for four.

  Mayonnaise of Celeriac with Sweet Pepper
  Crêpes de Boeuf à la Crème
  Coffee Mousse

Timetable

Before the guests arrive:
Celeriac and pimento mayonnaise are ready in the living-room.

Filled pancakes wait on a well-buttered roasting tray with a tablespoon of cream and a sprinkling of grated cheese on each.

Mousses are in refrigerator.

Oven is turned on at mark 3 (325°F).

During first break: eat hors d'oeuvre. Put pancakes in already-heated oven.

During second break: eat pancakes.

During third break: eat mousses.

Mayonnaise of celeriac with sweet pepper

1 medium-sized celeriac
2 sweet red peppers
2 egg yolks
1 dessertspoon lemon juice
1 teaspoon Dijon mustard
⅓ pint oil
salt and pepper
¾ pint water
1 coffeecup wine vinegar

Scrape the celeriac with a potato peeler and cut out black pieces with a knife. Cut in half and boil for 15 minutes (12 minutes if it is a small one) in well-salted water.

Make the mayonnaise by whisking together egg yolks, mustard, lemon juice and a tablespoon of the boiling celeriac water; add salt and pepper and drip on the oil and beat. Check for seasoning. Take celeriac from water and allow to cool; cut in slices and then in strips and blend with the mayonnaise.

Celeriac on its own has its addicts but is a rather rich, white, heavy hors d'oeuvre, which is why it may be a good idea to serve it with slices of red pepper. Cut the peppers in half, remove surplus pith and all pips and simmer in the water and vinegar for 20 minutes. Drain well, sprinkle with oil and salt, and let cool. Then cut into strips for decoration or blending in with the celeriac.

Crêpes de boeuf à la crème

2 oz. plain flour
2 oz. cornflour
1 egg
1 tablespoon oil
1 teaspoon curry powder
salt and freshly ground black pepper
1 clove garlic
a little milk and water

For the filling:
¾ lb. sliced roast beef or pork
3 oz. currants
1 oz. butter
1 tablespoon oil
¼ pint double cream

For the pancakes, take the first seven ingredients (pass the garlic through a garlic press), using enough milk and water to make a mixture the consistency of cream. Whisk well and leave to stand for a few minutes, or more. Using a 6–7-inch frying-pan, make thin pancakes of this mixture.

For the filling, heat the oil and butter in a saucepan, add the currants and then the meat, cut into strips. Stir as it cooks, and pour in cream. Boil together for a minute or two. Fill the pancakes with the meat and currant mixture. Place the filled pancakes in a buttered roasting tray. Pour over each pancake a tablespoon of double cream over which you sprinkle a teaspoon of parmesan cheese. Cook in a mark 4 (350°F) oven for 20 minutes, moving the pancakes to the top shelf on a higher temperature for a few minutes if you like them rather more browned.

Coffee mousse

    4 eggs
    2 oz. plain chocolate
    4 tablespoons strong black coffee
    2 tablespoons Tia Maria liqueur
    1 level teaspoon gelatine
    2½ oz. castor sugar
    1 oz. peeled almonds
    1 small nut of butter
    1 teaspoon water

In a basin engaged over a pan of boiling water melt the chocolate and gelatine in the coffee. Separate and beat the egg yolks and stir as you add the liqueur. Let this 'cook' for 3 or 4 minutes. Then remove the bowl from pan and let the mixture cool a little. Whisk the egg whites, add 1½ oz. sugar, and when the coffee mixture is no hotter than lukewarm fold in the beaten egg whites.

While you are waiting for the mousse to cool, heat the butter, the remaining sugar and water in a pan, and as it begins to caramelise add almonds, cut into slivers. When they are well coated, turn off the flame. Tip out the almond pieces on buttered paper, and when they are cool enough to handle cut them into small pieces. Mix these into the mousse and serve into individual moulds and put them in the refrigerator to set.

CENTRAL EATING

Since the beginning of time – a pleasantly loose phrase – man seeking inner warmth has sluiced his insides with 'nice hot strong cups of tea' or similar delicacies. A teapot, properly warmed; a spoonful or three of good tea; a gill of boiling water to inflate the leaves left in the pot for 15 seconds and then the pot filled with boiling water is a recipe from which so many tea-makers depart. It is time they went back to it.

Only recently did public opinion decree that warm, heavy food should be confined to cold, crisp days. I argue with this. I would as soon eat a plate of pease pudding on Midsummer's Eve as on New Year's morning. On the other hand I bow to the majority view in letting the menu:

Lentil soup

Moussaka

Steamed treacle pudding

be described as it is, rather than insist upon my original title SUMMER SUPPERS. On reflection, all three courses at one sitting might be an exaggeration; each is a highly satisfying meal in itself.

Lentil soup

1½ lb. lentils

1 carrot

2 large onions

3 pints water

1 soup cube

Salt, pepper, a bayleaf, cider vinegar

A piece of bacon rind or the rinds of a dozen rashers tied together

2 slices garlic-rubbed white bread

1 thick slice of gammon

Soak the lentils for about an hour in cold water, removing the bad ones – they rise to the top. Cut up the onions and carrot and put the drained lentils, carrot, onion and bacon rind into 3 pints of boiling water. Season with salt and pepper, and simmer to a pulp; remove bacon rind and liquidize or pass through a sieve. Dilute with a little more stock if it is too thick, and correct the seasoning. Serve the soup very hot, giving each guest some cider vinegar to mix into the lentils; and cubes of gammon and squares of garlic-rubbed white bread, fried golden.

Moussaka

is what might be described as vegetable with animal connections; Greek with Rumanian influence. There is no haute cuisine in Greece – so there's no definitive way of making this Mediterranean version of shepherd's pie.

1 lb. minced beef or mutton – cooked or raw
1 lb. aubergine – or marrow
1 lb. onions
1 large tin peeled tomatoes, well drained
1½ oz. butter
3 tablespoons oil
1 dessertspoon oregano

For the sauce:
¾ pint milk
2½ oz. plain flour
2 oz. butter
1 oz. parmesan cheese

Cook the minced meat with a little stock, 4 oz. of grated onion and herbs and seasoning. Peel the aubergine or marrow. If using marrow, cut lengthwise and remove the inside pulp, then slice ¼ inch thick; dust with seasoned flour and fry the slices gently in oil-and-butter. Lift them out of the fat when they are cooked. Slice the remaining 12 oz. of onion and fry in remaining fat. Now butter a large oven dish and put in alternate layers of meat, aubergine or marrow, tomato and onion until you run out of ingredients.

In a saucepan, melt the butter, and add the flour. Let this cook but not brown and then remove from the flame for a minute. Add milk, reheat gently as you stir until you have a very thick white sauce. Add seasoning and cheese and use this thick sauce as a top layer on the meat and vegetables, spreading it with a palette knife to act as a lid. Bake in a mark 3 (325°F) oven for an hour and then turn up the heat and let the top brown.

Steamed treacle pudding

8 oz. self-raising flour
½ teaspoon salt
4 oz. shredded suet
grated rind of 1 lemon
¼ pint water
10 oz. golden syrup
3 oz. soft white breadcrumbs
1 pint pudding basin, buttered

Sieve the flour and salt into a bowl, add the lemon rind and suet, mix and add water. Cut into the mixture with a knife until the flour is absorbed; turn the dough out on a floured board and knead lightly into a ball. Let this rest for 10 minutes. Divide the dough into five equal parts; roll one to fit the bottom of the pudding basin and cover this with golden syrup and breadcrumbs. Repeat the process, rolling out layers of pastry to fit the basin and covering these with syrup and breadcrumbs. Finish with a layer of pastry dusted with flour. Seal basin with kitchen foil and stand in a pan of boiling water.

Cover the pan and steam for 2 hours, adding boiling water as necessary. Then remove the basin, let it stand and turn it out.

If you are worried about your figure, try to serve the pudding without double cream, brandy butter and black cherry jam warmed up in cherry brandy.

BARBECUING

To barbecue is a way of life rather than a desirable method of cooking. There are those who, given the slightest excuse – such as the temporary absence of snow or rain – will race to the paved loggia, outside the double-glazed window of the kitchenette, and go to it wildly with charcoal, bellows and griddle pan. For these frustrated arsonists the end-product is incidental to the exercise. I hold no special brief for outdoor cookery as such; I prefer, if forced, to light a fire in the garden, feed onto it in turn herbs and onions, lumps of sugar and coffee beans, and bring out at the appropriate times veal cutlets that have been dusted in flour and salt, fried in butter, then simmered in cream and rosemary in a low oven; purée of chestnuts sweetened, blended with whipped cream and served with raspberry biscuits; and the cona machine.

The hardest thing to do with an outside stove giving off unpredictable heat is to gauge accurate cooking time. It is therefore essential to buy good meat – so that it can cheerfully be eaten under, moderately or well done . . . and to remove most of the fat – which can be very unpleasant when undercooked. Meat must be sealed, by cooking it on both sides over a hot flame, after which the fire should be banked down so that the meat will cook and retain its juices. In the case of sausages, which have a protective skin, the best results are achieved over a slow fire.

The most important thing about a barbecue is the sauce. This must enhance, disguise, or in the event of complete failure be spread on bread and butter and be consumed instead of the meat or fish of which so much was expected. This, obviously, must be cooked indoors. The sauce can be either an assembly job – a personalized blend of tomato chutney, mustard, finely chopped onion, Worcester sauce, pounded anchovy fillets, crushed garlic and maple syrup – or a manufactured sauce.

Barbecue sauce

4 tablespoons oil
4 oz. grated onion
1 tablespoon flour
2 tablespoons tomato purée
2 teaspoons dried tarragon
1 teaspoon salt
½ teaspoon Tabasco
3 tablespoons lemon juice
¼ pint soured cream

Fry onions in oil until the mixture starts to brown; turn down heat, add flour and allow to cook. Then add tomato, tarragon, salt, Tabasco and lemon juice. Let it simmer, add cream, check for seasoning and serve hot, cold or at temperatures in between.

Next in order of importance comes the basting liquid. This can be made in quantity and kept throughout the summer. Whatever you decide to use, the ratio should be about ⅔ fat to ⅓ flavouring.

The baste

½ pint cooking oil
3 tablespoons choy sauce
3 tablespoons sweet sherry

Shake well and apply with a brush before and during cooking. Don't baste too lavishly or the fat may catch fire and char the meat.

Spare ribs with beer and honey

Lamb may be used instead of pork, cuts from the middle neck being the most suitable. For eight people:

298

4 *trimmed ribs or two chops per person*
½ *pint brown ale*
¼ *lb. clear honey or golden syrup*
2 *level teaspoons dry mustard*
1 *teaspoon Tabasco*
1 *tablespoon mixed herbs*
1 *tablespoon lemon juice*
1 *dessertspoon salt*

Mix together all the ingredients and leave the ribs in the marinade for an hour or two. Thread the ribs on a skewer and place this over your barbecue fire, turning frequently and basting with the marinade as often as you like. The cooking time is long – provided you do not burn the ribs to a cinder it is almost impossible to overcook them – but 30 minutes on a rack three inches above the flame is the minimum. If you want to try the dish using an oven, allow 1¼ hours in a mark 4 (350°F) oven, basting frequently and putting up the heat for the last 15 minutes to glaze the ribs.

Kebabs

are an excellent barbecue standby. Prepare:

1-inch chunks of lamb cut from the shoulder
thickly cut strips of streaky bacon, cut in three
pieces of onion
pieces of sweet pepper
mushrooms
bayleaves etc.

and thread these onto a skewer in any order that you think will be delicious. (Bayleaf next to meat is clearly a better idea than to have it adjacent to the mushroom.) Brush with basting liquor and cook over a slow fire.

Apple fritters

But, simply because you have a fire with a rack, there is absolutely no reason why you should not use this as a portable stove and cook on your al fresco flames such delicacies as apple fritters. Your deep-fry pan is likely to get blacker and should be stronger than the indoor variety. Otherwise, the same good batter mixture:

8 oz. flour
2 tablespoons melted butter
a mixture of beer and water sufficient to make this into a
    paste of the consistency of cream
2 stiffly beaten egg whites

You can then bring out the pieces of peeled cored apples in a bowl of flour, and prepare a dish containing a thick layer of sugar on which the fritters can cool off after they have emerged from the hot fat.

Christmas

Those of us who write of cookery things have calendars annotated with snippets of useful aids to the memory: Shrove Tuesday, not surprisingly, is marked 'pancakes'; the Glorious Twelfth has grouse written by its side. The close season for beetroot, the day when salmon shooting begins, the first week of the early cucumber, all are duly noted. Guy Fawkes Night goes with Angel Cake and at Whitsun there is a note 'Easter eggs': they are so much cheaper by then.

Around December the Christmas meal looms realistically in the foreground and for this repast it is meat to start with the pudding (I may have got the spelling wrong here). When I find the calendar is marked Christmas Pudding, a confection sometimes spelt Xmas Pudding (I suppose this may be all right though I have heard that Columbus absolutely hated being called Xopher), two things worry me about this traditional dish. Firstly, the enormous quantities you are expected to eat, and secondly, that on this day, which is after all a family feast, you are presented a dish which is either matured with old Guinness and flaming with cooking brandy totally unacceptable to childish stomachs, or you are expected to eat a sort of watered-up nursery pudding wholly unsuitable to adult palates.

CHRISTMAS PUDDING

Let us begin by submitting the product to the 'what is' advertising technique which has done so much for Polo mints and mums. 'Excuse me,' you say, stopping people in a busy Wigan shopping arcade, 'what is a Christmas pudding?' The answers come straight back at you, fast and true: 'gooey . . . full of plums . . . heavy and black and hot . . . quite hard to make now that parking meters take all the small change . . .' Naturally it is none of these. Christmas pudding is mahogany coloured, luscious, on the crumbly side of solid. Somehow this manna-like confection is the ideal – possibly the only – base that thrives on being anointed with flaming brandy, heaped with liquorous butter and covered with double cream.

There are a number of pernicious untruths about Christmas puddings which may as well be laid: there is the idea that these should be made in late August – that if they are not ready by Guy Fawkes afternoon, all is lost. At a recent tasting some of the most sophisticated palates in the land were utterly unable to identify the pudding which had been made that week from those made the previous week, the previous month and even the previous year. What is likely to have happened is that some eminent Victorian hostess made too many puddings, decided to resteam some the following year and one of her guests said: 'Why, this is better than ever,' by which people mean it is no worse than it was.

There is the idea that puddings bought in shops could not possibly be as good as those made at home. This is totally untrue because, and I say this with what lawyers call respect, housewives are considerably more likely to louse things up than are food manufacturers. There is also the idea that a home-made pudding is uneconomical. Strictly from an economist's point of view, this is correct. Due to the supermarket age in which we live, it is no longer easy to purchase fruit, peel, flour and suet by the ounce. Therefore, a two-pint pudding involving sultanas, currants and raisins could land the housewife with three partially full packets of these commodities – which she might well consider wasteful. The alternative is to use your purchases to make puddings galore and serve them on high days and holidays throughout the year. This, in the strictest sense of the word, could not be called thrifty because a pudding properly made and decorated is a more costly confection than jelly and custard.

On the other hand, Christmas pudding making can be an occasion of beauty and social significance, and many a little woman has been able to hold her head up that much higher as a result of ministrations with sleeves rolled to the elbow and sturdy wooden spoon heaved through a mass of fruit, egg, treacle and suet.

Ingredients

A 2-pint pudding basin will accommodate 3 lb. of pudding and on the basis that you will need two of these, if only to give the other away or send it to me, you require 6 lb. of ingredients. These can be divided into four groups: stodge, fruit, seasonings, liquids.

Stodge. You need just under 2 lb., 12 oz. of which should be suet. For the rest use flour, soft white breadcrumbs, toasted breadcrumbs, breakfast cereals – or any mixture thereof.

Flour makes for a smoother more glutinous consistency; soft breadcrumbs produce crumblyness and toasted breadcrumbs, Weetabix, etc. give a drier finish.

Fruit: 3 lb. Any mixture of currants, sultanas, raisins, chopped apricots, prunes, apples, carrots, candied peel and not more than about 4 oz. of chopped almonds.

Possibly as a result of some long-forgotten edict by the Monopolies Commission, most books tell you to use ¾ lb. each of currants, sultanas and raisins. This is as pointless as it is generally accepted. Raisins are the most suitable fruit, though they are on the large side. Currants are the right size but they are much too hard and sultanas are a good middle-of-the-road choice, unfortunately of the wrong colour though black treacle or gravy browning will see to that.

Peel has a bitterness which is pleasant to counteract the overall sweetness and if money is of small importance, buy whole crystallized fruit, and chop these into strips; this is a far more desirable thing than the contents of small cardboard cartons labelled 'chopped mixed peel'.

Shredded apple gives you a lighter pudding, chopped prunes make for heaviness and there are those who insist on grated carrot. I have tasted puddings with and without and prefer the latter.

Seasonings. For a 6 lb. pudding mixture use about 8 oz. of sugar and, at the end result should be brown, use soft brown sugar. You need 1 teaspoon of salt to help the rising process and somewhere between 1 and 3 teaspoons of spice; whether you use cinnamon, nutmeg, cloves or a mixture thereof is not for me to dictate. If you have forgotten what spices taste like, sprinkle a little of each on a piece of white bread with unsalted butter.

Liquids. For every pound of mixture add 1 whole egg, beaten, and twice the volume of the eggs in other liquids – half of which should be black treacle, the rest lemon juice, rum, brandy, Guinness, Coca-Cola . . .

A pudding is really not much better because it contains more spirits; ultimately it is the brandy butter, the lighted spirit and the cream that count. What is important is to get the right amount of liquid – so that the pudding is of the proper consistency.

Making the pudding

Start with the stodge – and if the flour is very lumpy there is no reason why you should not sieve it. Add the fruit, then the seasoning and finally the liquid. There is no particular virtue, unless you number masochism as a virtue, for adding an egg at a time and beating this into the mixture before adding the next egg. Beat up the eggs with a whisk, pour them into a measuring jug and make a note of the amount. Half fill the measuring jug with melted treacle and the rest with booze of your choice.

Then stir the mixture and, if it appears too stiff, add some more liquid – wine or water – if too slack add white breadcrumbs. At this point it is also customary to add sixpences, though for the sake of peace and quiet I bring a small bowlful to the table and slip them unostentatiously into the plated portions.

The pudding basins must be well buttered before the mixture is put into them and just over two-thirds as full as you require because the pudding rises in cooking.

Cover the mixture with a circle of buttered paper, cover the top tightly with foil and then wrap the whole basin in a cloth, gathering the ends together over the basin and tying them with a piece of string (this enables you to pick the basins out of the pan without boiling your hand as you do so).

Cooking instructions

The best way to go about things is to make the mixture one evening, cover it, leave it to stand overnight and fill it into the pudding basins the next day. Place the prepared basins in a pan in which the water comes to within an inch of the rim, bring the water to the boil and then put on a lid. Steam puddings for 6 hours, topping up the pan with boiling water when significant amounts have boiled away. Let the puddings cool slowly, store them and resteam for 2 hours before eating.

Brandy butter
Soften the butter by leaving it in a warm place. To ½ lb. packet, add 3 oz. castor sugar, cream gently and add 2 tablespoons of brandy. Mix with a fork and set in a cool place until required. (Unless you have airtight jars, it is a mistake to make brandy butter too far ahead because brandy evaporates.)

Lighting the pudding
Gently heat brandy, rum or whisky in a saucepan. When warm incline the pan towards the gas – or light it with a spill if you use electricity or coal – and pour the flaming liquid over the pudding in full view of the guests. As this is more of a ritual than a gastronomic aid, use not very much, not very expensive spirits.

A SLICE OF CHRISTMAS

Many years ago, I advocated that more people should eat breast of lamb for Christmas; I was young, living with an erratic gas ring in Drayton Gardens and see now that I was wrong. Everyone should really try to have what everyone else has, all the time, but they should have it better than their neighbours.

Christmas is not Christmas without Christmas cake; but it must have at least two weeks to mature before cutting.

Christmas cake
A woman wrote to me once and asked why I never started with the words 'Take 12 oz. of butter'. In deference to her,

and to achieve the very best possible Christmas cake . . .
Take 12 oz. of butter. Also

> *12 oz. brown sugar*
> *6 eggs*
> *1 lb. plain flour*
> *a pinch of salt*
> *1 lb. sultanas*
> *1 lb. currants*
> *6 oz. raisins – stoned*
> *4 oz. candied peel*
> *4 oz. glacé cherries, quartered*
> *4 oz. chopped peeled almonds*
> *1 coffeespoon mixed spice*
> *2 tablespoons of black treacle*
> *1 wineglass brandy or rum*

You will need a 9-inch cake tin, which should be 4 inches
high – alternatively bake it in a basin that will take that
volume of cake mixture.

Cream the butter until it is soft, add the sugar and continue to cream while you add the eggs, one by one. To this
runny yellow mixture add sifted flour and all other ingredients. Mix well and get some other people to help you
with the mixing.

Line the cake tin with foil or greaseproof paper, butter it
well and transfer the mixture to the tin. Cover with a piece
of well-buttered foil, and fold on to this the protruding
edges of the original lining. Bake in a mark 1 (275°F) oven
for 6½ hours.

If mixing and cooking in one day is difficult, the cake
mixture can be left to stand in the tin overnight. If you
halve the quantities, use a 7-inch tin and allow 3¾ hours
in a mark 1 (275°F) oven, taking the top foil off for the
last half-hour. After baking, the cake should be kept for at
least a week, and preferably a fortnight before it is iced –
or eaten.

Almond paste. When the cake has matured for some time in a cool, dry place, it deserves a smooth coat of almond paste. If you don't care for marzipan, you can make this a token layer . . . just enough to fill in the crevices. For a good thick layer:

    12 oz. icing sugar
    3 oz. castor sugar
    8 oz. ground almonds
    1 egg and 1 yolk
    1 tablespoon rum
    1 teaspoon lemon juice

Sift the sugar and mix with ground almonds. Put 2 eggs, rum and lemon juice into a bowl, engage this over a pan of hot water and beat gently as the egg thickens slightly. Add this to the sugar and almond, mixing first with a wooden spoon, and then work the paste well with your hands until it attains a smooth consistency.

Roll out the paste – sprinkling the working surface with icing sugar. If you have worked it properly, there will be no cracks in it. Drape it over the cake, cut off the protruding edges and smooth with the tips of your fingers dredged in icing sugar. Let the almond paste set overnight. The cake is now ready for its final coat.

Royal icing
    12 oz. icing sugar
    1 teaspoon lemon juice
    whites of 2 small eggs

Mix the egg whites and lemon juice in a bowl, using a wooden spoon, and add the sifted icing sugar. Beat with a wooden spoon until the mixture is smooth and white – which will take 10 minutes.

Ice the cake, helping it to set smoothly with a knife dipped in hot water. Decorate.

TURKEY

It is just conceivable that you are going to need a turkey, and I recommend this, though it is possibly not essential. Brillat Savarin, that ultimate sage of the last century, wrote much about the turkey. He said that because of his foreign countenance: 'No wise man could be mistaken about them.' It should be hailed with appropriate gestures. Other writers on the culinary arts spend much time advising you to look for the beady eye, the firm spring black toes, and pastel-coloured beak. Well, those days are past; you buy your turkey from butcher or supermarket and you get what you pay for in the way of quality (page 315). A 12 lb. bird is the best size for a small to medium family. I presume that those who have always picked out their own turkeys at a friendly farmer's Guy Fawkes evening will still abide with Brillat S. and ignore me.

Turkey is boring but obligatory. The woman who dishes up minced beef at the Christmas feast is considered a kink rather than a pioneer – so turkey it is, almost without the option. Anyway, you buy your turkey, take him from his protective cellophane, or whatever covering, and remove from the inside such goodies as the packers have seen fit to put back. If you have no cats or dogs who need Christmas treats roast these with the bones and onions for the sauce – or mince heart and liver into the stuffing. It is not the greatest delicacy but will do no lasting harm.

Roast turkey

Fortunately, so long as you can say 'We had turkey' there is no rigidly prescribed method of preparation. There was a time when one recommended leaving the innards inside turkeys so that they attained some gameyness. Modern production methods do not permit this dash, so if you like a gamey bird either let it stand with its innards in a warm place (dangerous because when it goes it goes very quickly), or put into it an onion or two, an apple stuck with slivers of garlic, or some garlic-rubbed slices of bread, and rub inside and outside with a solution of salt and pepper and Dijon mustard. What is very important is to truss the bird. Left to its own devices, the white meat of the turkey would take far longer than the brown meat, so you compensate. Wrap some pork fat or fatty bacon around the legs, and another layer around the whole bird, so that the legs are doubly protected; then you get the legs as tight up against the body as you can and tie them into place. Now you can do any of the following and your turkey will be entirely acceptable: season it inside and out with salt and pepper; wrap it in foil; make some holes in the bottom of the folk so that the juices can escape; place the bird on a rack in the oven, place the roasting tray underneath it and cook it for 12 hours or so on mark ¼. What is especially good about this is that you end up not only with the handsomely cooked turkey but with over a pint of fabulous turkey consommé . . . once you have skimmed the juices of the demon turkey fat. If your sleeping habits so demand, cook it for 7 hours on mark ½. In both cases defoil, brush the bird with salted butter and give it a final 25 minutes on mark 6 (400°F) to get colour.

The fast roasting is best done in a roasting tray from which liquor is poured as it forms – about half-hourly. You season the bird well, inside and out, wrap it in protective fat and give it 3½ hours, basting now and then and removing the protective layer of fat 25 minutes before its cooking time is up.

Bread sauce

is optional. You take an onion, grate it, simmer it in ½ pint of milk, ¼ pint single cream and 2 oz. butter until the onion is soft, having added season of salt, white pepper and half a dozen cloves wrapped in a muslin bag. Let this mixture stand. A few minutes before serving the sauce, add to it enough soft white breadcrumbs to give it the consistency you require, and remove the cloves. There is nothing clever about adding the breadcrumbs earlier and letting them cook for half an hour.

Gravy

you have to have. Unless you do a fast roasting job on your bird there are going to be insufficient deposits in the tray to give the gravy very much quality. It is therefore better to create one, which also allows you to prepare and make the stuff on the previous day. Burn some bones and onions in a roasting tray at the top of a very hot oven. Pour off fat; plunge them into a pan with water and herbs, reduce, season, strain and thicken a little with cornflour, add to this gravy a gulp or two of sherry or other reinforced wine, also some of the liquor from the bird but as little of the fat as possible. There is something not very desirable about the taste of turkey fat. If you like sweetness in gravy, a tablespoonful of black cherry jam and a dash of Tabasco (to show that this is not the pudding) make a very good impression on it.

Stuffing

is not a packet of herbaceous reclaimed breadcrumbs stuck up a dead bird's recess; ideally it should be more than that. There is no great advantage in cooking the stuffing inside the bird. It is tricky to get in, ignominious to scoop out and if the stuffing is well constructed, roasting it inside or outside the bird will make to it not a jot of difference. The following recipe – which can be altered if any of the ingredients do not appeal – produces a forcemeat which can be roasted and sliced and even eaten with enjoyment instead of the turkey – should something nasty happen to it. The quantities are deliberately on the generous side because sandwiches of stuffing, served at elevenses on Boxing Day, will get you talked about and permit you to stay in bed until tea time.

Ask your butcher to mince together ¾ lb. lean pork, ¾ lb. ox liver and ¾ lb. veal. Finely chop 4 oz. rindless streaky bacon, add it to the mixture and stir into it 1 lb. of unsweetened chestnut purée, 3 beaten eggs, 1 medium-sized onion, grated, and 4 oz. of mixed, chopped peel. Add 2 teaspoons of salt and a coffeespoon of rough, crushed black peppercorns. Stir well. Fry a rounded dessertspoon-ful of the mixture in a pan, like a rissole, for 3 minutes on each side. Let it cool a little. Taste it, adjust the seasoning . . . add white breadcrumbs if you like a less meaty stuffing.

Wrap the stuffing in buttered foil, shape it to look like a tortoise and bake it when you bake the turkey. The cooking time is fairly unimportant, as is the temperature. Ideally, I suppose, 2½ hours on mark 5 (375°F) or longer on a lower mark. If you fast roast the bird, wrap an extra layer of foil round the stuffing and put it in the very bottom of the oven for 2 hours. It is a good thing to let the mixture stand for a day before cooking it – but this is not essential.

A COMFORTABLE COUNTDOWN METHOD FOR CHRISTMAS COOKING – Our Four Day Plan

On Christmas Day we can get up at 12.15 because we have lunch at 1.00. We shall be ten for lunch.

Salted Almonds

Giblet Soup

Rock Salmon in Aspic
Mayonnaise of Asparagus

Roast Turkey
Stuffing
Gravy
Cranberry Sauce
Buttered Potatoes
Brussels Sprouts

Watercress and Egg Salad

Christmas Pudding
Brandy Butter
Double Cream

Stilton Cheese
Bath Oliver Biscuits
Normandy Butter

Nuts
Raisins
Clementines

Coffee

On the 3rd day before Christmas

We make a shopping-list:
BUTCHER
One 16 lb. turkey
6 oz. each minced beef,
    minced veal,
    minced ox liver,
    minced pork
1 pig's trotter
1 lb. shin of beef

FISHMONGER
2 lb. rock fish

GREENGROCER

1 lb. old carrots
1 head celery
1 bunch parsley
3 lb. onions
2 lemons
1 cucumber
4 bunches watercress
2 large packets frozen Brussels sprouts
4 lb. small new potatoes
3 lb. mixed nuts, 2 packets raisins
3 lb. cooking apples
24 clementines

GROCER

1 soup cube
jar chervil
1 bottle tarragon vinegar
1 pint oil
9 eggs
1 tube French mustard
1 tin asparagus tips
1 tin red pimento
1 lb. tin chestnut purée (unsweetened, if possible)
4 oz. mixed peel
4 oz. sultanas
8 oz. peeled almonds
1 tin cranberry sauce
1 lb. sugar
3 lb. Christmas puddings
1 lb. ordinary and ½ lb. good butter
1 packet gelatine
2 lb. Stilton
1 packet Bath Oliver biscuits
½ lb. coffee

MILKMAN
½ pint double cream
¼ pint coffee cream

WINE MERCHANT
½ bottle Madeira
¼ bottle brandy

We choose a turkey: turkeys come in many sizes, two sexes, fresh or deep-frozen and oven-ready. All represent some sort of value for money. It is up to you to decide whether you want to spend your money on more slices of a tough Irish cock turkey, or on perhaps half the quantity of tender breast of a Norfolk hen from Harrods.

We prefer fresh turkeys. When a bird is frozen it is virtually impossible to tell how long it has been in that state until you get it home and thaw it out. It is then too late to do anything, except change your butcher. Moreover, oven-ready birds have their entrails removed mechanically at the time of plucking and dressing – within hours of being put to death – whereas fresh turkey, left to hang for a few days, takes on an agreeable gameyness that does much to enhance the otherwise bland meat.

A good bird should be broad of breast and comparatively small of frame. The meat visible through the outer skin should be pale – indicating a thin protective layer of fat – rather than purple. There is no reason why a butcher should not lightly flour the outside of a turkey to make it look more appetizing. There is every reason for you to check on just how much flour has been used and what it is hiding.

We decide about Christmas pudding: the reasons for making a Christmas pudding at home have ceased to be gastronomic. Those you buy are, with few exceptions, excellent and can be made still better with brandy butter, cream and vinous flames. But the production of home-made puddings can be a splendid social occasion (page 302).

On the 2nd day before Christmas

We make the stuffing: people used to feel that stuffing was improved by being cooked inside the bird. And when they were told that the stuffing would be just the same cooked in the bird's juices, they said the bird would be better if it took on the aroma of the stuffing. There is slightly more truth in this, but the exercise of putting stuffing inside a turkey and then fishing most of it out again is not worth the candle. Put, if you like, a couple of cooking apples stuck with cloves and garlic inside the turkey. But make the stuffing separately, cooking it when the time comes with a little of the fat from the turkey pan (page 310).

We make the brandy butter (page 306). Store the brandy butter in a basin and when needed roll it in greaseproof paper into a large sausage shape and cut into medallions.

We make the dressing for the watercress and egg salad:
  juice of one lemon
  1 teaspoon French mustard
  ½ teaspoon of salt
  some black pepper
  1 teaspoon sugar
  1 dessertspoon tarragon vinegar
  5 dessertspoons oil
Dissolve mustard, salt, sugar and pepper in the lemon juice and vinegar, add oil, and whisk well before storing. Whisk again before pouring over salad.

We check that we have plates for soup, fish, meat, sweet and cheese, glasses for whatever we are going to drink, and the right number of spoons, forks, knives, and coffee cups, not to mention pots and pans and oven trays and steamers.

On the day before Christmas
We make the soup:
  1 lb. old carrots
  1 lb. onions
  2 or 3 sticks celery
  parsley stalks
  watercress stalks
  1 lb. shin of beef
  1 pig's trotter
  the neck, legs, liver, heart and gizzard of the turkey
  1 soup cube
  2 oz. cooking fat
Clean and chop the onions, carrots, celery, parsley and watercress stalks. Fry these in fat until they begin to brown.

Add the shin of beef, and the turkey liver, gizzard and heart cut up and lightly dusted with seasoned flour. Cook on medium gas with lid firmly on the pan, stirring from time to time. Season well and after about 10 minutes add 3 tablespoons of plain flour. Let the flour brown and then add 4 pints of water, the soup cube, the pig's trotter and turkey feet. Boil slowly for 2 hours.

We hard boil 4 eggs for 12 minutes at least. The best way to peel eggs is to take them straight from the boiling water into a bowl of cold water. Peel them and keep them in cold water, which will prevent them from becoming discoloured.

We cook the potatoes in their skins, very slowly, so that the skins don't break. Peel them when they are still warm. Melt a little butter, toss the peeled, cooked potatoes in it and store them in a bowl in a cool place.

We make the mayonnaise:
  2 egg yolks
  1 teaspoon French mustard
  salt and pepper
  juice of half lemon
  ½ pint oil
  small tin of asparagus tips
Chop the asparagus tips, removing any hard parts of stalk. Drain well and pass through a sieve. To this purée add two egg yolks, the mustard, salt, pepper and lemon juice. Then add the oil, a spoonful at a time, whisking as you do so until the mayonnaise thickens. If it becomes too thick, dilute with a little of the juice from the asparagus tin.

We prepare the fish course: rock salmon is inexpensive and good. Take 2 lb. of rockfish and simmer for 4 minutes in a

318

well-seasoned stock containing a sliced onion, a chopped carrot, a tablespoon of tarragon vinegar and a bayleaf. Remove the fish from the bones and put it in a basin. Now return the bones to the stock, add a packet of gelatine that will set 1 pint of liquid and reduce the stock to ½ pint. Strain and add this to the fish. Dice a cucumber and boil it in salted water until tender. Drain and add to the bowl. Add also the contents of a small tin of red pimentos, chopped. Blend well and fill into small cocottes making sure that each one has enough liquid to enable it to set.

On Christmas Eve

We strain the soup and add 1 pint of water and some flour to what remains in the pan to give us a basis for the gravy. We let this simmer for 20 minutes. We put the stuffing into a dish in which we can cook it. We place the turkey in an oven tray, stuff it with a garlicky apple or two, melt ¼ lb. cooking fat and pour it over the bird. We salt it and pepper it and sprinkle the skin with paprika and have a large piece of oiled greaseproof paper ready to protect its breast and we put the pudding into a steamer – ready for the flames.

And we lay the table.

On Christmas Day

From time to time there are small chores to be done.

At **9.30** one of us slips out of bed to put the turkey in the oven (bottom shelf mark 3 (325°F)). Then back to bed.

At **10.15** we baste the bird and protect the breast if it looks like getting too brown. And we light the gas under the steamer for the pudding. And go back to bed.

At **11.15** we take a spoonful of turkey fat from the pan and anoint the stuffing, which is then put in the bottom of the oven. We also baste the bird and replenish the water in the steamer. We repeat the basting and replenishing of the steamer water at **12**.

At **12.15** we all get up. We open a packet of peeled almonds, toss them in ½ oz. of butter in a saucepan, salt them and put them in the oven.

At **12.45** we take the almonds out of the oven and bring them to the guests. As we go we light the flame under the soup and the water for the Brussels sprouts. We put the buttered potatoes into the oven.

When we come back to the kitchen, we turn out the fish in aspic, cook the sprouts, whip up the mayonnaise.

When the sprouts are cooked, we drain them. A dot of butter – and into the bottom of the oven.

We arrange cheese on a dish, surrounded by biscuits, flanked with Normandy butter decorated with watercress. We wash the cress, chop the hard-boiled eggs and mix them with the salad dressing.

Now the only thing to worry about is the gravy. We have some secondary stock from a reboiling up of the soup solids. We strain this into the emptied turkey tray when we take the bird out of the oven after drinking the soup. We replace the tray in the oven and strain the resultant gravy into a sauceboat.

That's all there is to it.

CHRISTMAS EXTRAS

Toffeed grapes

Take ¼ pint of water and 4 oz. sugar and boil this fiercely until the mixture begins to turn brown. Then turn off flame, wait a minute or so and pour the tacky toffee mixture over grapes – or slices of mandarin oranges – on a slightly greased surface. When set, which takes about a minute, gently prise from surface with a knife and serve.

Fruit jellies

I have never yet found a packet of nasty jelly – only lots and lots of different kinds of boring jellies. Use one of these, but dissolve it in very hot water using half the total quantity of water suggested on the packet. For the other half use the fruit and syrup of a tin of pineapple, white peaches, raspberries or whatever. If it is a jelly for adults, add a little liqueur – Cointreau is excellent with peaches, Grand Marnier with mandarin oranges.

Mince pies

I am in favour of buying these – because they are a bore to make. Like Christmas puddings, the best thing about mince pies is the temperature, the brandy and the cream. Reheat them in a low oven, and before serving lift the lid, pour in a little brandy, reassemble, douse with cream, and sprinkle with sugar.

If you insist, you can make them yourself by taking

¾ lb. stoned raisins
½ lb. candied peel (minced)
1 lb. peeled, cored apple
½ lb. sultanas
½ lb. currants
½ lb. chopped suet
1 lb. demerara sugar
rind and juice of 1 lemon
rind and juice of 1 orange
1 teaspoon ground nutmeg
1 teaspoon ground cloves
1 bottle stout
or a wineglass of brandy for the opulent

You can get the texture you want by discriminate mincing or chopping of apple and dried fruit. Add suet, sugar, fruit, spice and liquid, mix well and leave in a covered bowl, stirring daily for a week. Armed with this fragrant, matured end-product you may fill it into tarts made of pastry that is short or flaky.

Salted almonds

The disparity in price between sweet almonds bought in packets and salted almonds purchased in tins is so staggering that it is worth making your own; this is especially advisable because home-made hot salted almonds are what Wodehouse characters describe as very good news.

Put the almonds into a sieve and suspend this in boiling water for 10 seconds. You can then pinch the skin off the almonds in a matter of seconds. Melt a little butter and use a pastry brush to paint the base of a baking sheet; scatter the peeled almonds on this, paint them with a little more butter and bake in the top of a mark 2 (300°F) oven for 15 minutes. Shake from time to time so they all become golden, salt them and cool in a colander or sieve.

Pâté

which is a meat pâté. Ask your butcher to provide you with:

¾ lb. minced veal
¾ lb. minced pork
¾ lb. minced liver

Put this into a bowl and add 2 whole eggs, 1 tablespoonful of grated onion, salt, a fair amount of pepper and a glass of red wine.

Line a terrine, or other suitable oven dish, with rindless rashers of thin-cut bacon, pile the mixture on to the bacon and fold the slices over the top. Bake in a mark 4 (350°F) oven for 1½ hours, and then put a heavy weight on to the top of the pâté, which will have risen, thanks largely to the eggs. Fifteen minutes later remove the weight – which will have flattened the pâté and brought forth a fair amount of liquid. Pour off the liquid, skim the fat from it, dissolve in it some gelatine and pour back on to the pâté. Let this cool and serve in slices with fresh breakfast toast.

Taramasalata
which is a fish pâté: this is no more than an assembly job (page 24). Serve cold, with toast.

Cumberland sauce
which will do fantastic things for cold meat, though it was originally designed to accompany freshly cooked ham (page 127). Serve in small spoonfuls over slices of cold breast of turkey.

Cider cup
Buy a tin of white peaches and liquidize or sieve it – syrup and all. To this add three times the volume of dry cider, ice cubes and enough slices of orange to make the jug look irresistible.

Puff pastry anchovy straws
Roll out the pastry to a rectangle of thickness of ⅛ inch; place this on a board with the wide side nearest to you and paint the near ¼ inch lightly with cream.

Roll some anchovy fillets in flour and place these lengthwise on the pastry just beyond the cream-painted strip. Fold over the pastry to encase the fillets, using the cream as a seal.

Cut a long strip from the rectangle – which process you repeat until you run out of anchovies, pastry or desire – divide strips into 3-inch lengths, prick these a couple of times with a sharp knife so that the anchovy fillet can breathe during the baking, and paint with cream or egg yolk.

These will need 15 minutes on a baking sheet in a mark 6 (400°F) oven.

Cream cheese and ginger

This is naturally intended for ginger addicts; Sainsbury's sell it, or possibly test-marketed it at my local branch. I thought their version suffered from the fact that the ginger was too sweet – though they get ten out of ten for enterprise.

For a spread on canapés use preserved ginger chopped very fine, leave overnight in brine, pour through a sieve to regain the ginger and incorporate in a high-class cream cheese to which you may add a little grated onion.

The Sainsbury's version would be excellent served as a separate course, on small plates, with castor sugar sprinkled over the cheese, as a pudding.

CHRISTMAS LEFTOVERS

And so we move subtly to the carcass that stares back at you on Boxing Day. Hail to thee and all that lark, bird thou art going to be again. There is not, there really is not any way to re-employ what is left on the carcass of a turkey that is truly memorable unless you add what I consider to be dishonest additives.

By this I mean that you can make a sauce of cream and egg yolks and white truffles and slip into it some delicately carved slices of the bird. The end-product is like any other flaccid white meat overpowered by a *sauce mousseline aux truffes blancs*. *Larousse Gastronomique*, a book for which I usually have little time, dispenses one great truism: 'Cold Turkey. All recipes for cold chicken are suitable for cold turkey.' That man should have been a politician.

The powers in the land who on the one hand urge you to invite the aged and infirm to share your festivities – and then cease to operate public transport on Christmas Day – make it imperative for you to conjure up a collation for the benefit of those who failed to leave at the proper time. You yourself may want no more than a lightly buttered Alka Seltzer; they are more demanding. While it would serve them right to be given cold turkey, Daddie's sauce and buckled slices of pre-Christmas cut loaf, it is your reputation even more than their digestion that might suffer as a result. There is nothing for it but to don the new apron and pick your dainty way to the kitchen.

Face your carcass squarely, pick all the meat from its bones and chop this coarsely. Place it in a basin and add the remainder of the stuffing, also such gravy, bread sauce and cranberry jelly as may remain; stir this well.

Now make a thickish mayonnaise, incorporating in it as much garlic as you care to crush and add this to the bowl of turkey mixture in the proportion of one part to four. If this amount of mayonnaise makes the mixture too fluid, add a cupful of white breadcrumbs; if it is too firm, whisk the egg whites left from mayonnaise making, and blend this into the mixture.

For every pint that you have made, add ½ oz. of gelatine crystals, dissolved and simmered gently in a wineglassful of port. Stir this in, and let it set either in individual moulds or a communal pie dish. Serve with thick cream decorated with paprika, chopped parsley or sprigs of tarragon – which people really ought to plant in greater profusion.

Turkey hash

2 cups turkey meat and giblets
1 cup thick white sauce
1 cup grated raw peeled potatoes
1 tablespoon chopped onion
3 oz. bacon fat or dripping

Cook the potatoes and onion in a frying pan in the hot fat; when they are beginning to brown, add contents to the turkey and white sauce in a fireproof dish, mix well and bake in a hot (mark 7/425°F) oven for half an hour. Garnish with rashers of crisp, streaky bacon and blobs of cold butter and Maldon salt.

If you really feel that this is a rotten thing to do to the noble bird that caused such intakes of breath upon his first appearance – how does a chaudfroid grab you? This is possibly the most acceptable way of presenting the secondary version – but one has to remember that a turkey is a turkey is a turkey. Here is the sauce that might just make you forget.

Chaudfroid

Basically this is a white sauce, flavoured with an extract similar to that over which you intend to pour it (viz. meat, chicken, mushrooms, etc.). Chaudfroid sauce is enriched with double cream, laced with gelatine and given a small flush of sherry; it envelopes and sets around the object at which it was aimed, greatly enhancing the dish. If you are talented and imaginative, you can line the base of the bowl in which you prepare turkey chaudfroid with strips of sweet pepper or angelica so that on turning the thing out you obtain a cunning design at the top. You need:

2 tablespoons of turkey jelly . . . or
meat jelly . . . or a beef stock cube
½ pint milk; 1½ oz. butter
2 tablespoons flour
1 envelope of gelatine which promises to set 1 pint liquid
¼ pint double cream
2 tablespoons sherry

Put milk, butter and flour into a pan and whisk as it thickens over a medium flame, using an occasional wooden spoon to ensure there are no hang-ups in the bottom corners. When the sauce is nicely thickened, add jelly or stock cube, double cream, salt and pepper and gelatine and let this simmer away for 15 minutes. Taste and check for seasoning, then add sherry and incorporate with the meat before letting it set in a bowl around the meat.

Galantine of turkey

For every pound of roughly cut turkey meat you require 2 hard-boiled eggs; a small onion finely sliced, and soaked overnight in wine vinegar; a good sprig of parsley; 3 rashers of cooked bacon; and ½ pint of aspic achieved by boiling down 1 pint of wine/water/clear turtle soup mixture and adding ½ oz. of powdered gelatine.

In a glass bowl arrange slices of egg, then pieces of turkey . . . spaced out by small sprigs of parsley, bacon, onion and so on. Pour on the aspic at the end, and push down the top to create a pleasant shape. Put the galantine in a cool place; when it is well set, turn it out, cut into slices and serve with a sauce vinaigrette.

Cold Brussels sprouts

Cut up sprouts, warm them gently in milk or cream, and liquidize or pass through a sieve. Season with a little salt and quite a lot of freshly ground black pepper, put a good tablespoon into small, buttered oven dishes, make a depression in the middle and break into this a small egg. Bake in a medium oven (mark 5/375°F) until the white is just set. Pour a little cream over the egg and sprinkle with cayenne pepper.

Eating on the Run

MEALS ON WHEELS

If a man drives from A to B (the achievement of which appears to be one of the principal functions of a motor car) and A is some distance removed from B, the chances are that the motorist will require sustenance.

I should like to make it quite clear that with very few exceptions a picnic in a car is a plumb bad idea. When a man has been driving for a long time in the same cramped position, what he needs is a change of surroundings and the chance to shout back at new people. There are actually two proper reasons why one eats in the car – and I am discounting such quirks of fate as the seat belt inextricably caught up in your fly buttons: one is pressure of time; the other pressure of money. Here is some golden advice.

Equipment

Basically the equipment you have dictates the whole concept of your picnic. What science has achieved is a fantastic advance in kitchen ware and packaging, and it is depressing to see how little general use is made of this. Aluminium foil is probably the most important single

item. Hardy plastic bags come next. If you have plastic or Tupperware bowls with close-fitting lids then you can have a feast instead of a snack. If you have – or can induce someone to give you – a pair of Thermos jugs, you need not be ashamed to give a lift to a really discriminating gastronome.

Finally, if you have a wicker basket, you are made . . . though, frankly, the chances of someone being poor, busy, and coming by a lot of expensive impedimenta, are remote.

Drink

The disadvantages of fizzy drinks on picnics have been wildly exaggerated. I grant you that in the case of high gravity bottled beer loose in the boot of your car on a summer's day, the amount left in the bottle is likely to compare unfavourably with that which shot out when you removed the crown cork. Remembering that it is inadvisable to give a driving man vast quantities of alcohol, put lagers, pale ales, ciders and cans of soft drinks into a polythene bag containing ice cubes. The colder the cans are before you put them into the bag, the longer will your ice cubes remain intact. A hundred miles from home the beer will be at about the right temperature – even if the melted ice has eased the labels from the bottles. White Muscadet given the same treatment is good.

Or you can buy a tight-fitting box made of stuff that looks like fossilized cottonwool in which ice cubes remain frozen for two hours or more. Vodka and orange juice (known in the cocktail trade as a Screwdriver) has the advantage of being an all-family drink – children getting more ice and orange juice than vodka . . . but being made to feel part of the Happening. I am also a fan of fruit drinks such as they sell at the German Food Centre: apple juice, morello cherry juice, passion fruit cordial. Finally, on the subject of drink do not underestimate the thirst-quenching qualities of tea and coffee.

Food

If you have fresh, thin-cut bread, butter it generously with decent butter, give this a thin application of English mustard and then carve slices of York ham with a knife that has been given a quick wipe across a clove of garlic . . . all you then need is a couple of sprigs of fresh watercress and a sprinkling of Maldon salt to obtain what I consider to be a very acceptable sandwich. Somehow sandwiches are considered *passé* . . . mainly I suppose because of the abundance of those made with stale thick-cut bread, margarine, grated ripe cheese and raw tomatoes . . . though grated raw cheese and ripe tomatoes do little to make the confection more beautiful.

My car picnic menu consists of:

First Course – to be eaten with plastic cutlery (which you can throw away) and transported in sealed plastic boxes (which you keep):

Mushrooms à la grecque

Button mushrooms simmered in a mixture of three parts wine, one part tarragon vinegar for 10 minutes . . . after which you remove the mushrooms, add salt and crushed peppercorns to the wine/vinegar and then cool; stir in half its volume in sour cream, reduce by boiling, incorporate the mushrooms and serve in a communal plastic basin with individual spoons.

Or radishes, wrapped in foil, salt apart. Meat balls in a closed Tupperware container.

Meat balls

Take 1 lb. of minced beef, 1 beaten egg, 1 tablespoon grated onion, 10 peppercorns rough crushed, salt and ⅛ pint soda water. Mix well and divide into 24 pieces. Roll each in flour and bake on a greased oven sheet for 20 minutes in a mark 5 (375°F) oven.

Second course:

Rice and prawn salad

Pilaff rice . . . 1 cup cooked in 2½ cups of stock; 6 oz. peeled prawns – frozen ones, for tinned ones tend to have very little taste – tossed in sizzling butter seasoned with pepper and lemon juice; 2 tablespoons of mayonnaise.

Put the drained rice, prawns plus liquid in pan, and mayonnaise into a bowl. Blend and carry in a closed container.

Main dish:

Breaded lamb cutlets

Small cutlets, brushed with liquid mustard, then floured, dipped in beaten seasoned egg and dried in toasted bread-crumbs. Fry these in a mixture of half oil, half butter for 3 to 5 minutes on each side. Leave to cool on a rack and wrap very loosely in foil.

Bantam eggs and small good tomatoes are ideal picnic fare in spite of the fact that everyone else takes them on picnics. If you like tomato chutney it is probably the best single all-purpose relish for the main dish.

Pudding: car picnics need not actually be four-course affairs. Make syllabub (page 248) if you are rich and enter-prising. Otherwise take Lancashire cheese and Cox's apples.

FOOD FOR ONE HAND

After a minimum of twenty minutes hard driving, brush your cylinder head with edible oil and you can fry an egg on it without great difficulty though you should be careful to keep it clear of the plug indentations. A small tap at the base of your radiator will give you water hot enough to dis-solve a soup cube; with a little patience the car's cigar-lighter will cook your bacon. One can safely say that the resultant food will be fresher, better, often quicker, invariably nicer than the fare that is to be obtained at road-side eating places. Nevertheless, this does not solve the problem of feeding the man with his eyes on watch and speedometer and the natural reluctance of the tired statis-tician to spoil his sums by stopping and having to recalculate his ETA.

If you really love your traveller, here is a selection of motorway foods; the accent, of course, is on durable, varied and exciting things that you can eat with one hand.

Quails' eggs

According to an old Inverness recipe for this you need a tin of Japanese quails' eggs and ½ lb. of high-class sausage meat. The cheaper variety can be smartened up with chopped chicken liver or any other minced meat or offal that your good sense tells you will improve the basic – or base – mixture. To the meat, add a beaten egg and a small grated onion. Season well, pick up just under an ounce at a time in wet hands, mould this into a thin flat and wrap it around a quail's egg dusted with flour. Help the joints of sausage meat together with wet thumbs, reshape it by rolling in seasoned flour, dip in beaten egg and dry in breadcrumbs. Fry in deep fat for 2 minutes.

There are obvious rich standbys: spring chicken sharply roasted with cayenne pepper, jointed and allowed to drink in the sauce of seasoned butter as it cools; under-done slices of roast beef (14 minutes to the pound in mark 7/425°F oven), rolled around its filling of fresh horseradish grated into whipped double cream; sticks of fresh young celery, the concave side of the stalk filled with a mixture half gorgonzola, half butter, churned well with a fork; asparagus tips around which you roll very thinly sliced, generously buttered crustless brown bread.

If you really love your traveller passionately, get a long skewer and spike on to it a selection of his favourite things until it looks like a giant kebab, or an edible totempole. Start with a chipolata, a piece of pineapple, a rolled slice of ham, a stuffed olive, a wedge of cucumber, a piece of cheddar, a radish, a barley sugar spiked through the wrapper . . .

THE SANDWICH

Larousse Gastronomique, which many consider the standard culinary work, is unambitious in its definition of a sandwich: 'Foodstuff composed of two slices of buttered bread with some edible substance in between.' Too many people seem to have heeded this advice. There are three basic parts to a sandwich, and each has an important role. There is bread, which is the foundation. It can be brown, white or black . . . but it must be fresh. The thickness of the slices should bear some relation to the depth of the filling inside. Then there is butter. Its main function is not to enrich the bread but to preserve the filling. Spread it when it is malleable – as it might become in a cool room. Spread it generously and evenly, and to the very edges. In this way the buttered crusts, gently pressed, will seal the contents. Lastly, the filling. This should not be hot or the butter will melt and reset unattractively. It should not be too wet – or the bread will eventually become soggy. And finally, it must be perfectly seasoned because no one wants to have to prise open the two halves of his sandwich in order to add salt.

Fillings

Meat intended expressly for sandwiches is best cooked in a pot on top of the stove and left to cool in its juices; these, skimmed of fat, will set to give a rich meat jelly.

Poultry should be roasted for a long time in a cool oven and basted frequently. Skim the juices in the pan and use the jelly. Accompanying relishes and condiments must be chosen with care – and avoid lettuce unless sandwiches are eaten within 2 hours of making. (Use cos lettuce.)

Jelly is an excellent adjunct to a sandwich – unless the storage temperature is very warm. Use redcurrant jelly with red meat, mint jelly with lamb, crab-apple jelly with pork. If you salt your sandwich salt it on the unjellied side.

Anchovy paste is good with fish sandwiches.

Gammon, sprinkled with cloves and baked for an hour per pound on mark 4 (350°F) in company with ½ pint of pineapple juice and 3 tablespoons of brown sugar boiled together and used as a basting liquor, cut to the thickness of a 10p piece in slices big enough to cover and spill over the bread. At home we call this a ham sandwich and wonder how people dare to mature pre-cut slices of steam-baked bread, brush these with melted margarine, arrange between two of them a small round of machine-cut tinned ham and use the same name.

Fresh salmon. Drain the salmon well, and add a stiff mayonnaise flavoured with lemon juice rather than vinegar. Add grated cucumber, salt it and then squeeze out the water. Blend the mixture, season it and spread it on the bread over a gesture of anchovy.

Sardine. Mix the contents of a tin of sardines with a fork adding a teaspoon of Dijon mustard, some chopped chive or parsley, and a dash of Worcester sauce or tomato ketchup.

Tunnyfish. This fish should not be eaten unadulterated. A sieved hard-boiled egg is a good way of lightening an intrinsically heavy fish. Also lemon juice, mayonnaise and chopped herbs.

Crab is an excellent sandwich filler. But it should be mixed with a stiff mayonnaise and it needs to be spread generously; crab sandwiches will benefit much from a little anchovy.

Egg. There seem to me to be two acceptable approaches to producing an interesting egg sandwich:

1. Hard boil the eggs, then cool and chop them and mix them with mayonnaise, capers and herbs. The ideal herbs for this purpose are either dill or fennel.

2. Make a thin pancake-like omelette. Beat up with a fork:

2 whole eggs
1 tablespoon cream
1 tablespoon chopped sweet peppers simmered in butter
Salt and pepper

Fry on both sides in hot shallow oil in an omelette pan. Let it cool.

In all cases, put the fillings into the sandwiches; do not cut them; wrap them in foil. Take a bread knife, and when the time comes to eat them cut off the crusts and divide them into halves, quarters or fingers as you choose.

In time *Larousse* might even agree to upgrade its definition of a sandwich.

A RACEGOER'S PICNIC

One would be foolish to recommend any enterprise that is wholly dependent for its success on the British weather. In the case of a day at the races, however, the alternative to a picnic is as distressing a table d'hôte meal as ever got left out of the *Good Food Guide*. The racecourse luncheon usually consists of flakes of quick-frozen Pacific salmon with bottled salad cream and boiled potatoes, followed by ice cream, followed by cheese.

Racecourse sandwiches are small, expensive and almost invariably made the night before, as if caterers, like trainers, were bound by overnight declarations. Unfortunately, jellied eels, a traditional and delectable racecourse food, are considered socially undesirable. If you want them, you must go to the cheaper enclosures, where the bookmakers' odds are shorter, the queues at the tote windows longer, and there is a harder fight ahead of you if you want to buy a drink.

Which brings us back to picnics. A picnic, by definition, is an al fresco meal consisting of various items of food eaten in the fingers. Fingers can be amended to include spoons and forks, and plates need not be banned. But game pie with Cumberland sauce and baked potatoes, kept hot by being wrapped in foil and strapped to the cylinder block with Sellotape, is cheating. (Try it.)

MENU
Potted shrimps and wholemeal bread
Rolled slices of underdone topside of beef spread with whipped cream and horseradish
Salad of leeks
Mont Blancs
Lancashire cheese and Cox's apples
To be eaten after the third race: Scotch eggs
Drink: Pimm's No. 1

Potted shrimps   (per person)

1 oz. peeled shrimps or prawns (fresh, tinned or frozen)
½ oz. butter
⅛ lemon
white pepper

Home-made potted shrimps taste better and cost less than commercial ones. Toss the shrimps or prawns in a pan containing lemon juice and pepper, simmer, stir for a minute or two, and pour into a sieve to drain. Then put them into small individual dishes, press down, cover with 2 dessertspoons of clarified butter (page 17) and let them set in a cool place.

Whipped cream and horseradish spread

(for 8)

Take ⅛ pint each of double cream and top of the milk; whisk until it thickens and fold in a heaped tablespoon of freshly grated horseradish, a good pinch of salt and a coffeespoon of lemon juice.

Leek salad

4 oz. cleaned leeks per person

Cut leeks lengthways into halves or quarters and boil in salt water for 8–10 minutes so that they are cooked but firm. Drain well.

Dressing

(for 8)

1 heaped tablespoon chopped chives
1 heaped tablespoon chopped parsley
1 dessertspoon chopped capers
1 hard-boiled egg passed through a sieve
1 tablespoon lemon juice
1 tablespoon wine vinegar
5 tablespoons oil
salt and pepper

Mont Blancs

(per person)

½ meringue
1 oz. purée of chestnuts (available at most grocers)
1 coffeespoon Grand Marnier
1 oz. cream
sugar

Mont Blancs should be prepared in small individual bowls. Break up the meringue to cover the bottom, blend liqueur with chestnut purée, and squirt through the smallest opening of a piping bag. Prepare whipped cream, sweetened and beaten fairly stiff and add a good dollop to each dish as you serve it.

Scotch eggs   (per person)

  1 egg
  1½ oz. sausage meat, to which may be added some extra
    ground mace and grated onion
  Flour
  Beaten egg
  Breadcrumbs

Boil the eggs for 8 minutes – longer if you like them really hard – cool, peel and roll them in the flour. Take the ball of sausage meat between wet palms, flatten it and place the floured egg in the middle, folding the sausage meat evenly around it. (This can be done properly only if your hands are wet.) Coat the Scotch egg in flour, beaten egg and toasted breadcrumbs and fry in hot, deep fat for 3 minutes, turning it to prevent the breadcrumbs from burning.

Pimm's No. 1

Prepare a cocktail stick spiked with a slice each of apple, orange, lemon and cucumber peel, a maraschino cherry and a couple of mint leaves. Wrap bottles of fizzy lemonade and of Pimm's in a tarpaulin with crushed ice, in the ratio of ½ pint of lemonade to ¹⁄₁₆ of a bottle of Pimm's. To serve, put a liqueur glass of Pimm's in a ½ pint tankard, add lemonade, top up with another liqueur glass of Pimm's (adults only), and finally add the decorated cocktail stick.

Index

A Feast of Freud

Clement Freud

CLEMENT FREUD, who died suddenly in April 2009, was a man of many parts. His life embraced a variety of careers, including TV chef, gambler, owner of a night club and several racehorses, radio broadcaster, adventurer and – not least – Member of Parliament. Yet, as his son Matthew declared at his funeral, it was Freud's writing that brought us closest to the man.

In addition to several books - notably the children's book *Grimble* (1968), *Freud on Food* (1978), *The Book of Hangovers* (1981) and a volume of autobiography, *Freud Ego* (2001) he wrote on a vast range of subjects for newspapers and magazines, including the *Observer*, the *Sun*, *Financial Times*, *Sporting Life*, *Daily Mail*, *Tatler*, *Guardian*, *New Yorker* and *Racing Post*.

A Feast of Freud presents a generous helping of Clement Freud's best and most humorous writing on a broad sweep of topics, including his consuming passions of food, sport, politics and the absurdity of the human condition, reflecting his extraordinarily varied life through the prism of his distinctive deadpan humour.

From the pen of the man who once joked of being 'out-grandfathered' by the younger Winston Churchill comes this richly stocked volume that every Freud fan, no matter in which of his many lives they encountered him, will treasure.

9780593065402

Now available from Bantam Press